Just Right

American Edition

Jeremy Harmer
Ana Acevedo
Carol Lethaby
Ken Wilson

Student's Book

Marshall Cavendish
Education

Acknowledgments and sources

The authors and Publishers are grateful to the following for permission to reproduce copyright text materials. Every effort has been made to trace and contact copyright holders; please notify the publishers of any omissions which will be rectified at the earliest possible opportunity.

Page 16 Taken from *The man who mistook his wife for a hat* and other stories, by Oliver Sacks, Touchstone Books (Simon and Schuster), 1998; Page 20 Based upon www.blindekuh.ch; Page 40 Reprinted by permission of Donadio & Olson, Inc., Copyright Mario Puzo, 1969; Page 58 Adapted from www.cozay.com; Page 62 Reproduced by permission of Penguin Books Ltd; Page 64 Taken from *The Lighthouse*, by P.D. James, reproduced by kind permission of Knopf Publishing Group; Page 95 From *The Ghost* by Robert Harris, published by Hutchinson, reproduced by permission of The Random House Group Ltd.; Page 98 'Fire and Ice' by Robert Frost from *The Poetry of Robert Frost* edited by Edward Connery Lathem, Henry Holt and Company, reprinted by permission of The Random House Group Ltd.; Page 104 © KidsHealth.org; Page 105 Republished with permission from AllAboutVision.com; Page 108 (Sexual Attraction) Reproduced by kind permission of *The New Scientist*; Page 108 (A-C) Based on www.californiaphysics.com; Page 109 Taken from *The Time Traveler's Wife* by Audrey Niffenegger, Harcourt, 2003; Page 112 Adapted from www.financial-inspiration.com; Page 113 Adapted from www.unmuseum.org/doyle.htm and www.pbs.org/wgbh/amex/houdini/peopleevents/pande02.html; Pages 120-122 Based upon information from The Canadian High Commission, UK; Audioscript Page 36 and CD Excerpt from *O Go My Man*, copyright 2006 Stella Feehily, reprinted by permission of the publishers, Nick Hern Books: www.nickhernbooks.co.uk; Audioscript Page 38 and CD 'Two Cures for Love' and 'Bloody Men' reprinted by permission of United Agents on behalf of Wendy Cope; Audioscript Page 38-39, 40 and CD 'Fire and Ice' and 'The Road Not Taken' from *The Poetry of Robert Frost* edited by Edward Connery Lathem, Henry Holt and Company, Copyright 1916, 1923, 1969 by Henry Holt and Company. Copyright 1951 by Robert Frost, reprinted by arrangement with Henry Holt and Company, LLC; Audioscript Page 40 and CD 'In Two Minds' by Roger McGough from *Everyday Eclipses*, copyright Roger McGough 2002, is reproduced by permission of PFD, www.pfd.co.uk on behalf of Roger McGough

Marshall Cavendish Education
5th Floor
32-38 Saffron Hill
London
EC1N 8FH
www.mcelt.com/justright

Designed by Hart McLeod, Cambridge

ISBN: 978-0-462-09885 2

Printed and bound by Times Offset (M) Sdn. Bhd. Malaysia

Photo acknowledgments

Cover image © JUPITERIMAGES / Comstock Images / Alamy; p6 © Chuck Babbitt; p8 both Mike Ruzen; p11a © Design Pics Inc. / Alamy, p11b © Visual&Written SL / Alamy, p11c © blickwinkel / Alamy; p12a © Steve Bloom Images / Alamy, p12b © Lions Gate / Everett / Rex Features, p12c © Peter Barnes / Rex Features; p14 António Miguel de Campos / Wikipedia; p15a&b Hart Mcleod; p16 Rex Features; p22 © Scott Houston / Corbis; p24 Stephanie Paschal / Rex Features; p28 Tony Gutierrez / AP / PA Photos; p29 © Daniel Stein; p30a © Helene Rogers / Alamy, p30b © Chris Schmidt, p30c © Alec Pytlowany / Alamy, p30d Greg Meeson / hitandrun / Alamy, p30e © Heiko Bennewitz, p30f © Image Source Black / Alamy; p31 © Rob Barker; p33a © Brett Rabideau, p33b © Andrew Holt / Alamy; p34 pixelorb; p36a © Joan Vicent Cantó Roig, p36b © Lise Gagne, p36c © Aldo Murillo; p38a © Tom Wood / Alamy, p38b Canadian Press / Rex Features, p38c © ImageState / Alamy, p38d Sipa Press / Rex Features, p38e Jan Rihak, p38f © Terry Fincher.Photo Int / Alamy, p38g © Arco Images GmbH / Alamy, p38h © Patryk Galka; p40 © Pictorial Press Ltd / Alamy; p41a © Ken Weingart / Alamy, p41b © Brownstock Inc. / Alamy; p43a © The Print Collector / Alamy, p43b © North Wind Picture Archives / Alamy; p46a Reg Wilson / Rex Features, p46b Everett Collection / Rex Features, p46c © Bettmann / Corbis, p46d Sipa Press / Rex Features, p46e Time & Life Pictures / Getty Images, p46f Everett Collection / Rex Features; p47 CSU Archv / Everett / Rex Features; p48a © Interfoto Pressebildagentur / Alamy, p48b © Bettmann / Corbis; p49a © Sunset Boulevard / Corbis, p49b Everett Collection / Rex Features, p49c c.Warner Br / Everett / Rex Features; p50 Everett Collection / Rex Features; p51a © Trinity Mirror / Mirrorpix / Alamy, p51b Ilpo Musto / Rex Features; p52a AFP / Getty Images, p52b © Trinity Mirror / Mirrorpix / Alamy; p53a © Bettmann / Corbis, p53b © Michael Ochs Archives / Corbis; p54a © Alex Segre / Alamy, p54b © AGB Photo / Alamy, p54c Lauri Wiberg, p54d © Redferns Music Picture Library / Alamy, p54e © i4images - premium / Alamy, p54f Justin Horrocks, p54g © Look Die Bildagentur der Fotografen GmbH / Alamy, p54h © Tom Gundelwein / Alamy; p55a © David R. Frazier Photolibrary, Inc. / Alamy, p55b © niceartphoto / Alamy, p55c © Kevin Foy / Alamy; p56a © avatra images / Alamy, p56b © AA Pix / Alamy, p56c © Gabe Palmer / Alamy, p56d © Mary-Ella Keith / Alamy, p56e © Image Source Black / Alamy, p56f © Mark Baigent / Alamy; p58a Raido Väljamaa; p62a Popperfoto / Getty Images, p62b © Marvin Koner / Corbis, p62c ITV / Rex Features, p62d © Pictorial Press Ltd / Alamy; p62e&f © Photos 12 / Alamy; p64 © Arts & Authors / Alamy; p68a © Hulton-Deutsch Collection / Corbis, p68b NILS Jorgensen / Rex Features, p68c 2008 AFP, p68d © By Ian Miles-Flashpoint Pictures / Alamy, p68e ©Kudos Film and Television, p68f © Pictorial Press Ltd / Alamy; p70 © Fabrice Coffrini / Staff / AFP / Getty Images; p71 WireImage; p72a © Istockphotos, p72b © Jakub Cejpek, p72c © Ben Blankenburg, p72d © Matej Michelizza, p72e © Daniel Cardiff, p72f Jeff McDonald; p73a © Helle Bro Clemmensen, p73b © Toby Burrows / Digital Vision / Alamy, p73c © Leigh Schindler; p75a © Izabela Habur, p75b Bojan Fatur, p75c Ann Marie Kurtz, p75d Caroline Schiff, p75e Agata Malchrowicz; p76 © bilderlounge / Alamy; p77a © Allstar Picture Library / Alamy, p77b Charles Sykes / Rex Features; p78a © keith morris / Alamy, p78b © neilsetchfield.com / Alamy, p78c © The Photolibrary Wales / Alamy, p78d © Andrew Fox / Alamy; p80a © The City Project, p80b 2008 Getty Images; p82 JUPITERIMAGES / PolkaDot / Alamy; p83a © Devinder Sangha / Alamy, p83b PhotosIndia, p83c © Nikki Bidgood, p83d Rex Features, p83e © Nikreates / Alamy, p83f © Mc Pherson Colin / Corbis; p84a © Elisabeth Coelfen People / Alamy, p84b © Blend Images / Alamy; p86a © imagebroker / Alamy, p86b © Thinkstock Images / Jupiter Images / Alamy, p86c © LeeStrickland / Taxi / Getty Images, p86d © chris stock photography / Alamy, p86e © Michael Willis / Alamy, p86f © Design Pics Inc. / Alamy, p86g © Jeff Greenberg / Alamy, p86h © Corbis, p86i © Ronnie McMillan / Alamy, p86j © Tom Stewart / Corbis, p86k © Ariel Skelley / Corbis, p86l © JUPITERIMAGES / Creatas / Alamy; p87 Rienna Cutler; p88a © Nir Alon / Alamy, p88b © Jacques Sarrat / Sygma / Corbis; p94a © Manfred Konrad, p94b © Alistair Scott, p94c © Greg Nicholas, p94d © Simfo, p94e © Rockcoast sports / RCS Graphix, p94f © Brett Hillyard, p94g Peter Holloway, p94h © Christophr O'Driscoll, p94i ©Kronick; p95 © Geoffrey Swaine / Rex Features; p99 © JUPITERIMAGES / Comstock Images / Alamy; p104 © Jacob Wackerhausen; p105 © Cristian Ardelean; p106 © NILS Jorgensen / Rex Features; p108 © Jacom Stephens; p112 © Hulton Archive / Getty Images; p113 © Bettmann / Corbis; p115a © World Pictures / Alamy, p115b © Peter Adams / Photographers Choice / Getty Images; p116a © Hulton Archive / Getty Images, p116b © David Levenson / Getty Images; p118a © Nick Laham / Getty Images, p118b © Hamish Blair / Getty Images; p123a © JUPITERIMAGES / BananaStock / Alamy, p123b © Emmanuel Dunand / AFP / Getty Images; p127a © Zoran Kolundzija, p127b © Ales Veluscek, p127c © MBPHOTO; p131 © Ronald Grant Archive

Contents

Skills		Language

Skills

Skills

Language

UNIT 1
Shark attack

→ inversion
→ dangerous creatures
→ expressing fears and phobias

Speaking: frightening creatures

1 **First impressions** Discuss these questions with other students.

a What were the first thoughts that came into your mind when you looked at the picture on this page?

b What would you do if you were in the water and you saw this creature coming towards you?

c Do you know any stories about shark attacks?

2 **In pairs** Try to answer these questions about sharks. Then Student A turn to Activity Bank 1 on page 127. Student B turn to Activity Bank 16 on page 134. Read the information there and then discuss the answers.

a How many species of sharks are there?

b What is the risk of being attacked by a shark?

c How many people are killed by sharks every year?

d Why do people hunt sharks?

3 Read the sentences and answer the questions.

a I'm absolutely fascinated by sharks, but also absolutely terrified of them.

Fascinated and *terrified* describe extreme feelings. Can you think of adjectives to describe **less** extreme feelings?

b Can you explain why this sentence is different?

I find sharks absolutely fascinating and also absolutely terrifying.

4 Read the conversation and choose more extreme adjectives to replace the words in bold. What other changes do you have to make to the sentences?

SARAH: Did you see that program about sharks on TV last night?

ANDY: Yes.

SARAH: What did you think of it?

ANDY: I thought it was very **interesting**.

SARAH: Me too. And I thought the woman who presented it was very **good**.

ANDY: Yes! She looked a bit **scared** when the shark suddenly appeared.

SARAH: I know. I would have been the same. But she also looked very **pleased** when she got out of the water.

ANDY: Yes. In fact, I thought she looked rather **unhappy** when the shark swam away.

SARAH: Right. I think I would like her job.

ANDY: Really? I think working like that must be very **tiring**.

Vocabulary 1: dangerous creatures

5 **Look at this list of creatures and discuss the questions.**

  a Have you seen any of these creatures in the wild? Describe the experience and answer questions from the rest of the class.

  b What kind of danger do the different creatures pose? Use these words to describe the dangers if you can: *bite, sting, poison, crush, attack, destroy.*

  c When might you be in danger from these creatures?

  d How can you protect yourself from attack or help people who have been attacked?

alligator	locust
bear	mosquito
crocodile	scorpion
eagle	snake
elephant	stingray
fox	tiger
jellyfish	wasp

Vocabulary 2: mind map

6 **Copy the mind map into your notebook. Add as many words and phrases as you can. Then compare notes.**

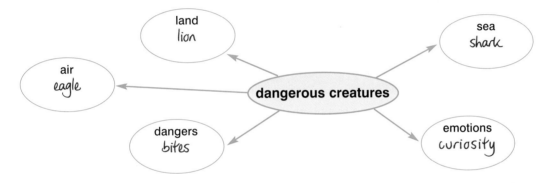

Vocabulary 3: extreme adjectives

7 **Look at the two lists of words. Find pairs of words with similar meanings using a word from each box.**

8 **Complete these sentences using a word from one of the boxes.**

  a I'm feeling **a bit** .... after that meal.

  b I was **absolutely** .... when the boat turned over in the storm.

  c She was **rather** .... when I finally arrived at the cinema.

  d My parents will be **very** .... when they meet you.

  e We were all **extremely** .... with the result.

  f The crowd at the baseball game was **absolutely** .... with the decision.

boiling	angry
delighted	cold
exhausted	good
fascinated	happy
freezing	hot
incensed	hungry
miserable	interested
parched	scared
starving	thirsty
terrified	tired
wonderful	unhappy

9 **Noticing language What's the rule? Discuss these questions.**

  a What is the difference between the words in the two lists?

  b What is the rule about the **modifiers** (*a bit, absolutely,* etc.) that can be used with each list of words?

  c Add other words to the two lists.

  Read 1A–1B in the Mini-grammar. Do you want to change your answers?

Reading: great white sharks

10 Before you read Work in pairs. Look at the photo with the text. Imagine you are having a phone conversation.

STUDENT A: You've just seen this photo in a magazine. Describe it to your partner.

STUDENT B: Ask for more details about the magazine photo and article.

11 Background Read about Mike Rutzen.

Mike Rutzen is an expert on great white sharks and an outspoken champion of shark conservation. He has become notorious for his exploits swimming with the animals without a cage. He has traveled the world lecturing on sharks and filming documentaries about them.

12 Scan the magazine article and find the information.

a In paragraph 2: two words that are used to describe sharks
b In paragraph 4: something potentially dangerous that happened
c In paragraph 5: an example of how sharks treat Mike Rutzen differently now

The Sharkman of Cape Town

Great white sharks are awe-inspiring. **Anyone** who has been lucky enough to see one, even if only through the bars of a cage, **will tell you so.** They are the world's largest predatory fish, can reach up to 20 feet in length, and weigh more than 2 tons. They are the sovereigns of the ocean, magnificent but also deadly. So what happened when someone stepped into the white shark's world—further than anyone else has gone before?

Read on ...

Mike Rutzen is a South African fisherman who describes himself as an average guy, although **clearly he is not**. About 15 years ago, he became interested in great white sharks, the scariest of ocean dwellers, and decided to spend a little time studying their behavior. Little did he know that this interest would turn into an all-consuming passion. For the past 15 years, he has spent all day every day engaging with these astounding creatures, monitoring their behavior and learning about their role in the ecology of the ocean.

When Rutzen got bitten by the white shark bug, he realized that watching was no longer enough. Not only did he start playing with them, albeit from the safety of his boat, he then graduated to full-on communication, which meant making the potentially life-threatening decision to swim with them without the protection of an underwater cage. This is called freediving.

Freediving with great white sharks is a serious business. **When you do it**, the important thing is to show maximum respect but no fear. Mike's initial encounters with them were tentative, and progress was slow. It was, he admitted, a steep learning curve. There were times when he made a wrong move or came across a dominant, pushy shark. One even pushed him to the bottom of the sea, leaving him flat on his back. But, thankfully, Mike has never had an encounter too dangerous to deal with.

Mike discovered that great white sharks convey their moods to each other by using subtle body positions and movements. They use a sophisticated language that experts are only beginning to translate. **Mike has keyed into this language**, and little by little is learning to speak it. By controlling his movements, he has learned how to use his body in the same way as white sharks do, and so interact with them. Now, the sharks seem to accept Mike's presence among them, seeing him neither as prey nor as predator. In fact, some of the ones he has befriended have even allowed him to hold on to their dorsal fins, so that he can swim with them.

"Anything that moves fast in the ocean is either chasing something or being chased," says Mike. "The movements of other individuals tell a white shark what is going on around it. **If you can fit into this system**, you can be accepted as part of it, and everything around you, including white sharks, will behave as normal."

Did you know?

The White Shark Café

The popular belief is that great white sharks are solitary predators. Not so, say the experts. In fact they like to gather at "hotspots" on the ocean floor. One of these hotspots, somewhere between Mexico and Hawaii, has been called the White Shark Café. "Sharks are just like people," says a shark researcher. "They like to hang out and chew the fat with their friends."

Do you know something unusual about the behavior of creatures in the wild?

13 **Words in context** Are the meanings of these words clear? If not, look them up in a dictionary. Use the words to complete these sentences. You may need to change the form.

> awe-inspiring (para 1)
> astounding (para 2)
> pushy (para 4)
> tentative (para 4)
> subtle (para 5)
> sophisticated (para 5)

a Experts will tell you to approach any wild animal ....

b The changes in the animal's body language were so .... that none of us noticed them.

c Swimming with sharks is scary, but also the most .... thing in the world.

d The .... tourists managed to get the three places on the boat.

e My grandfather was .... when I told him how much the trip would cost.

14 Explain these references in the article. (The words are in bold type.)

a Anyone ... will tell you so. *Tell you what?*
b ... clearly he is not. *Not what?*
c When you do it, ... *When you do what?*
d Mike has keyed into this language, ... *Which language?*
e If you can fit into this system, ... *Which system?*

Language in chunks

15 These expressions are used in the passage. Can you think of other ways of expressing the same idea?

a an **all-consuming** passion
b the white shark **bug**
c **full-on** communication
d a **steep learning curve**
e seeing him **neither as prey nor as predator**

16 Choose the best way to complete these sentences to show the meaning of the phrases in Activity 15.

a The first time, he stopped short of full-on communication and
  1 contented himself with swimming around the sharks.
  2 simply tried to put his arm around the shark's neck.

b My friend Luke has caught the surfing bug and
  1 avoids going to the beach as much as he can.
  2 spends all his time on the beach now.

c His interest in the sea is all-consuming and
  1 I really think he would prefer never to return to dry land.
  2 he finds time for several other hobbies as well.

d His first month in the job has been a steep learning curve
  1 because he's done many similar jobs before.
  2 as he had no previous experience of live broadcasting.

17 **Reaction** After Mike Rutzen was seen on TV free-diving with sharks, this criticism appeared on a diving website. Do you agree? Give your reasons.

Riding sharks like domesticated ponies for a half-baked television program is both disrespectful and a disservice to sharks. Please take this man off the air!

Grammar: inversion

18 Study the examples of inversion.

Little did he know that this interest would turn into an all-consuming passion.
Not only did he start playing with sharks, he also then graduated to full-on communication.
No sooner had we started than it began to rain.
At no time did they explain the problem.
Only when I saw the news on TV did I realize.
I've never seen a shark, nor have I seen a whale.

Now rewrite these as inverted sentences. Read 2A–2C in the Mini-grammar to help you.

a He studied marine biology and then started his own research project.
b We had no idea that the shark was following the boat.
c We had just arrived back at port when it started to rain.
d They never told us that we had to pay more for the boat trip.
e It wasn't until my friend called me on the phone that I heard the news.
f I've never been to Mexico and I've never been to Brazil.

Write three more inverted sentences.

19 Study the examples of conditional sentences.

If you get bitten by a poisonous snake, there isn't much you can do.
Should you get bitten by a poisonous snake, there isn't ...

If you saw a great white shark, what would you do?
Were you to see a great white shark, what ...?

If we had known what the weather would be like, we would have stayed on the island.
Had we known what the weather would be like, we would ...

Now complete these sentences. Read 2D in the Mini-grammar to help you.

a Imagine you were alone in a forest full of wild animals. .... , what would you do?
b It was much colder at sea than it had been on land. .... , we would have worn warmer clothes.
c I think what Mike does is fascinating. .... the opportunity, I would definitely do what he did.
d The sharks were not interested in Mike when he remained motionless. .... , that would have been a different story.
e Apparently, there was a story about the shark attack in a newspaper the day before. .... , I probably wouldn't have gone for a swim.

Functional language: fears and phobias

20 Complete the word box. What is the grammatical class of the words in each column?

?	?	?
fear		fearful
	terrify	
		scared
	frighten	

21 Complete these sentences, using a form of the word in brackets.

a I must admit I was .... of going in the water. (fear)
b We were all .... when the shark appeared. (terrify)
c Sea creatures don't .... me at all. (scared)
d The noise gave me the most dreadful .... (frighten)
e I am .... of heights. (terrify)

22 Rewrite the sentences so that they are true for you or someone you know.

a My sister is **scared** of spiders.
b Everyone in my family is **frightened** of flying.
c I **get a fright** every time I hear a police siren.
d I **got the fright of my life** when I went to the Ghost Museum.
e My best friend is **terrified of** taking exams.
f I was **scared stiff** when I saw the snake.
g It **scared the living daylights** out of me.

23 **In pairs** Read this quotation. What kind of human situations does it make you think about?

"The only thing we have to fear is fear itself—nameless, unreasoning, unjustified terror which paralyzes the effort needed to convert retreat into advance." Franklin D. Roosevelt, 32nd American President, in his inaugural address, March 4th, 1933

Listening: the most dangerous place on Earth

24 Brainstorm You are going to hear about the place where the most dangerous creatures in the world live.

a Where do you think the most dangerous place on the planet is? What do you know about it?

b What is the most dangerous place you know personally? Why is it dangerous?

25 Look at the photographs and answer the questions.

A saltwater crocodile

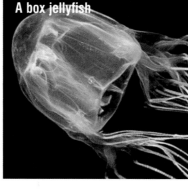
A box jellyfish

A taipan

a Where do they live?
b What can they do to you?
c Do you think you would survive?
d What would be your reaction if you saw one?

26 Listen to Track 1 and decide who is speaking. Choose from this list:

a an expert on wildlife giving a lecture at a university
b an Australian lifeguard talking to tourists
c someone giving advice to visitors to a summer camp
d some students asking questions before they set off to another country

27 Now listen to Track 2 and answer these questions.

a What do you find out about the snake population of the area?
b What part does the taipan play in the environment?
c Name some of the creatures that saltwater crocodiles eat.
d What is the attitude of the government to taipans and crocodiles?
e What's the difference between Canadian and Australian jellyfish?
f What effect does the sting of a box jellyfish have?
g Which of these creatures is the most dangerous?
h What is Graham's final message?

28 Discuss these questions.

a How does Graham give information to the visitors?
b Do you think he changed the attitude of the listeners?
c Would you want to take a vacation there?

Pronunciation: statement questions

29 Read and listen to Track 3. They all have a question mark at the end. What exactly is the speaker trying to convey?

– do you understand what I mean?
– disbelief or amazement
– uncertainty

a A: The venom of a taipan is very useful, so we collect it.
   B: You collect the venom?

b A: Can anyone tell me why no one is swimming?
   B: They're frightened of being eaten by a saltwater crocodile?

c A: How big were the jellyfish that you saw?
   B: Uh ... quite big. About the size of a pizza?

30 In pairs Identify the type of exchange and practice them. Then listen to Track 4 and check.

a A: I'm a vet dentist. I specialize in sharks.
   B: You're a shark dentist?

b A: Why do you think the dolphins finished up on the beach?
   B: They were confused by some radio signals from a submarine?

c A: I love scuba diving off the Australian coast.
   B: You like diving where there are saltwater crocodiles?

d A: What color was the fish?
   B: The color of wet grass?

e A: How do you think sharks communicate with each other?
   B: By making noises?

Writing: news report

Police close roads after lion escapes from zoo

Roads around Los Angeles Zoo were closed yesterday after a seven-year-old male lion named Hercules escaped.

31 You are going to write a news report for your local newspaper about a dramatic incident. Here are some suggestions, but you may choose your own topic:

someone has been attacked by a shark
an animal has escaped from the zoo
a series of attacks on people by dangerous dogs

32 Write your news report. Follow these instructions.

a   Read the Writing Tips on the right and make notes about your article.
b   Write a draft. Exchange it with a partner and give each other suggestions for improving your drafts.
c   Write the final version of your article.

Speaking: debate

Should we interfere with the way animals live in order to protect them?

33 Read the information about Steve Irwin and Timothy Treadwell.

Steve Irwin was an Australian zoo owner famous for doing daring things with wild animals, especially crocodiles. Once he fed a crocodile while holding his baby son, a stunt that was criticized by parent groups. He made TV programs where he played with poisonous snakes. Irwin was eventually killed by a stingray while he was being filmed underwater.

American environmentalist Timothy Treadwell spent 13 summers living with grizzly bears in Alaska. He famously described them as "harmless party animals." At the end of the summer of 2003, when a pilot arrived to pick 46-year-old Treadwell and his girlfriend up, he found that the couple had been eaten by the bears.

34 Reacting Read these opinions. Discuss them with other students. Which (if any) do you sympathize with?

People like Steve Irwin and Timothy Treadwell dare to do what other people only think about in an otherwise gray and predictable world.

They bring to our attention the importance of understanding and respecting the creatures we share this planet with.

They are dangerous eccentrics who cause as much trouble to other people as they do to themselves.

They are obsessive self-publicists, who have found an unusual way to become rich and famous.

35 Preparing a discussion Work in three groups.

Group 1: Make a list of the *positive* things people like Irwin and Treadwell achieve.
Group 2: Make a list of the *negative* things about their work.
Group 3: Make a list of adjectives, positive or negative, to describe people like Irwin and Treadwell.

Then each group presents its list to the rest of the class.

36 Debate Is the class for or against the kind of work done by people like Irwin and Treadwell?

Review: grammar and functional language

37 Read the conversation. Rewrite the lines in italics, replacing the inverted sentences with something less formal.

TOURIST: Well, I decided to take a boat trip to see the sharks.
INTERVIEWER: And what happened?
TOURIST: Well, *little did we know* that storms were forecast. *No sooner had we started the trip than* a thunderstorm started.
INTERVIEWER: But thunderstorms aren't a problem on a boat.
TOURIST: Well, it's easy for you to say that. *Had I known* there was going to be a storm, I would definitely NOT have gone.
INTERVIEWER: I see. Go on.
TOURIST: So, in the middle of a storm, the engine stopped.
INTERVIEWER: Oh no!
TOURIST: Yes. So now, *not only were we* in the middle of a storm, but we also had no power. And then …
INTERVIEWER: What?
TOURIST: There was a flash of lightning and the boat caught fire.
INTERVIEWER: Wow! That sounds dangerous!
TOURIST: Yes. Well, it was easy to put the fire out but things got worse. I asked the captain to radio for help. *Only then did we discover* that the lightning strike had also knocked out the radio.
INTERVIEWER: Goodness! So what happened next?

38 Complete the story with a partner by continuing the interview.

39 Answer these questions about your fears and phobias (or lack of them). Compare your answers with other students.

How would you feel if …
a you were about to make a speech in English to a thousand people?
b you had to spend the night in a haunted house?
c you had to wade across a river which might contain snakes or crocodiles?
d you were in a plane flying through a thunderstorm?
e you jumped from a plane with a parachute?

Review: vocabulary

40 Fridge, trash can, suitcase Look at the word lists. Decide if they are words you would use regularly (fridge), never (trash can), or in the future (suitcase). List them in your notebook.

41 Describe the most amazing thing you have ever seen or done. Use as many words as you can from the Word List.

Word List

astounding	life-threatening
awe-inspiring	notorious
boiling	outspoken
daring	parched
delighted	predator
exhausted	prey
fearful	pushy
freediving	sophisticated
freeze	starving
frighten	stunt
full-on	subtle
incensed	tentative
key into	terrify

Word Plus

a serious business
a steep learning curve
out of control
scare the living daylights out of someone
scared stiff
the white shark bug
to chew the fat
to hang out
to maul to death

Can you believe your eyes?

→ negative prefixes
→ expressing degrees of certainty
→ modal verbs

Listening: optical illusions explained

1 **In pairs** Look at these three images and answer the questions. Compare your answers in groups.

a What word do you see?

b Can you see black dots here? What happens when you try to count the black dots?

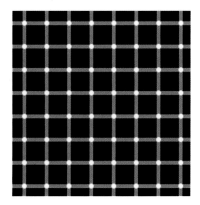

c Are the table tops the same size? Which is longer? Which is wider?

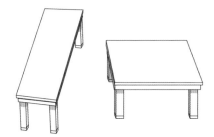

2 Listen to Track 5, an interview with an expert on optical illusions, and answer these questions.

a What causes an optical illusion?

1 The eyes see something the brain doesn't see.
2 The brain thinks it sees something that isn't there.

b Which of the examples in Activity 1 is a *physiological* illusion and which is a *cognitive* illusion?

c What explanation does Changizi give for optical illusions?

1 The brain sees things before the eye.
2 The brain generates images from the future.
3 Perception and reality are always the same.

3 Now listen again to Track 5. Match the definitions a–d to the terms 1–4 and complete the sentences e and f.

1 optical illusion   2 physiological illusion
3 cognitive illusion   4 neural lag

a When we receive too much stimulation of a particular type in the eye, it causes us to see something that isn't there.

b The space of time the brain takes to catch up with what the eye is seeing.

c When we look at something and think we see something that isn't actually there.

d When we make assumptions about something we see based on what we already know.

e When light hits the retina, about one-tenth of a second goes by before the brain translates the signal into a .... of the world.

f Changizi asserts that the human .... compensates for these neural delays and produces images of what will occur one-tenth of a second into the future.

4 **In pairs** Now try these three puzzles. Explain them using the information from Activities 2 and 3.

a Can you read what this says?
It's prttey fnuny how we can raed tihs einrte snetnece wtih all tehse ltteres all out of palce, and we can cnotniue to keep raednig and sitll mkae snese of waht we are raeding. No mttaer how mnay tmies you raed tihs oevr and oevr you can sitll mkae snese of it. How is taht pssoible?

b What do you see here?

c Look at the chart below and say the COLOR of the word, not the word itself.

YELLOW BLUE ORANGE
BLACK RED GREEN
PURPLE YELLOW RED
ORANGE GREEN BLACK
BLUE RED PURPLE
GREEN BLUE ORANGE

Functional language: expressing degrees of certainty

5 Listen to Track 6. The people are discussing one of these photographs. Which one?

6 Listen again and complete the expressions with the words you hear.

a KATIE: I .... it's some kind of technological device.

b JAMES: There's .... it's part of a toaster.

c KATIE: I .... it might be something to plug something into, because of the holes.

d KATIE: Yes, ... be little pins that go into those holes.

e KATIE: Hmm... .... be the back part of something connected to a computer?

f JAMES: You're right— .... the hard drive for a computer.

g KATIE: Yes, ... that's what it is!

7 Draw a table and put these expressions in it according to the degree of certainty.

it might be ...	do you think it could be ....?
it could be ...	I'm sure it's ...
it must be ...	it may be ...
it can't be ...	I think it's ...
it has to be ...	I have a feeling it's ...
there's no way it's ...	I bet it's ...
it couldn't be ..., could it?	

certain (yes)	uncertain	certain (no)

Say the sentences below in as many ways as you can, expressing different degrees of certainty.

a They're French.
b Karen and Richard don't like John.
c Jack stole my car.
d Rachel didn't eat the cake.

Pronunciation: stress and intonation to express degrees of certainty

8 Listen to Track 7. Put a check mark by the sentence in which the speaker sounds *more* certain.

1a I think she went to her piano lesson. ☐
1b I think she went to her piano lesson. ☐
2a He might be watching TV. ☐
2b He might be watching TV. ☐
3a I'm pretty sure it's the guy from the fruit store. ☐
3b I'm pretty sure it's the guy from the fruit store. ☐

Now underline where the main stress falls in the sentence in each case.

9 Practice saying the sentences in Activity 7 with different stress and intonation to show the degree of certainty.

10 Look at the pictures on page 127 and discuss what you think they are. Make at least ten guesses. Use the expressions in 7.

Reading: case histories

11 Background Read about the writer Oliver Sacks.

   a What is the story going to be about?

   b What does a neurologist do?

   c Do you know any people with unusual mental abilities?

Oliver Sacks was born in 1933 in London, into a family of physicians and scientists. He earned his medical degree at Oxford University. Since 1965, he has lived in New York, where he is a practicing neurologist. In 2007, he was appointed Professor of Clinical Neurology and Clinical Psychiatry at Columbia University. Sacks is perhaps best known for his collections of case histories from his experience as a neurologist, *The Man who Mistook his Wife for a Hat* and *An Anthropologist on Mars*, in which he describes patients struggling to live with unusual neurological conditions.

12 Read this extract from a case history.

The Man who Mistook his Wife for a Hat

In this case, Dr. Sacks is interviewing a highly educated musician, Dr. P., who has been referred to him after the ophthalmologist concluded that there was nothing wrong with Dr. P.'s eyes, but that he clearly had problems "seeing."

"Can I help?" I asked.

"Help what? Help whom?"

"Help you put on your shoe."

"Ach," he said, "I had forgotten the shoe," adding, sotto voce, "The shoe? The shoe?" He seemed baffled.

"Your shoe," I repeated. "Perhaps you'd put it on."

He continued to look downwards, though not at the shoe, with an intense but misplaced concentration. Finally his gaze settled on his foot: "That is my shoe, yes?"

Did I mishear? Did he missee?

"My eyes," he explained, and put a hand to his foot. "This is my shoe, no?"

"No, it is not. That is your foot. There is your shoe."

"Ah! I thought that was my foot."

Was he joking? Was he mad? Was he blind? If this was one of his "strange mistakes," it was the strangest mistake I had ever come across. I helped him on with his shoe (his foot) to avoid further complication. Dr. P. himself seemed untroubled, indifferent, maybe amused. I resumed my examination. His visual acuity was good: he had no difficulty seeing a pin on the floor, though sometimes he missed it if it was placed to his left. He saw all right, but what did he see? I opened a copy of the *National Geographic Magazine* and asked him to describe some pictures in it. His responses here were very curious. His eyes would dart from one thing to another, picking up tiny features, individual features, as they had done with my face. A striking brightness, a color, a shape would arrest his attention and elicit comments—but in no case did he get the scene-as-a-whole. He failed to see the whole, seeing only details, which he spotted like blips on a radar screen. He never entered into relation with the picture as a whole—never faced, so to speak, its physiognomy. He had no sense whatever of a landscape or scene.

I showed him the cover, an unbroken expanse of Sahara dunes.

"What do you see here?" I asked.

"I see a river," he said. "And a little guesthouse with its terrace on the water. People are dining out on the terrace. I see colored parasols here and there." He was looking, if it was "looking," right off the cover into mid-air and confabulating nonexistent features, as if the absence of features in the actual picture had driven him to imagine the river and the terrace and the colored parasols.

I must have looked aghast, but he seemed to think he had done rather well. There was a hint of a smile on his face. He also appeared to have decided that the examination was over and started to look around for his hat. He reached out his hand and took hold of his wife's head, tried to lift it off, to put it on. He had apparently mistaken his wife for a hat! His wife looked as if she was used to such things.

I could make no sense of what had occurred in terms of conventional neurology (or neuropsychology). In some ways he seemed perfectly preserved, and in others absolutely, incomprehensibly devastated. How could he, on the one hand, mistake his wife for a hat and, on the other, function, as apparently he did, as a teacher at the Music School?

Taken from *The Man who Mistook his Wife for a Hat and Other Clinical Tales* by Oliver Sacks published by Touchstone Books (Simon and Schuster) 1998

13 Fact check Who or what ...

a thought at first that Dr. P. might be crazy?
b is not worried at all by Dr. P.'s condition?
c was Dr. P. not able to "see"?
d did Dr. P. look at instead of the picture from the magazine?
e was not surprised by Dr. P.'s behavior?
f was Dr. Sacks surprised about Dr. P. being able to do?

14 Now read the extract again and answer these questions.

a What are the mistakes that Dr. P. makes with these things?
   – a shoe
   – a desert scene
   – a hat
b What is Dr. Sacks' explanation for these mistakes?

15 Vocabulary What do these words in the text mean? Match the words with their meanings.

a sotto voce
b misplaced
c indifferent
d striking
e dart
f physiognomy
g confabulate
h conventional

1 to invent things unconsciously from memory
2 in a low voice
3 the human face, facial features
4 without interest
5 traditional, normal
6 to move quickly
7 put in the wrong place
8 noticeable, fascinating

Language in chunks

16 Use these expressions from the text in the sentences below. Change the form where necessary.

> to look downwards   to settle one's gaze on something
> visual acuity   to elicit comments   to arrest one's attention
> a hint of a ...   to look aghast   to look as if   to make sense of

a She .... when he suggested that she should naturally be able to cook because she was a woman. How could people think like that in the 21st century?

b John opened the instructions and tried .... the impossible diagrams and technical words he saw.

c There was something about the photograph that .... She .... on one person in the back row. She knew she had seen him somewhere before, but where? Suddenly, her face changed and she .... she had seen a ghost. The room fell silent.

d The eye doctor gave me a test to determine my .... There was .... a smile on his lips when he realized that I had memorized the chart before the test.

e The students .... , staring intently at their books, when Ms. Collins asked for the answer to the first homework problem. She tried .... by asking questions, but no one raised their eyes to risk answering her.

Now use at least four of the phrases in sentences of your own.

17 In pairs Which of these would you rather have? Put a check mark in the boxes.

a perfect vision? ☐
b great hearing? ☐
c the ability to cook well? ☐
d the ability to write music? ☐
e the ability to play a musical instrument well? ☐
f the ability to draw well? ☐

Rank them in order and note your reasons. Then compare with another pair.

Vocabulary: negative prefixes with *mis-*, *un-*, *in-*, *dis-*, *im-*, *de-*

18 Word formation Use your dictionary. Choose the correct word.

a She was *untroubled / introubled* by his reaction.
b He was *indifferent / undifferent* to her dog. He really didn't care much for animals.
c What you feel is *irrelevant / unrelevant* to me.
d That's *impossible / unpossible*.
e Her statements are completely *illogical / unlogical*. What she says does not make sense.

19 Draw a table, make these adjectives negative, and place them in the correct row.

un-	unambiguous
im-	improbable
in-	
ir-	
il-	

articulate	familiar	pleasant
audible	friendly	polite
believable	happy	rational
comfortable	healthy	reliable
complete	legal	responsible
conscious	legible	sane
cooked	mature	successful
correct	modest	tidy
edible	necessary	usual
expected	perfect	well

Can you see any rules? Look at the first letter of the adjectives. Try to add as many adjectives as you can to the table.

20 Complete this paragraph with the negative adjectives from Activity 19. Sometimes more than one answer is possible.

She looked around her. She was in a .... surroundings—she didn't recognize anything. She tried to speak, but her voice was b .... —no sound came out. What had happened to her? The last thing she remembered, she had been eating a rather c .... meal with her brother Joe. The fish was d .... , almost raw, and the vegetables were completely e .... , because they were burned. Joe had been f .... , talking about strange things that made no sense—as usual he had been g .... , talking about how great he was all the time. Had he drugged her? This was h .... , but not i .... For some time now he had been acting strangely and she was beginning to think that he was j .... Sarah felt as if she had been k .... for several hours—in a deep sleep. She rubbed her eyes and saw a note on the table—it was in Joe's almost l .... handwriting.

21 Read these sentences. Discuss the different meanings of the prefixes.

a She *dis*connected the computer during the storm.
b The policeman quickly *dis*armed the robber.
c Thousands of people were *dis*placed by the war.
d She had *mis*placed her hat and couldn't find it.
e They *un*wrapped the gift and found it was a food processor.
f He looked dangerous, but he held up his arms to show that he was *un*armed.
g She had one minute to *de*activate the alarm before the bell started ringing.

22 Form new verbs with the prefixes *dis-*, *mis-*, *un-*, *de-* and complete the sentences below with a suitable form of the verb.

activate	*deactivate*
code	
hear	
satisfy	
wrap	
agree	
connect	
infect	
speak	
appear	
continue	
judge	
stabilize	
believe	
do	
like	
understand	

a I think I .... her. I thought she was selfish and cold, but she's actually a very good person.
b You must have .... me. I said you should be here at 7, not 11!
c George was very .... with his new computer. It was slow and kept crashing.
d I'm afraid that line of products has been .... We no longer make them.
e That's a nasty cut on your leg. You should clean it carefully and .... it.
f They sat down and started to .... the message. They had been trained very carefully to do this.
g The assassination of a political leader often .... a nation.

Speaking: police lineup

23 In pairs Look at these photos for one minute and try to remember what the people look like. Then close your books and describe the people in as much detail as possible.

24 Now turn to Activity Bank 3 on page 128. Can you find the two people in Activity 23 in the lineup of people?

25 Role play

In pairs Yesterday there was a bank robbery. Student A is an eyewitness and Student B is a detective. The detective wants to know what the robber looked like.

STUDENT A: Go to Activity Bank 5 on page 129.
STUDENT B: Go to Activity Bank 17 on page 135.

How many people identified the correct person?

26 In groups Read this statement and discuss the questions below.

"Misidentification by eyewitnesses was the leading cause of wrongful conviction in more than 75 percent of 183 cases of people who were freed from jail based on DNA evidence."—US government report

a Do you think police lineups are worthwhile or a waste of time? Why?
b Do you think you would be a good eyewitness? Why or why not?

CONVERSATION TIP

Paraphrasing
If you don't know the exact word, try to paraphrase and describe the thing with other words that you do know. This will give you time to think of the actual word and will give the person you are talking to the chance to help you.

Example:
A: He is quite tall and he is, uh, he has no hair.
B: You mean he's bald?
A: Yes, he's bald.

Grammar: modal verbs—meaning and use

27 Read this sentence and put the modal verbs into four groups from most certain (yes) to most certain (no). You can use 3B in the Mini-grammar to help you. The first one is done for you.

a		must have been		1
b		can't have been		
c		might have been		
d	She {	could have been	}	tired
e		may have been		
f		will have been		
g		should have been		

28 Write these sentences in a different way using the correct modal verb. You can use 3A–3B in the Mini-grammar to help you.

a It's not possible that Kevin wrote that paper.
b Perhaps Katie went to the show.
c I'm pretty sure she was there, because her teacher told her to go.
d I'm certain that Martin sent that email, because it came from his account.
e Maybe Janet has already gone to the party.

29 Match 1–7 with the sentences a–g. You can use 3C in the Mini-grammar to help you.

1 permission
2 ability
3 lack of ability
4 recommendation/mild obligation
5 strong obligation
6 no obligation
7 prohibition/lack of permission

a You mustn't speak English. Mr. Watanabe doesn't understand.
b Rebecca can touch her nose with her tongue.
c The children must be in bed by 8:30.
d We don't have to get up early tomorrow. We're on vacation.
e You can all go outside and play now.
f Kevin can't play the piano very well.
g You should listen to my new CD—it's cool.

30 In pairs For each of sentences a–e there are *two* possible sentences which explain the context.

a You must speak Spanish.
b Janet could have gone to the party.
c She should have eaten her spinach.
d Lucy can play the piano.
e Juan may stay up late.

STUDENT A: Turn to Activity Bank 4 on page 128.
STUDENT B: Turn to Activity Bank 18 on page 135.

Writing: an online restaurant review

31 Read this information about an unusual restaurant in Switzerland. Would you like to eat there? Why or why not? Make a list of reasons. Then compare your answers in groups.

DINING IN THE DARK

They say the eye is as important as the taste buds when it comes to food. Not here. At *blindekuh*, the pleasures of the palate are experienced by other senses that are sharpened by the darkness. Let smell and taste, hearing and touch, be your guides as you eat in complete darkness. You don't need your eyes to enjoy *blindekuh*! We don't want you to feel lost in our world of darkness, so our professional staff is always there to help. Our team is made up of blind and partially sighted people who will take the very best care of you, making your visit to *blindekuh* an unforgettable experience.

Review	A	B	C
overall			
food			
service			
ambiance			

32 Now read these three online reviews of the restaurant and give it stars according to what they say. Compare your answers.

☆☆☆☆ fantastic
☆☆☆ good
☆☆ average
☆ not very good

A The **blindekuh** has good food—but the experience of eating in the dark was truly out of this world. My partner and I went with two friends and we noticed that whenever a group arrived they were very loud and very nervous. Once people settled down, the experience became much more sublime. I would definitely go again! The blind waiters are wonderful—they are very helpful and really know how to help you enjoy the experience.

B The world's first dark restaurant—doesn't that sound exciting? When I first heard about it I just knew I had to pay a visit. It's definitely an unusual, but not necessarily enjoyable, experience. **blindekuh** is run very efficiently by blind staff and the guests eat in a pitch-black environment to experience how it would feel to be blind. After being guided to a table by the waiters, you can order, and as you eat you will see neither the interior nor your own food. The food is very good, but eating in the dark creates an atmosphere that is uncomfortable and unpleasant. Just for your information, the restaurant's bathroom is not pitch-black. And neither is the kitchen.

C Although I was quite disturbed at first, I quickly grew accustomed to the surroundings. Every gesture has to be made with the greatest of care so as not to tip over the drinks ... or get too close to the people at the next table. Fortunately the excellent wait staff are there to help you. Eating is fun, with the only problem being that there is no way to know how much food is left on the plate. Probing with the fingers is the best solution. And anyway, nobody will complain about your bad table manners, since nobody can see you! In all, it was a very entertaining evening, a rare experience in life, and way less scary than I thought at first. Of course, it was expensive for rather plain food, but this is Zurich after all and one doesn't get to eat in complete darkness every day. It was fun!

33 Groups of four Choose four restaurants that you are all familiar with. Each of you write a short online review about all four of them. Comment on:

a food
b service
c ambiance
d overall impression

On a second piece of paper, give a score for each aspect and an overall score. Don't show your scores!

34 Exchange your reviews. Try to guess the scores that the other group members gave based on the review they wrote.

Review: grammar and functional language

35 Complete these sentences so that they mean the same as the original using the word given.

a It's not possible that Maria recognized me from so far away.
CAN'T
Maria .... me from so far away.

b Perhaps she eats a lot of carrots.
MIGHT
She .... of carrots.

c Kevin's definitely going out tonight.
MUST
Kevin .... tonight.

d Joe and Lucy aren't allowed to stay up past 9 PM.
MAY
Joe and Lucy .... 9 PM.

e Why didn't you tell me you were tired?
SHOULD
You .... you were tired.

f I'm sure you were terrified.
MUST
You .... terrified.

g She'll probably be here later.
THINK
I .... later.

h I'm pretty sure she's gone already.
SHOULD
She .... by now.

36 In groups Discuss these things about your life. How sure are you about these things? Find different ways to say these things to express degrees of certainty.

a You will pass your English course.
b You will go on vacation in the summer.
c Your country will win the next World Cup.
d Life will be found on Mars.

Talk about two more things that you are sure of in your life and two things you are not sure of.

Review: vocabulary

Word List

a hint of a smile	illogical	to dart
conscious	inference	to disconnect
conventional	irrelevant	to infer
deceptive	misleading	to make sense of
elicit	perception	to misplace
excess	sense	to perceive
excessive	striking	unarmed
eyewitness	to arm	untroubled
police lineup	to compensate	unwrap

Word Plus

neural lag	deactivate
physiognomy	displace
confabulate	disarm
visual acuity	neurologist
to raise one's eyes	optical illusion
to settle one's gaze	indifferent
to look aghast	

37 Read the story and use the correct form of the word given to complete the text.

She knew her anger was a .... (rational), but she couldn't help it. It's true that the meeting was b .... (important), but nevertheless, she hated it when her manager made her feel c .... (adequate). He had asked her for the latest sales figures, which she had spent four hours preparing, and then he had told her that they were d .... (accurate). Sally was e .... (satisfy) with her job and she felt deeply f .... (happy) and wanted to change jobs. This wasn't the first time this had happened. Her manager frequently g .... (understand) her and she felt he was very h .... (connect) from his employees and even seemed to i .... (like) them. She couldn't wait to get home and relax and j .... (wind) from her nightmare day.

38 Fridge, trash can, suitcase Look at the word lists. Decide if they are words you would use regularly, never, or in the future. List them in the appropriate part of your notebook.

UNIT 3

Throw away the key

→ causative verbs
→ prison and other punishments
→ giving both sides of an argument

Speaking: ways of punishing offenders

"The United States has 5 percent of the world's population and 25 percent of the world's prison population. We rank first in the world in locking up our fellow citizens."

Ethan Nadelmann, The Drug Policy Alliance, New York

Women prisoners in Arizona preparing for chain gang duty

1 In groups Discuss the following questions with other students.

a What is your initial reaction to the photo on this page?
b Can you imagine what "chain gang duty" involves?
c Can a punishment like this happen in your country?

2 In pairs

STUDENT A: Read the information below.
STUDENT B: Read the information in Activity Bank 6 on page 129.
STUDENT C: Read the information in Activity Bank 7 on page 129.
STUDENT D: Read the information in Activity Bank 8 on page 130.

Prison statistics for the U.S.
1 There are now 1.6 million people in prison in the U.S. This is 0.5 percent of the population, and 1 percent of the adult population of the country.
2 In total, seven million people—or 1 in every 32 American adults —are behind bars, on probation, or on parole.
3 Drug offenders account for about two million of the seven million.
4 One in every 36 Hispanic adults is currently behind bars, while the number for African-American men is 1 in 15.
5 One in every nine African-American men aged 20 to 34 is now serving time.

3 In groups Discuss what you have read. Make notes about what you hear from the other students in your group.

4 Work together to answer these questions.

a Which group of people is most likely to be in prison in the U.S.?
 1 Hispanic adults
 2 drug offenders
 3 young African-Americans
b What has happened to the UK prison population since 1993?
 1 It has remained the same.
 2 It has reduced by half.
 3 It has nearly doubled.
c What percentage of Russian adult males have been in prison before?
 1 25
 2 35
 3 50
d What do the Chinese prison figures not include?
 1 people who have committed an offense
 2 people who have been charged but not put on trial
 3 people who have offended before
e What difference is there between Chinese prisons and American and British prisons?
 1 Prison numbers are going up more slowly in China.
 2 There are more people in each cell in China.
 3 The prison population in some areas of China is getting smaller.

5 Discussion What do you think?

a What does the information tell you about different countries' attitudes to crime and punishment?
b Do you know any comparable statistics about the prison population in your country?

6 Read this list of crimes and
answer the questions.

arson	kidnapping
assault	manslaughter
blackmail	murder
burglary	robbery
drug trafficking	smuggling
fraud	treason
identity theft	vandalism

a Which of the crimes are
  – against people?
  – against property?
  – against businesses?
  – against the state?
  (Some could be more than one, or none of them.)

b Which of them do you think are serious crimes, and which are
  not so serious? What do you base your opinion on?

c What kind of punishment do people who commit these crimes
  receive in your country?

Vocabulary 1: crime

7 Match the news items with the crimes in Activity 6.

a They were accused of setting fire to the office where they
  worked.
b He was sentenced to two years' imprisonment for the attack on
  his neighbor.
c The gang took the ambassador's children and kept them in the
  forest for three days.
d When the border guards opened the trunk of the car, they found
  several cases of whisky.
e The two youths were sentenced to a year's community service
  and told to clean the walls that they had painted.
f She attempted to open a bank account using her employer's
  personal details.

8 Complete these crime reports. Think of details yourself.

a Simpson was arrested and charged with assault the day after
  he …
b The environmental campaigner was charged with vandalism after
  she was seen …
c He was accused of arson after he …
d She was arrested on suspicion of identity theft when she tried
  to …
e The three men were convicted of treason because of …

9 Describe what is happening in the illustrations. What is the crime?

Vocabulary 2: punishment

10 Explain what the following
types of punishment involve.

a a fine
b confiscation
c community service
d a custodial sentence
e corporal punishment
f capital punishment

11 Read the information about
punishments that people
received. What kinds of
punishments are they? Do
you think they are fair?

a He had to pay $5,000
  after his dog ran into the
  road, causing a collision
  between three vehicles.
  No one was hurt in the
  accident.
b When he was 14, he was
  paddled by the school
  principal for repeatedly
  failing to do his
  homework.
c She was sent to prison for
  six months when she
  refused to pay her local
  taxes. She claimed that the
  authorities were not
  providing adequate
  services.
d When she arrived in the
  U.S. with some rare
  plants, they were taken
  away from her.
e The three men were
  executed for selling drugs
  to children.

Courage of their convictions ...

The house **lights go down**, the hum of audience conversation dies away. In the darkness, the orchestra starts playing. The stage lights fade up to reveal 12 women dressed in black, singing and dancing the opening number of the musical *Chicago*.

Even though the music is clearly being played by professionals, it is immediately obvious that the singers and dancers are amateurs. But this is no ordinary musical theater event. It is not being performed in London's West End or on Broadway in New York, but **behind locked doors** in a high-security women's prison!

We are at Bronzefield Prison near London and the women on stage are all inmates. Some of them have been convicted of violent crimes. They are performing a musical about two women who end up in prison after committing murder.

Welcome to the amazing world of Pimlico Opera, a London-based company that spends six weeks a year working in prisons, **culminating in** public performances of musicals in which inmates share the stage with professionals. The company has worked with almost one thousand prisoners, who have performed to more than 25,000 members of the public.

Last year, Pimlico Opera put on a production of the musical *Les Misérables* at London's Wandsworth Prison, where the inmates are men. Again, the musical is about a crime. The story begins when a convict is released from a French prison after serving 19 years for stealing a loaf of bread and for **subsequent attempts** to escape.

Most of the Wandsworth cast were long-term inmates. I spoke to one of the cast, a 22-year-old man who was serving a life sentence for murder, which he was six years into. "Working on this show has helped me learn how to control my anger, and it's made me listen to instructions without shouting back," he said. "**I come from a violent background** but doing this has helped me to express myself more calmly."

Although artistic projects such as these are becoming more common in British prisons, not all prison officers agree with them. In spite of opposition from among his own staff, the governor of Wandsworth **gave the project his blessing**. "We have to encourage prisoners to see what they're capable of. Some of them have never been praised and we must let them have some **positive feedback**."

Even so, he admits that this is not enough justification for these programs. "I have to convince the director-general of the prison service that it improves the behavior of the prisoners," he added. "Being part of this project must motivate the prisoners to change the way they behave. It can't be just fun for them."

You can find out more information about Pimlico Opera at http://omtf.org.uk/pimlico

Quotes from the Bronzefield cast of *Chicago*:
*names have been changed

"I turned 24 during rehearsals and am currently serving a seven-year sentence for smuggling drugs. Working on a production with Pimlico Opera is really good as it has given me a chance to prove I have talent. My sentence has had a lot of downs but I'm able to look back at this and feel proud."
Ainslie*

"I'm 21 years old, and this is my first conviction. I've been here since October, and can truly say that being in this play has been one of the best experiences of my life and I've learnt so much about my abilities and myself. This project shows me there's nothing we can't achieve if we put our minds to it. I have never done anything like this before but I've had a great experience."
Terry*

"I'm 19 years old and English is not my first language, but I used to be a nightclub dancer in my country. When I took part in *Chicago* I really enjoyed myself, especially the 1920s dancing. We had a ball and I made nice friends. I felt as if I were in a warm family. It was a great project which made us really happy and we forgot about depression and stressful times. Now I'm looking forward to becoming a professional dancer in the future." Lina*

12 Read the text on page 24 quickly. Which paragraphs contain the following information?

a general information about Pimlico Opera

b information about a previous production by Pimlico Opera

c the feelings of prison staff about theatrical activities

d the atmosphere at the beginning of the show

13 Answer these questions and give details to support your answers.

a Are all the members of the *Chicago* cast in prison?

b Does the musical have any connection with the lives of the performers?

c Does Pimlico Opera work with prisoners all the time?

d Is this the first time the company has worked with prisoners?

e Are there similarities between the shows at Wandsworth and Bronzefield?

f Is there any evidence that performance changes the way prisoners behave?

g Does the governor of Wandsworth have everyone's support?

h The title of the text is a play on words, because *conviction* has two meanings. Explain the meaning of the title.

14 Read the quotes from the Bronzefield cast and find words and expressions to describe the following:

a Someone who had a birthday while working on the show

b People enjoyed working on the production

c Someone who has never been in prison before

d someone has had problems during his or her time in prison

e Someone felt very happy working with other people.

Language in chunks

15 Choose the correct meaning for these expressions. They are in bold in the text.

a (the) lights go down ...
1 the lights go out
2 the lights become less bright

b ... behind locked doors ...
1 in the prison cells
2 with the exterior doors locked

c ... culminating in ...
1 ending in
2 adding to

d ... subsequent attempts ...
1 later attempts
2 unsuccessful attempts

e I come from a violent background ...
1 I live in a violent street
2 I was surrounded by violence

f ... gave the project his blessing.
1 agreed to the project
2 prayed for the prisoners

g ... positive feedback.
1 applause from the audience
2 a good reaction to what they do

16 Read these extracts from letters to newspapers. Are they for or against the company's work? What are your views?

... and there is no doubt that such activities are beneficial for the rehabilitation of prisoners, some of whom have known nothing but criticism and punishment throughout their lives.

The cast of *Les Misérables* are there because they have committed serious crimes. People like this don't deserve to be treated with respect. I know it's a cliché, but I think we should put them in a cell and throw away the key.

A murderer in the cast was quoted as saying that being in the show was the most wonderful thing he had ever done. I wonder what the families of his victims think.

Congratulations to, the prison service! It is a well-established fact that prisons are colleges of crime, and most inmates come out better equipped to reoffend than when they went in. Anything that shows them there is more to life than crime is to be encouraged!

Grammar: causative verbs; present continuous passive

17 Complete these sentences using one of the causative verbs at the end. Sometimes the second blank does not need to be filled in.

Examples:
*We must **let them have** some positive feedback.*
*It's **made me listen** to instructions without shouting back.*
*We have to **encourage prisoners to see** what they're capable of.*
*This project must **motivate the prisoners to change** their behavior.*

a When I was young, my parents .... me .... do whatever I wanted. *let/force*
b The prison governor failed to .... the authorities .... allow the performance to take place. *make/persuade*
c This has .... me .... understand how the victim of a crime feels. *help/permit*
d Doing this show has .... her .... study acting when she is eventually released. *motivate/get*
e The director .... him .... join a theater company when he completes his sentence. *encourage/force*
f Working on the show .... inmates .... enjoy themselves in their otherwise dull routine. *allow/persuade*
g Nobody .... me .... commit a crime. It was my own decision, and I have to live with that. *make/motivate*
h The police officer .... me .... get out of the car and stand with my hands above my head. *order/help*

Look at 4A–4C in the Mini-grammar.

18 Present continuous passive

Active or passive? Complete the questions with the active or passive form of one of the verbs in the box.

build	hold	rehearse	spend
force	perform	send	waste

a But this is no ordinary musical theatre event. It ***is not being performed*** in London's West End.
b Is the show .... by professional actors?
c The prisoners .... the show for an hour every day for three weeks before the first show.
d How many people .... in prison in the Netherlands?
e The state government .... more than $50 million on prisons.
f A lot of the money that is intended to help prisoners .... on unsuccessful literacy programs.
g As a result of the cost of prisons, not enough new schools ....
h Five hundred prisoners .... to prison every week in this country.

Look at 5A–5B in the Mini-grammar.

Functional language: expressing two sides of an argument

19 Choose the best expression to complete these opinions.

whereas
on the other hand
although
despite/in spite of
even though
even so
nevertheless

a The UK, France, and Germany have prison populations of 1 percent of the total population of those countries, *whereas* the U.S. figure is 1.5 percent.
b *In spite of* opposition from among his own staff, the governor of Wandsworth gave the project his blessing.
c Some U.S. states still have the death penalty for murder, ... it has been abolished in countries that belong to the European Union.
d The number of crimes that are being committed has fallen. .... , our prisons are overcrowded.
e .... there are more police in the streets, graffiti continues to be a problem.
f People feel safer when dangerous criminals are in prison. .... , they may be even more dangerous when they come out.
g .... pleading guilty he was sent to prison for ten years.

20 Discussion Complete the quotation using one of the words in Activity 19. Then discuss Chekhov's opinion with other students.

Capital punishment kills immediately, ... lifetime imprisonment does so slowly. Which executioner is more humane? The one who kills you in a few minutes, or the one who wrests your life from you over the course of many years?

Anton Chekhov (1860–1904),
Russian short story writer
and playwright

Listening: opinions on prison

21 You are going to hear the following five people giving their opinions about prison. Before you listen, try to guess what each will say.

a prisoner currently doing time	the victim of a crime
an ex-convict	a campaigner for penal reform
a prison guard	

22 Listen to Track 8. Decide who each speaker is. What words or expressions tell you who is speaking?

23 Listen again and answer these questions.

a What prevented the ex-convict from learning as much as he wanted when he was in prison?

b What does the prison guard think is the main cause of trouble among the prisoners?

c Apart from the problem of overcrowding, what does the campaigner think is wrong about the number of people who are in prison?

d What kind of crime does the victim describe?

e Why did the prisoner think it was beneficial to get involved in a fight?

24 Explain what the prison guard means by the following.

a Most of the people here just want to keep their noses clean, ...

b ... we've got some tough guys with really short fuses, ...

c ... if something happens, they can lose it big time.

d There have been three lockdowns.

e It's a dog's life for most of them.

Pronunciation: keeping your listener interested

25 In pairs Listen to these extracts on Track 9 of people giving their opinions about prison. The speakers use some fixed expressions to keep their listeners interested. Complete the sentences below.

a I thought it would help me become a better person ....

b That's all they're interested in, ...

c ... they think they've done a good job, ...

d .... , if I'd spend any more time in that place, I would have gone crazy.

e .... , I'd been locked up during the trial, ...

f Then they brought me here, and it was really the pits, ... ?

g .... I shouldn't have done it, ...

What expressions in your language do speakers use to keep the listener interested?

Writing: discursive essay

26 Read the prison case histories of these three people. Discuss the differences between their prison experiences.

CASE 1

William Bessant, who is 52 years old and comes from a village in Norfolk, England, has spent 35 years of his life in prison. He has never committed a serious offense in his life. Almost all his convictions have been for driving offenses, often for driving without paying his road tax and insurance. The most serious offense that he has ever committed is damage to other vehicles. He has never caused injury or death to anyone. Bessant admits that he has probably become so used to living in prison that after a short time in the outside world, during which he usually lives with his sister, he behaves in a way that lands him back in prison.

CASE 2

On January 3rd, 2008, Charles Chatman (right) was released from prison in Dallas, Texas, after spending 27 years behind bars for a crime he did not commit. The African-American was convicted of rape in 1981 and sentenced to 99 years in prison. He was finally exonerated by a DNA test, the fifteenth person to be exonerated in Dallas in the last seven years. In the following three months of 2008, two more Dallas prisoners were cleared after DNA evidence proved they were innocent.

At the time of his arrest in 1981, Chatman could not afford a lawyer. "The DA (District Attorney) offered me a 12-year sentence if I agreed to plead guilty," he said. "But I would not accept that because I was innocent. At the time, I trusted the legal system would find out the truth."

CASE 3

In 1994, John Henry Claiborne kicked in the back door of the home of Homer and Vivian Allbritton in Little Rock, Arkansas, held them at gunpoint, and robbed them. He even took Mrs. Allbritton's wedding ring from her finger as she lay on the ground. Claiborne then stole the Allbrittons' car and drove away. He was soon arrested, put on trial, and sentenced to 375 years behind bars. Claiborne remained in prison until 2004, when Governor Mike Huckabee commuted his sentence and he was released.

Greg Allbritton, the son of Homer and Vivian, says that his mother isn't the same person she was before this happened. "She's afraid Claiborne will come back and hurt her again," he said. Claiborne was arrested again for drug dealing in 2007. He is currently free on bail and still lives in Little Rock.

27 Write a "for and against" essay with the following title: *Is prison always the best solution?* Use the case histories on this page, and any other cases that you know about.

Review: grammar and functional language

28 Complete the news item, using each verb in the box once in the right form.

agree
allow
encourage
force
help
motivate
order

The jails in Ventura County, California, are overcrowded. Built to accommodate about 1,500, they now house nearly 1,900 inmates. Some inmates are **a** .... sleep on beds in spaces formerly used as common rooms. Last month the city's mayor **b** .... the prison authorities **c** .... do something about it. At the same time, the sheriff's department has been trying to find ways to **d** .... inmates **e** .... improve themselves through education.

Convicted offenders can now reduce their sentence if they **f** .... spend more time in class. Inmates sentenced to 45 days or more in jail can earn up to ten days of credit by passing high school graduation tests or taking courses such as English as a Second Language and Introduction to Computers.

There is also an in-service training program that **g** .... certain inmates **h** .... work during the day and return to jail at night. Ellen Worthy, who teaches ESL and computers at one of the Ventura jails, is excited about the new program. "Inmates have to feel **i** .... study and become better people. This new program **j** .... them **k** .... feel better about themselves, which is the icing on the cake," she said.

29 Complete this conversation by adding an alternative opinion.

ANDY: I don't think prisoners should be allowed to perform in musicals.
DORA: I agree. It's making their life too easy.
YOU: ....
ANDY: Prison is a punishment and prisoners should know they are being punished.
DORA: That's right. If you make it too soft for them, they don't want to leave!
YOU: ....
ANDY: If it goes on like this, prisons will be more like vacation spots!
DORA: Yes! They'll be standing in line to get in!
YOU: ....
ANDY: Look! There is absolutely no evidence to suggest that prisoners benefit from this kind of thing.
DORA: Right! I bet when they leave prison, they just pick up where they left off.
YOU: ....

Review: vocabulary

Word List

arson	kidnapping
assault	manslaughter
blackmail	murder
burglary	offender
to commit a	robbery
crime	smuggling
drug trafficking	suspicion
evidence	treason
fraud	vandalism
identity theft	victim
imprisonment	

Word Plus

to be cleared of a crime
behind bars
behind locked doors
capital punishment
community service
to commute a sentence
corporal punishment
custodial sentence
to exonerate
to give something your blessing
inmate
on bail

30 Fridge, trash can, suitcase Look at the word lists. Decide if they are words you would use regularly, never, or in the future. List them in your notebook.

31 Read the list of crimes in the Word List and decide which are the three most serious and the three least serious.

UNIT 4

Modern love

→ love and romance
→ looking back and looking forward
→ grammar: conditional structures

Listening: how we met

1   In groups Look at these different ways of meeting a potential mate. What are the advantages and disadvantages of each of them?

2   You are going to listen to Karen and Jake talk about how they met. First listen to Karen on Track 10. Then answer the questions.

a   Where was she living?
b   What was she doing before they met?
c   Why was she online?
d   How did she feel when she met Jake online?
e   What attracted her to him?
f   How did the relationship develop?
g   When did they meet in person?
h   Was he how she had imagined him to be?

3   Now listen to Jake's story on Track 11.

a   What had he been doing the night they met?
b   Why did he go online?
c   What attracted him to Karen?
d   Where did they choose to meet and why?
e   Was she how he imagined she would be?

4   Compare Karen's and Jake's stories. What are the similarities and differences in the things they talk about?

5   Listen again and note down how many times they use these different "fillers":

	Karen	Jake
a um	....	....
b uh	....	....
c you know	....	....
d I don't know	....	....
e kind of	....	....

Complete their final sentences:
KAREN: ... it's weird to think that if I .... online that night, we ....
JAKE: if .... for that one night/ early morning, seemingly a random meeting, um that we .... met and, uh, and now we're married.

6   In pairs Imagine you are Jake or Karen the day after you met online. Tell your friend about what happened. Your friend can choose whether to encourage you or discourage you.

7   In groups Do you think this is a good way to get to know someone? Why or why not?

Grammar: conditional structures

8   Read these conditional sentences. Which type of conditional are they? Put the right letter in the box. You can use 6A in the Mini-grammar to help you.

a   If she hadn't gone online, they might never have met.
b   I would tell you who he was if I knew.
c   She'll help you if you ask.
d   If he likes someone, he always asks her out immediately.

zero conditional ☐
first conditional ☐
second conditional ☐
third conditional ☐

9 Complete with a conditional structure.

a You won't meet anyone if you .... (not go out)!

b If she .... (not gone) to the party, she wouldn't have met Jack.

c If it rains tomorrow, we .... (not go) for a picnic.

d If they hadn't met, they .... probably .... (live) with their parents right now.

e You wouldn't have missed the party if you .... (read) your emails regularly.

10 Decide which type of the conditional sentences a–e are and write the number in the box. Use 6B in the Mini-grammar to help you.

1 **A past event that has happened or has been happening that may affect the future.**

2 **A real or unreal situation in the present that is related to the past.**

3 **An unreal past action that may affect the present.**

a If I had moved to Paris, I would be speaking French now. ☐

b If you have been paying attention, you'll understand this. ☐

c She would never have married him if he weren't rich. ☐

d They won't be hungry if they have already eaten. ☐

e I wouldn't be in this mess if I had listened to my mother. ☐

11 Write mixed conditional sentences for these situations, using the words given.

a Kristen and Ted didn't get married this year because they don't have enough money at the moment.
If they had ...

b Emily and Steve don't know Harry very well so they didn't introduce him to Rachel.
They would have ...

c Christine didn't call Jake back, so she doesn't have a date tonight.
If she had ...

d Martin waited all night for Jenny and now he's feeling sad.
He wouldn't be ...

e Josh is confident that Carmen will go on a date with him tomorrow if she received his flowers yesterday.
If Carmen ...

Pronunciation: *would* in conditional sentences

12 Listen to Track 12 and write the sentences out in full.

13 Listen again and notice the different ways of saying the abbreviation of *would*. Now practice saying the same sentences in different ways.

14 Look at the sentences in Activity 11 and practice saying them in different ways.

15 **In pairs** Read this story and make at least five conditional sentences about it.

Example: If Anthony Hopkins hadn't gotten the role in the movie, he wouldn't have been looking for the book.

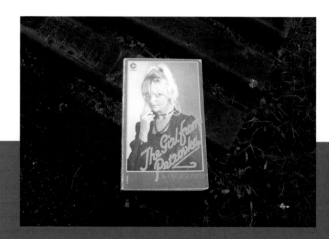

The actor Anthony Hopkins was very happy in 1971 to hear that he had gotten a role in a film based on the book *The Girl from Petrovka* by George Feifer, a love story between a Russian ballerina and an American reporter. A few days after signing the contract, Hopkins went to London to buy a copy of the book. He looked in several bookshops, but he couldn't find the book anywhere. While he was at Leicester Square station, waiting for his train home, he noticed a book that had been left on the bench—it was *The Girl from Petrovka*. Two years later, in the middle of filming the movie in Vienna, Hopkins was visited by George Feifer, the author. Feifer mentioned that he did not actually have a copy of the book himself. He had lent his copy—with all his notes in it—to a friend who had lost it somewhere in London. Hopkins handed Feifer the book he had found. "Is this the one?" he asked, "with the notes scribbled in the margins?" It was the same book.

Do you know of any strange coincidences?

16 Listen to the people on Track 13 talking about their hopes, wishes, and regrets. Which ones are expressing hope about the future (H), wishes for the future (W), regrets about the past (R)? Write the letters in the boxes.

a ☐   b ☐   c ☐   d ☐
e ☐   f ☐   g ☐

17 Listen again and complete the expressions.

a I wish you .... me about the party sooner. I .... Saturday night at home and I don't want to change my plans now.

b I'm really excited about the game next week. I ....—they really deserve it.

c If only we .... more money, then we .... that new car that we really need.

d What a shame that Marco .... last year. He .... to college if he'd gotten better grades, but now he'll have to try again.

e I wish you .... about the wedding. Do you want it in the city or in the country?

f If only Jason and Carly .... to this country. They've been living abroad for way too long.

g I wish you .... the car. If only you .... in the garage when I asked you to. I'm sorry .... it to you.

18 Now put these expressions in the table.
If only + past perfect
If only + would
If only + past simple
I wish + past perfect
I hope …
What a pity/shame that …
I'm looking forward to + -ing
I'm very excited about …
I regret + -ing/having + past participle

Hopes about the future
Wishes for the future
Regrets about the past

19 In pairs Imagine you are siblings. How would you react in this situation?

STUDENT A: Go to Activity Bank 9 on page 130.
STUDENT B: Go to Activity Bank 19 on page 136.

20 In groups Talk about your hopes for the future and regrets about the past. Think about these topics, or find your own.

a your studies
b your English classes
c your next vacation
d global warming
e overpopulation

Speaking: speed dating

21 Read about speed dating.

How speed dating works

People who are looking for romance register and arrive at the allotted time. They are rotated to meet each other over a series of short "dates," usually lasting from three to eight minutes depending on the organization running the event. At the end of each interval, the organizer rings a bell or clinks a glass to signal the participants to move on to the next date. At the end of the event participants submit to the organizers a list of who they would like to give their contact information to. If there is a match, contact information is forwarded to both parties. Contact information cannot be given during the initial meeting in order to reduce the pressure to accept or reject someone to his or her face.

a How long do speed dates last?
b What do participants do if they would like to meet one of the speed dates again?
c What must you not do? Why?

22 Think of a *new* personality and complete the profile below.

Name:
Age:
Profession:
Interests:
What you want in a relationship:

Think of five questions to ask your partner.

23 Form two circles, one inside the other, with the people in the inner circle facing the people in the outer circle. You have three minutes to find out as much as you can about the person you talk to. After three minutes one of you moves over to the next person. Talk to everyone in the circle. Note the names of those whom you want to contact later.

24 In groups Compare your lists. What do you think about speed dating? Is it an effective way to meet someone? Why or why not?

CONVERSATION TIPS

Starting a conversation
- Take care when you begin a conversation not to be too direct or intrusive, e.g., **Where are you from?**
- Try to begin a conversation with an indirect comment that attracts the person's attention but is not too direct:
  A: *Wow! It's warm in here, isn't it?*
  B: *Yes, it is.*
  or
  A: *Those flowers are pretty.*
  B: *Yes, they are.*

Ending a conversation
Be careful, too, when you close a conversation. Don't just say "goodbye" and leave. Use a polite expression to show that you are getting ready to finish:
  A: *Well, I'd better get going.*
  B: *OK, well, good to see/meet you.*
  or
  A: *Well, it was very nice talking to you.*
  B: *Yes, good to see/meet you.*

Vocabulary: love and romance

25 Look at these words. Make as many expressions about love and romance as you can.

be	single	pregnant
get	married	in love
fall	divorced	children
have	engaged	

26 Read this story and make a mind map about love with words from the story.

Gavin was madly in love with Jenna. He had met her at a party and it was love at first sight for him. He had gone over to talk to her and had felt tongue-tied and nervous. He had asked her out and now he was head-over-heels in love with her! They had been dating for about six months and he still had butterflies in his stomach every time they met. He loved her deeply and in his pocket he carried the engagement ring that he was going to surprise her with.

Jenna walked slowly to the date with Gavin. Yes, Gavin had swept her off her feet and she had fallen in love with him, but now she wasn't so sure. She knew that he was a flirt; he was always looking at other women and often seemed to be hitting on them. He had even admitted that he had cheated on his ex-girlfriend. Jenna had always been a jealous person but she had been infatuated with Gavin, who had been so different from her ex-fiancé. Now she felt like her crush on him was over and she didn't know if he was the kind of person she wanted to have a long-term relationship with. She felt like it might be a good idea to break up with him.

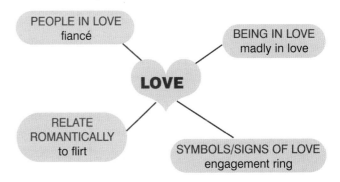

PEOPLE IN LOVE
fiancé

BEING IN LOVE
madly in love

LOVE

RELATE ROMANTICALLY
to flirt

SYMBOLS/SIGNS OF LOVE
engagement ring

Compare your mind map with others. Add as many other words and expressions as you can.

27 In groups Do you think their relationship will last? Why or why not?

28 In pairs Role play the conversation between Jenna and Gavin when they meet for the date.

29 **In groups** Discuss these questions:

a What is virtual reality?

b Do you have any "friends" that you have never met in person?

c Do you need to meet someone in person to be their friend?

d Do you know anything about multiplayer virtual reality games like Second Life?

30 **Now read the article and match these headings to the sections:**

Growing confusion between real life and virtual reality

Taking second place

A fantasy marriage

Together but in separate worlds

Why he traded reality for fantasy

31 **Read again and complete this table with the biodata.**

Real world
Name: *Ric*
Age: ....
Married to: ....
Occupation: ....

Second Life
Name: ....
Age: ....
Married to: ....
Occupation: ....

Real world
Name: *Janet*
Age: ....
Occupation: ....

Second Life
Name: ....
Age: ....
Married to: ....
Occupation: ....

Is this cheating?

Clare Marshall

a

In May 2008, Ric Hoogestraat, 53, a call center operator from Phoenix, Arizona, married Janet Spielman, 38, a Canadian, in a ceremony that was attended by a small group of close friends. The two own a private island, they have two dogs, they have a joint mortgage, and they spend weekends together going on long motorcycle trips. Nothing unusual about any of this, it seems at first, but actually there is. First of all, the two people have never met in person, never even spoken on the telephone, and secondly, Ric Hoogestraat was already married to Sue Hoogestraat, 58, an export agent who works for a shipping company. Ric Hoogestraat and Janet Spielman married in the virtual reality online fantasy game known as Second Life, where Ric controls an online character (an avatar) called Dutch Hoorenbeek and Janet controls an avatar named Tanej Jackalope—Tanej is an anagram of Janet and a Jackalope is a famous fictional animal, which is, arguably, what Tanej Jackalope is.

b

Ric Hoogestraat is a rather burly man with long, thick sideburns and a big gray mustache. He looks like a typical motorbike enthusiast wearing old Harley-Davidson T-shirts and sporting a long, gray ponytail. He was never really into games of any kind until he started playing Second Life six months ago. Since then he has been going online every day for six hours and staying for up to 20 hours at a time as Dutch Hoorenbeek. It's not difficult to see the attraction of the online world for Ric Hoogestraat. First of all, online he can be young again—Dutch looks like a more muscular, more youthful version of Ric. Avatars often look like physically enhanced versions of the people who control them. Secondly, in Second Life he's a successful business man. In real life Hoogestraat has a job that pays $14 an hour, while in Second Life he has 25 people who work for him and he's a wealthy man worth about 1.5 million lindens (the currency of the game), which is about 6,000 US dollars. In Second Life, Dutch owns a mall and various clubs on his island. He also designs and sells fancy swimwear and lingerie, which is worn by the "exotic dancers" at his clubs. Earlier this year Hoogestraat needed real-life surgery that left him unable to move for five weeks. During that time he was in Second Life for up to 20 hours a day. Often Ric Hoogestraat has had little control in his real life, while in Second Life Dutch Hoorenbeek has had total control.

c

Meanwhile, his real-life wife, Sue, sits alone. She says that being married to someone who plays Second Life can be devastating—it is like being widowed. She wonders how long it will take her husband to snap out of his obsession with his fantasy life and come back to real life and to her. At the same time she recognizes the pull of his fantasy world where no one gets old and where your dreams can come true, and stay true.

d

Ric Hoogestraat doesn't know what all the fuss is about, because for him it's just a game. However, research is showing that more and more people are becoming involved in Second Life and other similar games and that the boundaries between the virtual world and the real world are becoming more and more fuzzy. Dr. Nick Yee from Stanford University found that 40 percent of men and 53 percent of women considered their online friends as equal to or better than their real-life friends in a survey he conducted of 30,000 gamers. Perhaps Sue is right to be concerned when there are over 30 million people involved in these types of games from all over the world and when more and more people are squandering their real lives in favor of their online lives.

e

But life (and Second Life) goes on, and on a typical scorching summer day in Arizona, where the temperature can reach 120° F, you'll find Ric Hoogestraat sitting at his computer in his shaded bedroom, and his wife, Sue, watching TV in the living room. On Ric's screen Tanej plays with Jolly Roger, one of their dogs. On Sue's screen is a daytime drama show. Ric is in his fantasy world as Dutch with his online wife and his other friends, while Sue is in hers. They continue to argue over which one is worse.

32 Vocabulary What do these words from the text mean? Complete the sentences with one of these words in the right form.

argue	enthusiasm	scorch
burly	fuzzy	squander
devastated	lingerie	widow

a Her husband died and so she became a
....
b The sun was so hot that it began to
.... the grass, which turned brown.
c He inherited a fortune from his grandparents, but quickly .... the money on new cars and things he didn't need.
d Jackie's eyes could not focus on the letters and everything looked .... just before she fainted.
e She loved painting and went to her new class with great ....
f I don't want to .... with you, but I don't agree with what you are saying.
g A new underwear store opened at the mall and women lined up to buy the latest .... styles from Europe.
h There was one table left in the restaurant, but the .... man had trouble fitting into the space between two tables around it.
i The news was a big shock and he left her feeling ....

What different parts of speech are the words (1) in a–i and (2) in the text? Make definitions and compare them.

Example: A _widow (noun) is a woman whose husband has died. Widowed (adjective) means that your husband has died._

33 In pairs Do you think the man in the text is cheating on his wife? Why or why not? Imagine you are his wife or girlfriend. What would you do or say to him to encourage him to spend more time with you? Compare with another pair.

34 Read the ads on the right.
Where would you see them?
Match the photos with the ad.

Looking for a single dad

Unfortunately, life doesn't always go as planned. I had hoped that when I got married and had a family it would last forever. But it didn't —so here I am.

I'm a fit, intelligent, nice-looking, fun-loving professional. I have a fantastic 4-year-old daughter and I'm looking for someone similar who enjoys life, has kids of his own, and adores them.

I'm not looking for love at first sight—it would be great to be friends first—but I'm looking for that special chemistry that suggests we would be good together. Do you think that could be you?

Please send me a picture and we'll take it from there!

Looking to meet someone new?

Let me tell you something about myself. I'm 20 and have a great job. My only complaint is that I work nights, so I don't always get to go out and do stuff normal 20-year-old guys get to do and I don't always get the opportunity to meet new people. As far as spending my free time is concerned, I'm a movie fan, I also like a good party and I love to travel when I get the chance. I'm very independent, so you won't have to worry about my being needy—I'm not. I actually enjoy having fun by myself, although in my experience it's even better to have someone to share adventures with. Do you think you've got what it takes? Tell me about yourself and let's see.

35 Which ad or ads fit(s) the following statements?

a This person doesn't necessarily want someone who has a lot of money. ....

b This person is a single, white female looking for a long-term relationship. ....

c This person doesn't like people who are too sure of themselves. ....

d This person likes being by herself or himself sometimes. ....

e This person has a job that prevents her or him from meeting people. ....

f This person would like to have a friendship before a romance. ....

g This person is looking for someone who has children. ....

SWF seeks LTR

I'm seeking a long-term relationship with a smart, nice guy—a nonsmoker between the ages of 43 and 51.

I'm a good person, but I'm not very good at marketing myself to others. I enjoy hanging out with my family and going to movies, clubs, and all kinds of museums. I like to play board games and I'm really intimidated by people who are overconfident. I exercise, but I wouldn't call myself athletic. I'm 5'9" tall, in good shape, and I love being an aunt, but I'm not interested in having children. I work hard but I'm not particularly ambitious and I don't need material things to be happy.

As for my personality, I'm shy, but as you get to know me you'll find that I have a lot of love to give and I want to feel loved in return. I always pay for myself and I've learned to stand on my own two feet. Money can't buy what I'm looking for: a man with a lot of integrity who wants to find a relationship that brings out the best in both of us.

36 Identify the sections in each ad that:

a describe appearance
b describe personality
c say what the person is looking for

37 Now write an ad about you or a person you know.

38 In groups Put the different ads together and see which ones would make a good match.

Review: grammar and functional language

39 Change these sentences using the word or words given.

a I wish I hadn't eaten that pie. I feel nauseated.
Example: If I hadn't eaten that pie I wouldn't feel nauseated.

b We always get hungry when we go on long car trips.
If …

c Kevin regrets falling in love with Jane because now he can't concentrate on his work.
If …

d Katie is going on vacation and she's very excited about it.
looking forward

e Larry is sad that he broke up with Angie.
regret

f Kristina has always wanted to learn French.
wish

g Jack didn't get the job he wanted.
pity

40 Look at Crystal's summary. Then imagine you are Crystal. Write an email to a friend about your regrets, hopes, and wishes.

Jan 1st

Last year	This year
failed my exams	Retake my exams.
out with friends too much	See friends less.
Lost job at pizzeria – late all the time	Find a new job.
Rob left me, because I cheated on him.	Find a new boyfriend.
Dog, Rusty, ran away.	Rusty might come back.

Dear Mandy,
Well I really messed up last year! I wish I hadn't gone out with my friends all the time …

Review: vocabulary

Word List

blind date	single
boundary	speed dating
burly	to adore
divorced	to bond
enthusiasm	to break up with someone
excited about something	to date
fiancée/fiancé	to fall in love
fuzzy	to flirt
if only	to go out with
infatuated	to have a crush on
jealous	to look forward to
lingerie	to regret
married	to scorch
online dating	to squander
pregnant	virtual reality
real-life	what a pity/shame!
relationship	widow/widower

Word Plus

butterflies in your stomach	single, white female (SWF)
devastating	to ask someone out
engagement ring	to be madly in love
head-over-heels	to click a glass
long-term relationship (LTR)	to hit on someone
	to sweep somebody off their feet
physically enhanced	tongue-tied

41 Choose one of the words or expressions from the Word List and Word Plus to complete this text. Sometimes more than one answer is possible.

By 1955 Marilyn Monroe was established as a sex symbol and wanted to become a serious actress. Around the same time she began .... Arthur Miller, the great playwright. They .... in the summer of 1956 and Miller became her third husband. She had .... Joe DiMaggio, the famous baseball player, in 1954. Marilyn really wanted to get .... with Miller, but she had two miscarriages and never had a child. Miller and Monroe seemed to be an unlikely couple—she was beautiful and vivacious while he was serious and intellectual, but they seemed to be .... Miller even wrote a play for Marilyn to star in, which shows how .... he was with the star. The couple .... in 1961.

UNIT 5

Absolute power

Speaking: What is power?

1 **Look at the photos and share any information you have about the people, places, and objects.**

   Example: Ferrari cars have been made in Italy since 1929.

2 **Discussion Think about these questions.**

   a In what way does each photo represent the concept of power?
   b Which of the images do you think is the strongest representation and why?

Ferrari Enzo

Chinese weightlifter, Cao Lei

Mount St. Helens volcano eruption

American President Barack Obama

Challenger tank

American dollars

Koeberg Nuclear Power Station, South Africa

Iguaçú waterfalls, Brazil/Argentina border

Power tends to corrupt; absolute power corrupts absolutely.
   Lord Acton, British historian, 1834–1902

3 **Now try to disagree that the photos represent the concept of power. Say what else you think they stand for. For example:**

   In my opinion, the Ferrari represents style rather than power …
   A weightlifter makes me think of strength, not power …

Vocabulary: abstract nouns

4 **Review Complete this list of abstract nouns and their related adjective forms.**

Noun	Adjective
power	powerful
strength	
love	
	hateful
kindness	
	sad
	cruel
	furious
	violent
	respectful
pride	
pleasure	
	relieved
disappointment	
anger	
	courageous
charity	
	lonely
happiness	
charisma	
	stylish
	embarrassed
	joyful
beauty	
mischief	
	lucky
boredom	
surprise	

5 Complete the sentences using a word from the list.

a My failing the exam was a great .... to my parents.

b The firefighters showed tremendous .... when they went into the burning building.

c Although I live alone in the city, I never feel ....

d The woman was extremely .... when her three-year-old daughter told the mayor that he was fat.

e It was late, I was getting nervous, so I felt a great sense of .... when the bus finally arrived and I was able to leave that part of town.

f Bowing low is a sign of great .... in Japan and other Asian countries.

g He built up the firm from nothing and he takes great .... in its success.

h There's a very .... scene in the film when several people are attacked by a mob.

6 Read the poem about happiness. Rewrite it with your own images.

HAPPINESS is …
Happiness *is purple*
It smells *like sea air*
It tastes *like strawberry shortcake*
It sounds *like a choir of angels*
It feels *like a new T-shirt*

Now write a similar poem about POWER.

Reading: *from The Godfather*

7 **Read the information about *The Godfather* and answer the questions.**

The Godfather is a novel written by American author Mario Puzo and was first published in 1969. It tells the story of Don Vito Corleone, a fictitious Sicilian Mafia leader based in New York City. The novel is set between 1945 and 1955, with flashbacks to Corleone's earlier life.

The plot deals with a gang war fought between the Corleones and five other New York Mafia families. After Don Vito is shot, two of his sons, Sonny and Michael, take over the family "business." Michael is a studious young man and a decorated war hero, but when he takes over the family business he proves to be even more ruthless than his father.

The novel comes to a dramatic climax when Michael has his two main enemies assassinated. Michael then sells all his business interests in New York and moves to Las Vegas, where he attempts to live as a legitimate businessman.

The novel was an immediate and unprecedented success for a well-respected but not widely known writer. It is one of the biggest-selling crime novels of all time and stayed at or near the top of the *New York Times* bestseller lists for 69 weeks.

It formed the basis for a 1972 film of the same name, directed by Francis Ford Coppola, with screenplay by Puzo and Coppola. It stars Marlon Brando as Vito Corleone and Al Pacino as his son Michael.

Two film sequels, with new contributions made by Puzo, were made in 1974 and 1990. The first and second films are widely considered to be two of the greatest films of all time. *The Godfather 1* was voted the second greatest film in American cinematic history, after *Citizen Kane*, by the American Film Institute.

a Have you seen *The Godfather* films? What did you think of them?

b If you haven't seen the movies, does the story appeal to you? Give reasons.

c Do you know any extra information about *The Godfather* book and films?

Before you read Read the sentences from the passage in the novel on the right. Is sentence 1 or 2 closer to the meaning?

a "Brasi's reputation for violence was awesome."
  1 He had a big reputation for violence.
  2 His reputation for violence was a mistake.
b "His kind was a rarity."
  1 There were many people like him.
  2 There were few people like him.
c "Brasi held himself stiff with respect."
  1 He stood like a soldier.
  2 He was very embarrassed.
d "He stuttered over the flowery congratulations he offered."
  1 He didn't speak his words fluently and confidently.
  2 He spoke his words fluently and confidently.
e "He had to be handled as gingerly as dynamite."
  1 He had to be treated carefully.
  2 No one should go near him.

Backstory *It is the wedding day of the daughter of New York Mafia boss Don Vito Corleone. During the wedding, Corleone allows certain guests to visit him in his office to ask for favors. One of the visitors is Luca Brasi, a man who wants to give something rather than receive ...*

Luca Brasi was indeed a man to frighten the devil in hell himself. Short, squat, massive-skulled, his presence sent out alarm bells of danger. His face was stamped with a mask of fury. The eyes were brown but with none of the warmth of that color, more a deadly tan. The mouth was not so much cruel as lifeless; thin, rubbery and the color of veal.

Brasi's reputation for violence was awesome and his devotion to Don Corleone legendary. He was, in himself, one of the great blocks that supported the Don's power structure. His kind was a rarity.

Luca Brasi did not fear the police, he did not fear society, he did not fear God, he did not fear hell, he did not fear or love his fellow man. But he had elected, he had chosen, to fear and love Don Corleone. Ushered into the presence of the Don, the terrible Brasi held himself stiff with respect. He stuttered over the flowery congratulations he offered and his formal hope that the first grandchild would be masculine. He then handed the Don an envelope stuffed with cash as a gift to the bridal couple.

So that was what he wanted to do. Hagen noticed the change in Don Corleone. The Don received Brasi as a king greets a subject who has done him an enormous service, never familiar but with regal respect. With every gesture, with every word, Don Corleone made it clear to Luca Brasi that he was valued. Not for one moment did he show surprise at the wedding gift being presented to him personally. He understood.

The money in the envelope was sure to be more than anyone else had given. Brasi had spent many hours deciding on the sum, comparing it to what other guests might offer. He wanted to be the most generous to show that he had the most respect, and that was why he had given his envelope to the Don personally, a gaucherie the Don overlooked in his own flowery sentence of thanks. Hagen saw Luca Brasi's face lose its mask of fury, swell with pride and pleasure. Brasi kissed the Don's hand before he went out the door that Hagen held open. Hagen prudently gave Brasi a friendly smile which the squat man acknowledged with a polite stretching of rubbery, veal-colored lips.

When the door closed Don Corleone gave a small sigh of relief. Brasi was the only man in the world who could make him feel nervous. The man was like a natural force, not truly subject to control. He had to be handled as gingerly as dynamite. The Don shrugged. Even dynamite could be exploded harmlessly if the need arose.

9 Read the first paragraph and decide which of these photos could be Luca Brasi.

10 Now read the whole text and answer these questions. Quote from the text to support your answers.

a Is Brasi short and strong, or tall and thin?
b Is he an enemy of Don Corleone?
c Is he unhappy about his relationship with Corleone?
d Was his wedding gift given in the normal way?
e Did Brasi think much about his wedding gift?
f Does Corleone's reply have a positive or negative effect on Brasi?
g Was Corleone pleased or disappointed to see Brasi go?
h Is Brasi important to Corleone?

11 Meaning check Answer the questions about these lines from the text.

a *... one of the great blocks that supported the Don's power ...*
   Does this make Brasi sound reliable or not?
b *Ushered into the presence of the Don ...*
   Did Brasi simply walk into the room?
c *The Don received Brasi as a king greets a subject ...*
   How do you think a king receives a subject?
d *... a gaucherie the Don overlooked ...*
   What kind of mistake did Brasi make and what was the Don's reaction?
e *Hagen prudently gave Brasi a friendly smile ...*
   Why did Hagen think it was "prudent" to be friendly towards Brasi?

12 Read these sentences from the passage and give the descriptions asked for.

Example: The mouth was ... thin, rubbery and the color of veal.

Give a more attractive description of a mouth.

The mouth was full, soft, the color of roses.

a *Luca Brasi was indeed a man to frighten the devil in hell himself.*
   Describe a man whom everyone likes and no one is afraid of.
b *Brasi held himself stiff with respect.*
   Describe a less respectful way of standing in front of someone.
c *The Don received Brasi as a king greets a subject who has done him an enormous service.*
   Describe how the Don would receive someone in a less respectful way.
d *When the door closed Don Corleone gave a small sigh of relief.*
   Imagine what the Don would do if the visitor was less threatening than Brasi.
e *He had to be handled as gingerly as dynamite.*
   Describe how to handle someone who is easier to control.

13 Discussion Work in groups and discuss these questions about the style and content of the passage.

a The first two paragraphs describe Brasi's frightening power. Which words indicate this?
b The fourth and fifth paragraphs describe how Don Corleone behaved towards Brasi. Which are the key words in this description?
c Explain the meaning of the last sentence in the text.

Language in chunks

14 Read the following sentences and think of situations or details to make the meaning clear.

Example: As soon as she walked in, I heard **alarm bells** ringing.
I knew that there would be an argument between her and her ex-boyfriend.

a I opened the briefcase and found that it was **stuffed with cash.**
b Tom wasn't very pleased when his boss gave **flowery congratulations** to one of his colleagues.
c Seeing the notice on the wall always makes me **swell with pride.**
d When the plane landed, everyone gave a **sigh of relief.**
e He's like a **natural force,** which is good in some ways but a real problem in others.

Grammar: zero article (–) and definite article (the)

15 Study the examples of zero and definite articles with abstract concepts.

*His presence sent out alarm bells of **danger**.*
*We were made aware of **the danger of an attack**.*
*Hagen saw Brasi's face swell with **pride** and **pleasure**.*
*I can't describe **the pride I felt** when I received the award.*
*Nothing can compare with **the pleasure of a great rock concert**.*

Now decide whether these sentences need a definite article or not.

a I am always impressed by .... power of a thunderstorm.
b It takes more than .... strength to climb Mount Everest.
c "I've always depended on .... kindness of strangers." Blanche Dubois, *A Streetcar Named Desire*
d She found it hard to suppress .... frustration she felt when he ignored her.
e It's important to show .... respect when you visit another country.
f This examination wouldn't test .... intelligence of a five-year-old child.
g Her face didn't show .... surprise she was feeling.
h Forget about .... love. I'd rather fall in chocolate!

Look at 7A–7C in the Mini-grammar.

16 Choose an abstract noun that can be used in all three sentences. Decide if the sentence also needs a definite article.

Example:
He was sentenced to *life* imprisonment.
She never got used to the *life* of a secretary.
Life is much more fun if you have an interesting job.

a CARE is a .... that works extensively in Africa.
  They say that .... begins at home.
  He gave 10 percent of his earnings to ....
b Puzo's writing .... creates a marvelous tension.
  I really don't like .... of this year's fashions.
  Brad Pitt has more .... in his little finger than I have in my whole body.
c The organization is committed to preventing .... to animals.
  The Don was famous for his .... but also for his fairness.
  The police were astonished by .... of the attackers.
d It came as a .... to hear that she had decided to emigrate.
  A good ambush needs an element of ....
  .... he showed when he got the prize was charming.
e Hercules had .... of ten men.
  I hope she has .... to get over the terrible news.
  The weightlifter's .... was phenomenal.
f .... is in the eye of the beholder.
  Looking at the flowers in the garden makes me realize .... of nature.
  Aristotle believed that .... was in the object, not in the mind of the person looking at the object.

Look at 7E in the Mini-grammar.

17 Functional language: describing emotions.

Read the examples of ways of describing positive and negative emotions. Can you add examples to either list?

Positive emotions
I'm on cloud nine.
I'm as happy as a lark.
I'm high as a kite.
I feel like a million dollars.
I'm walking on air.
I'm on a high.

Negative emotions
I feel sick to my stomach.
I feel as sick as a dog.
I feel down.
I feel like death.
I feel as if my whole world has collapsed.

Now answer the questions using the expressions. Then think of more situations when you would use them.

a How do you feel when you win something—a race or a prize, for example?
b How do you feel when you wake up and know that you can stay in bed all morning?
c Can you define the feeling you get when your favorite team loses?
d How would you feel if a doctor told you that you could never eat your favorite food again?
e How would you feel if someone gave you two free tickets to see your favorite band live on stage?

The
ROMAN EMPIRE
about the middle of the 2ⁿᵈ Century A.D.
by Karl Wolf.
Scale 1:20 000 000

18 Background Read the information about Julius Caesar. How much of it did you know already?

Julius Caesar was a Roman soldier and politician whose armies were loyal and devoted to him, and with whom he extended the boundaries of the Roman Empire north and west to the Atlantic Ocean and Britain, killing more than a million people in the process. Back in Rome, Caesar made bitter enemies amongst those who felt that his ambition and desire for absolute power were against the principles of the Republic. He was murdered on March 15th (the Ides of March) by a group of senators led by Caesar's former friend Brutus.

19 A lecture You are going to hear a lecture about Julius Caesar. Which of the following words do you expect to hear? Underline them.

charisma ☐   courage ☐   dictatorship ☐   disappointment ☐

disintegration ☐   glory ☐   love ☐   loyalty ☐   pleasure ☐

popularity ☐   poverty ☐   power ☐   relief ☐   wealth ☐

20 Listen to the lecture on Track 14. Put a check mark after the words in Activity 19 that you hear. Compare your list with another student's.

21 Listen again and answer these questions.

a Who is Professor Harding giving the lecture to?
b What does he think the audience already knew?
c What are his two main arguments?
d How does the audience member misunderstand him?
e What does the Chair suggest after the interruption?
f What did Caesar achieve as a soldier?
g What happened after the first civil war?
h What was the long-term consequence of the assassination?

22 Rewrite these lines from the lecture, changing the nouns in bold to adjectives.

Example: The armies gave him complete **loyalty**.
The soldiers were completely **loyal** to him.

a He knew that success would give him **wealth**.
b Land was given to the soldiers who had fought with such **courage**.
c Someone with Caesar's **charisma** makes lots of enemies.
d It would also lead to **popularity** amongst the common people.
e The people who assassinated him probably breathed a huge sigh of **relief**.

Pronunciation: shifting stress

23 Read the list of words aloud. Is there a change of stress between the noun and adjective forms? Underline the stressed syllable.

charisma	charismatic
loyalty	loyal
possibility	possible
responsibility	responsible
territory	territorial
courage	courageous
popularity	popular
repetition	repetitive
success	successful
wealth	wealthy

Now listen to Track 15 and check.

Writing: a film review

24 Read the review of *The Godfather* Part 1 and answer these questions.

   a Look at the headline first. What do you expect to read in the review?

   b Was the review written when the film was first released? How do you know?

   c What does the writer do in the first paragraph?

   d What does he do in the second paragraph?

   e What are the third and fourth paragraphs about?

Coppola's Mafia drama is a masterpiece. Hank Groves takes a twenty-first century look at a Hollywood classic.

The Godfather, the first in a trilogy of films about the Corleones, a New York Mafia family, was released in 1972. Directed by Francis Ford Coppola, and based on the novel by Mario Puzo, the film starred Marlon Brando as Don Vito Corleone and gave Al Pacino his first starring role as Corleone's youngest son, Michael. The film won three Oscars, including Best Picture and Best Actor for Marlon Brando.

Vito Corleone is a family-loving but ruthless businessman whose family is drawn into a Mafia gang war when they refuse to participate in the drug business. After Vito is shot, his hot-headed son Sonny (James Caan) becomes acting head of the family, but the violence escalates. Youngest son Michael returns home to take control and becomes embroiled in the violence himself.

The film is almost faultless, with unforgettable performances from Brando, the brilliant Pacino, and a terrific ensemble cast. The pace is perfect, moving dramatically between moments of calm and intense violence. It was also the first in a sequence of films and TV programs that took a deeper look at the Mafia culture (*Goodfellas*, *The Sopranos*, etc.).

Hollywood took a gamble when they selected the relatively unknown Coppola to direct this film, and Coppola may have done the same when he persuaded Brando to play the part of Don Corleone. At the time, Hollywood producers considered Brando to be box office poison. How wrong they were! The role secured his reputation as America's greatest film actor.

---

25 Write a review of a film, a TV program, or a computer game. Check the Writing Tips box for content ideas.

WRITING TIPS

Writing a review

Before you start, consider the following:

- Remember that you are writing the review for someone who may or may not have seen the film or TV program.
- It is important not to give away too much detail about the story and certainly not about the ending.
- There are three parts to a review: (1) some factual information (the director, the stars, etc.); (2) a summary of the plot/storyline; (3) your personal opinion about the film.
- If you can, add any extra information you have heard about the film. (See paragraph 4 of *The Godfather* review.)

Now make notes for your review:

- What are the key pieces of information for the three parts of the review?
- What are the most attention-grabbing details?
- What headline would you write if the review was appearing in a newspaper or magazine?

Extras:

- Can you find a photograph on the Internet for the article?

Review: grammar and functional language

26 Read the conversations and choose the best reply: 1, 2, or 3. If you don't like any of them, think of another example.

   a A: How did you feel after you failed the exam?
      B: 1 I felt as happy as a lark.
         2 I felt as if my world had collapsed.
         3 I felt a bit down.

   b A: What do you feel just before you make a parachute jump?
      B: 1 I feel as if I'm being sent to prison.
         2 I feel as high as a kite.
         3 I feel OK.

   c A: What's it like when you eat your favorite food?
      B: 1 I feel very guilty—as if I shouldn't be doing it.
         2 I don't feel anything at all.
         3 I'm in heaven.

d A: Describe how you feel when you're talking to your best friends.
  B: 1 I feel relaxed and on top of the world.
    2 I feel nervous and inarticulate.
    3 I feel empty.
e A: How do you feel in your English classes?
  B: 1 I feel like a soldier in the army.
    2 I feel uncertain and afraid.
    3 I usually feel a little frustrated.

Word List

awesome	hate	sadness
beauty	intelligence	stiff
boredom	joy	strength
charisma	kindness	style
charity	loneliness	subject (person)
confidence	loyalty	success
courage	mischief	surprise
cruel	popularity	territory
disappointment	power	to acknowledge
embarrassment	pride	to be subject to
familiar	prudent	to shrug
fury	relief	to stutter
generous	repetition	violence
glory	respect	wealth
happiness	responsibility	

Word Plus

acting head	mask of fury
alarm bells	natural force
based on (the novel by...)	prudently
	regal
box office poison	sigh of relief
bridal couple	squat
Caesar was no fool	stuffed with (cash)
embroiled in (the violence)	swelled with pride
	took a gamble
gaucherie	to usher in
in the presence of	

27 Read these examples of images relating to the abstract concepts in the Word List.

a Charity isn't just giving money to people; it's showing a real interest in making people's lives better.
b Respect is listening to someone speak, and not nodding your head and saying, "Yeah, right" or "I know, I know" every ten seconds.
c Pleasure is chocolate ice cream.
d Charisma is walking into a room and stopping the conversation.
e Relief is a long, deep exhalation of air when something dangerous or difficult is over.
f Success is seeing your name in the newspapers.
g Boredom is gray and cold.
h Embarrassment is going to a party in a costume and then finding out it isn't a costume party.

Now write your own images of some of the concepts. Use the same ones or different ones.

28 Complete these sentences with an expression from the Word Plus box in the right form.

a I ran back to the café, saw my phone on the table, and gave a huge ....
b In the 1990s, various states in the former Yugoslavia became .... a conflict with each other.
c We didn't know which tour to go on, so we .... and went with the driver with the nicest smile. It paid off—he was a great tour guide.
d The Harry Potter films are .... stories that were written by J. K. Rowling.
e My dad said his chest .... when he saw me receive the prize.
f I was really puzzled. My suitcase was .... old newspapers. Who could have put them there?
g I must say that when the stranger said he had to come into my apartment to check something, ... started ringing in my head.
h He really has no idea what's going on. He's .... of the company until they appoint a new chief executive.

29 **Fridge, trash can, suitcase** Look at the word lists. Decide if they are words you would use regularly, never, or in the future. List them in your notebook.

Gone, but not forgotten

→ synonyms and antonyms
→ using discourse markers
→ narrative tenses

Speaking: What was their legacy?

1 In groups Match these names to their pictures. What do you know about them?

Eva Perón ☐   Malcolm X ☐   Dian Fossey ☐

Bruce Lee ☐   Jacqueline du Pré ☐   Yuri Gagarin ☐

Where was she or he from?
What did she or he do?
How did she or he die?

2 In groups of six Each student reads about one famous person then tells the others the answers to Activity 1.

STUDENT A: Turn to Activity Bank 10 on page 130.
STUDENT B: Turn to Activity Bank 20 on page 136.
STUDENT C: Turn to Activity Bank 22 on page 137.
STUDENT D: Turn to Activity Bank 24 on page 138.
STUDENT E: Turn to Activity Bank 26 on page 139.
STUDENT F: Turn to Activity Bank 31 on page 142.

3 Who made the biggest contribution to the world? Rank them in order. Consider:

a what they had already done.
b how old they were when they died.
c what they would have achieved if they had lived longer.

4 Compare your order with other groups. Think of other people who have contributed to the world. Rank them and add them to your list.

CONVERSATION TIP
Taking turns
In a conversation, look for signals that tell you when to speak.
Also give people signals that you want them to join in the conversation.
For example:
- Falling intonation This is often a signal that the speaker has finished and you can speak:
  So, we went to the party and saw Jody, Kevin, Rob, and ...
- General questions These give other speakers a chance to speak:
  What do you think about X? or just *What about you?*
  But be careful, too, that you don't lose your turn because you hesitate too long before you say something.
- Time to say more Use phrases like these to give you more time to think:
  There's one more thing I want to say, ...
  Another thing is, ...
  Well, ...
  Um, ...

Listening: What happened to Amelia Earhart?

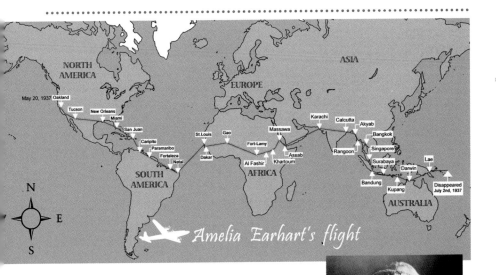

Amelia Earhart's flight

5 Look at the map. You are going to hear the trailer for a TV program about a person. Who is she? Can you guess what she was famous for? Listen to Track 16 and check your answer.

6 Listen again and say whether these statements are true or false.

a Nobody had ever made the journey that she was making.
b She was alone in the plane.
c Most people think that the plane crashed into the ocean.
d Her airplane was never found.
e Radar was used to detect her plane.

7 Complete this synopsis of the program using these words.

search
castaways
theories
Equator
disappearance
crash
survive
spy
2,500

7 PM THURSDAY

What happened to Amelia Earhart?

A new documentary that looks at the famous aviator as she attempts to be the first person to fly around the world along the .... What happened to her on the .... mile third-to-last leg? The show looks at the 16-day .... for Earhart and Noonan in the days following their ....
The show will then examine the four .... about what happened to her. Did she really .... and die in the accident or did she .... and return to the U.S.? Was she a .... for the U.S. or did she and Noonan die on an island as .... ?

Which of the theories do you think is the most probable and why?

Pronunciation: reading a prepared script

8 Listen to part of the script on Track 17. The marks in the first sentences show how the speaker adds drama to his reading.

ˈ= stress

‿ = links between words

The disaˈppearance of ˈAmelia ˈEarhart has reˈmained‿a ˈmystery for‿over ˈ70ˈyears. Many think that the so-called "crash and sink" conclusion is actually wrong. Immediately after her disappearance there are reports of SOS calls from her radio and people begin to hope that she is still alive. There is no radar in 1937 so authorities rely on radio news for information about her whereabouts. There are conflicting messages all through the day and all through the night, but no sign of Earhart or her plane.

9 Listen again. Finish marking the sentence stresses and the links between words. Notice the intonation.

10 **In groups** Now practice reading the script in the same way using your marks to help you.

11 **In groups** Find information about another mysterious disappearance that has never been solved. Record a trailer for a program about it.

Grammar: narrative tenses

12 Read the extracts below and match them to 1–7. You can use 8A–8H in the Mini-grammar to help you. Comment on the structures used in each case.

a By the time I was 12 my parents had already gotten divorced. They had never really been in love and had tried to make it work for the sake of the children.

b Martin was going to be a lawyer. He knew he would never be able to stand the sight of blood, so he was planning to go into the only other profession his father would approve of.

c She's working in a bank at the moment and she lives in a little apartment. She works out three times a week and goes to the movies once a month.

d By the time we meet again, next year, we will have known each other for ten years and I'll have lived in this city for 11 years.

e After I've finished this novel next week, I'm going to start on my next book, which is going to be a non-fiction book.

f In 2006 Caroline went to Greece for the first time. She worked as a journalist in Athens and stayed for four years.

g She's planning to travel to South America in the summer. First she's going to fly to Lima and then she'll travel overland to Chile.

1 talking about the present
2 talking about the past
3 talking about the future
4 talking about the past from the past
5 talking about the future from the past
6 talking about the past from the future
7 talking about the future from the future

13 Now write the numbers 1–7 on this timeline

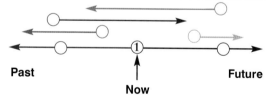

Past   Now   Future

14 Look at these sentences and comment on the use of tenses and the time reference. You can use 8A–8H in the Mini-grammar to help you.

a So I get to the party last night and Lucy tells me Jason's already gone home.

b I wish you cleaned up your room more often.

c I'm having dinner with Suzy. / I'm having dinner with Suzy later.

d My bus leaves at 9 PM tonight. / The bus leaves at 9 PM every day.

15 Read this story and number the events in the order they happened.

Marie Curie, née Maria Skłodowska, was born in Warsaw in 1867. She received a general education in local schools. After becoming involved in a students' revolutionary organization she left Warsaw for Cracow before going to Paris in 1891. While at the Sorbonne she met Pierre Curie, and they were married a year later. By the time she earned her Doctor of Science degree in 1903 she had already succeeded her husband as head of the physics laboratory at the Sorbonne, and following the tragic death of Pierre Curie three years later, she took his place as Professor of General Physics in the Faculty of Sciences. In 1911 Marie Curie won her second Nobel Prize, this time for chemistry, eight years after having been honored with the Nobel Prize for physics with her husband. After visiting Poland for the last time in 1934, Marie Curie died from a disease caused by exposure to radiation.

☐ She went to Cracow.
☐ She went to Paris.
☐ She became involved in a students' revolutionary organization.
☐ She met Pierre Curie.
☐ She got married.
☐ She won the Nobel Prize for physics.
☐ She won the Nobel Prize for chemistry.
☐ Pierre Curie died.
☐ She became Professor of Physics.

16 Tell the story of Harold Holt using these notes.

Harold Holt, b. 1908, Sydney, Australia. Began law degree 1927 in Melbourne, graduated 1930. Joined United Australia Party, 1933. Met Zara Dickens 1934, elected to House of Representatives, 1935. Married Zara, 1946. Became Prime Minister of Australia, 1966. Disappeared while swimming, Dec. 17, 1967. Search for body lasted three weeks. Holt was never found.

Reading: famous actors die young

17 In groups Look at these three photos. What do you know about these people? Answer these questions about each one.

What's his name?
What was his profession?
What is he famous for?
How old was he when he died?
How did he die?

18 Now read the text and check your answers.

Warning—acting can damage your life

Zena Lubowsky compares three young actors and asks: Is acting a dangerous profession?

After the tragic death of Heath Ledger in 2008 by accidental overdose, attention has been drawn to other actors who also died young but left an indelible impression on the world through their screen work. Journalist Bob Thomson remembers interviewing Heath Ledger when he was playing Bob Dylan in the movie *I'm Not There*. Thomson says, "Ledger, friendly enough, was pasty and thin as he spoke—almost manic. Phoenix looked and talked in the exact same manner when I interviewed him a few weeks before he died of an overdose on Halloween night, 1993." Thomson is referring here to River Phoenix, who like Heath Ledger had a reputation for being obsessive about his work, preparing for roles by immersing himself completely in the character and world he was portraying. Phoenix was just 23 when he overdosed on heroin and cocaine after visiting Johnny Depp's club, The Viper Room, on Sunset Boulevard. He was in the middle of filming a movie called *Dark Blood*, which was never completed, but which dealt with the theme of nuclear testing and its effects. Phoenix was a committed animal rights and environmental activist and is probably best known for his role in the movie *Stand by Me*. Like Ledger, Phoenix's public image was mainly that of a clean-cut, responsible, and hard-working actor. Little was known about the depression and compulsivity the young man suffered prior to his death.

Ledger, on the other hand, had completed his now infamous portrayal of the Joker in *Dark Knight*, and many say that the role had affected him deeply. Jack Nicholson, who had also played the Joker in an earlier Batman movie, is famously quoted as saying "I warned him," when hearing of Ledger's death. It was said that Ledger was an insomniac and had admitted to having trouble switching off from his role as a psychotic, murderous clown. At the same time, Ledger had recently split from his longtime girlfriend, Michelle Williams, with whom he had had a child named Matilda, and was said to be suffering from anxiety over the separation from his daughter.

But, of course, Phoenix and Ledger are not the first promising actors to die young and tragically. Decades earlier a young actor named James Dean was making a name for himself, both as a bright new star in the film industry and as a tortured soul prone to depression, and with a less than healthy penchant for drugs and alcohol. Dean had made just three movies in his short life when he died at the age of 24 in a car accident as he made his way to Salinas, California, to take part in a sports car race. Car racing was a passion of Dean's, and when Dean introduced himself to the British actor Alec Guinness outside a restaurant, Dean asked Guinness to take a look at his car, a Porsche 550 Spyder. Guinness thought the car appeared "sinister" and told Dean: "Please never get in it. If you do, you will be dead within a week." This happened on September 23rd, 1955, exactly seven days before Dean's death in the car crash.

Being an actor requires achieving a delicate balance between your professional life and your private life, between who you really are and who you want to be. Unfortunately, it's often hard for young actors who are thrust to stardom to maintain that balance.

19 Fact check Who ...

a ... played Bob Dylan in the movie *I'm Not There*?
b ... is Bob Thomson?
c ... looked similar to River Phoenix?
d ... was obsessive about his work?
e ... warned Heath Ledger about playing the Joker?
f ... loved car racing?
g ... predicted that Dean would die in his car?
h ... often find it difficult to separate their work from their real lives?

20 Complete the sentences with one of these words from the text.

outlet	penchant	insomniac	manic
sinister	longtime	pasty	

a I have a .... for very sweet desserts. I really love chocolate cake and lemon mousse.
b Because of his financial worries he wasn't sleeping well, but he would not normally qualify as an ....
c She was a .... accountant who had decided to become a social worker. After 22 years with the accountancy firm Johnson and Maddox, she went to study for a master's in social work.
d After the wedding she went from feeling ecstatically happy to feeling very sad, and she didn't understand where this .... behavior was coming from.
e He had nothing to do, but he needed an .... for his feelings of aggression, so he took up boxing.
f After two weeks without going outside, he felt very unhealthy and he looked very pale and ....
g There was something very .... about the fact that the door to the office was left open and some papers had been moved. Had someone broken into the office?

Language in chunks

21 In pairs Follow these instructions and make notes. Use the expressions in bold. Then tell your partner your answers.

a Write one thing that you are **prone to**.
b Name someone who has **made a name for herself or himself** as a singer.
c Name a famous person who has **split** from another famous person recently.
d Do you know any **committed environmental activists**?
e Name a scientist who has left an **indelible impression** on the world.
f Name a person you think is a **tortured soul**.
g Name someone who has been **thrust into the limelight** recently.

22 Talk about famous people using the expressions.

23 In groups Discussion

a What problems do famous people have in their private lives?
b Are famous people more likely to be "tortured souls"? Why?

Vocabulary 1: antonyms

24 Find opposites in these two groups of words. Sometimes more than one answer is possible. There is not a match for every word.

> indelible   detached
> thin   manic   obsessive
> committed   responsible
> infamous   psychotic
> murderous   tortured
> delicate   unfortunate

> relaxed   sane
> loving   robust   scruffy
> famous   lucky
> fortunate   unknown
> chubby   laid-back
> strong   calm   forgettable
> dirty   unmotivated
> irresponsible   organized
> compassionate   placid
> involved

25 Use the words above to describe these people.

Albert Einstein
a mass murderer
Mother Teresa of Kolkata
Angelina Jolie
Mahatma Gandhi
Adolf Hitler
Pelé

Vocabulary 2: synonyms

26 Read these two descriptions of the same person and list the different ways of describing the same thing.

Example: not very good-looking / the most handsome man in the world

A He was not very good-looking, a little chubby, and a mediocre singer. He had dark hair, which he swept back in a ridiculous style, and his eyes always looked tired. His nose was fairly large, and he had a crooked mouth and fat lips that made him look unpleasant.

B He was one of the most handsome men in the world, tall and slim. He was also one of the most talented singers, with a totally unique, sexy style. He had thick black hair and dark, moody eyes. He had a very attractive straight nose and full lips that smiled seductively.

Can you guess who they are describing? Turn to Activity Bank 11 on page 131. Which description do you agree with?

27 In pairs Write a description of a person.

STUDENT A: Write from a positive perspective.
STUDENT B: Write from a negative perspective.

Compare your descriptions.

Functional language: using discourse markers

28 Listen to this extract from a radio program about Anita Roddick on the first part of Track 18. Put a check mark after the discourse markers that you hear from the list.

after that ☐	during ☐	second ☐
although ☐	first ☐	then ☐
and ☐	furthermore ☐	therefore ☐
because ☐	however ☐	though ☐
before ☐	in 1976 ☐	thus ☐
besides ☐	in spite of ☐	when ☐
but ☐	meanwhile ☐	whereas ☐
by 1991 ☐	moreover ☐	while ☐
by 2004 ☐	nevertheless ☐	
despite ☐	on the other hand ☐	

Now write them in this table according to the meaning.

Contrasting ideas	Adding something	Cause/reasons	Time

29 Now listen to the rest of the story on the second part of Track 18 and find more discourse markers. Add them to your table.

Add all the discourse markers from Activity 28 to your table.

30 Look at these sentences from the radio script and the discourse markers in brackets. Choose the correct marker and say each sentence again, making any changes necessary.

a On March 17th, 2006, L'Oréal purchased Body Shop for £652 million starting a controversy **due to** L'Oréal's involvement in animal testing. (**because / meanwhile**)

b **In addition to** this the company is part-owned by Nestlé which has been criticized for its treatment of third-world producers. (**thus / furthermore**)

c **However,** Anita Roddick countered this by insisting on having direct input into decisions made by the company. (**besides / nevertheless**)

d **Despite** the enormous wealth accumulated from the Body Shop, Roddick was not interested in money and **so** chose to give away her fortune to charity in 2006, leaving nothing for her daughters to inherit. (**although, therefore / moreover, on the other hand**)

e Roddick was also involved in activism, campaigning for environmental and social issues, **and** founded **Children On The Edge** in 1990, ... (**as well as / in spite of**)

f Roddick had contracted Hepatitis C **as a result of** a blood transfusion she had received following the birth of her second child and she died of liver disease in 2007. (**whereas / due to**)

Writing: a biography

31 Read the story of Dorothy Stang. Which paragraph(s) contain these parts of her biography?

- description of her death
- information about her birth and childhood
- description of what she did
- description of her personality

Important people of our times: Dorothy Stang

Dorothy Stang was born in Ohio in 1931, and after leaving high school she decided to become a Roman Catholic nun. She was a strong believer in social justice, and her beliefs took her to the Brazilian rainforest in the 1960s, where she began to work with poor and disempowered farmers and peasants in the Brazilian Amazon. She later became a naturalized Brazilian citizen.

Stang's work involved two main goals: first, she was concerned about the protection of the rainforest and the serious threat to it from loggers, who were carrying out illegal deforestation. Second, she was fighting to protect the rights of rural farmers who were being killed or thrown off their land in battles with large landowners. In addition, Stang was working to promote small-scale sustainable agriculture that would not damage the forest.

Because of the nature of her work, Dorothy Stang was not without enemies. Loggers and landowners saw Stang as a serious threat to their plans to take over and exploit the land for commercial purposes. But Dorothy Stang was courageous and dedicated and refused to be intimidated by the threats to her life, believing that her age and the fact that she was American-born would protect her. She was wrong, and on February 12th, 2005, Dorothy Stang was assassinated in Anapu as she walked to a meeting in the jungle. She was 73 years old.

32 Complete this timeline of Dorothy Stang's life:

1931
1949
1960s
1970s
1980s
1990s
2005

33 Now choose a famous person and draw a timeline of the events from her/his life.

34 Write a biography using the information from your timeline and organize the information into three paragraphs like the biography of Dorothy Stang.

Review: grammar and functional language

35 Complete the text using the correct form of the verb.

Natalie Wood (1938–1981) was an American film actress. Wood .... (begin) appearing in movies when she .... (be) five years old, ... (have) parts in successful Hollywood films and .... (star) in films like *Rebel without a Cause* (1955) with James Dean and *West Side Story* (1961). By age 25 she .... (be nominated) for three Oscars: for *Rebel without a Cause*, *Splendor in the Grass*, and *Love with the Proper Stranger*. Natalie Wood .... (marry) actor Robert Wagner in 1958. They .... (be married) for four years when they .... (divorce). She .... (remarry) Wagner in 1972 after she .... (marry) and .... (divorce) Richard Gregson and .... (have) a child with him (the actress Natasha Gregson). Her second marriage to Wagner .... (last) nine years until she .... (die) in an accidental drowning off the family yacht when she .... (be) 43 years old.

36 Look at this information about Maria Montessori and complete the paragraph using the appropriate discourse marker.

Maria Montessori was the first woman to graduate from the University of Rome, La Sapienza Medical School. **a** .... she was a member of the University's Psychiatric Clinic, she became intrigued with trying to educate the "mentally retarded" and the "uneducable" in Rome. In 1898 she gave a lecture in Turin about the training of the disabled. **b** .... it was the first time he had ever seen her, the Italian Minister of Education was so impressed by her arguments that he appointed her as director of the Scuola Ortofrenica, an institution devoted to the care and education of the mentally retarded. She accepted **c** .... put her theories to the proof. Her first notable success was to have several of her eight-year-old students apply to take the state examinations for reading and writing. The "defective" children not only passed, **d** .... had above-average scores.

    e .... her success with these children, she was asked to start a school for poor children in Rome, which opened on January 6th, 1907. She was focused on teaching the students ways to develop their own skills at a pace they set, which was a principle Montessori called "spontaneous self-development." **f** .... the success of this school, many more were opened and there was a worldwide interest in Montessori's methods of education. Maria Montessori died in the Netherlands in 1952, **g** .... a lifetime devoted to the study of child development.

a 1 Meanwhile	2 While	3 During	4 As
b 1 In spite of	2 Despite	3 Although	4 Whereas
c 1 in order to	2 so	3 therefore	4 thus
d 1 but	2 however	3 nevertheless	4 even
e 1 Due	2 Because	3 As a result of	4 Owing
f 1 Because	2 Due	3 As a result of	4 Besides
g 1 then	2 before	3 finally	4 after

37 In groups Look back at the people mentioned in this unit. Who has left the most important legacy? Why?

38 Complete this paragraph using suitable discourse markers. Practice telling the story of John Lennon. Then write the story.

John Lennon was born on October 9th, 1940. He was a singer, songwriter, artist, and peace activist. John started his first band in 1957 with his friends from school, including Paul McCartney, George Harrison, and Pete Best. Pete Best was replaced with Ringo Starr by George Martin. Lennon left the Beatles in 1969. He made several albums by himself. He was shot in 1980 in New York City by Mark David Chapman.

Review: vocabulary

Word List

castaway	obsessive
caused by	outlet
clean-cut	overdose
committed	pasty
compassionate	placid
furthermore	psychotic
insomniac	robust
irresponsible	scruffy
laid-back	sinister
longtime	skinny
manic	to intimidate
meanwhile	well balanced
moreover	whereas
murderous	

Word Plus

conflicting messages
disempowered
environmental activist
exposure to
indelible impression
no sign of somebody/something
penchant
solitude
to be prone to something
to be thrust to stardom/into the limelight
to maintain a balance
to make a name for oneself
to put something to the proof
to split from
tortured soul

39 In pairs Find (a) synonyms and (b) antonyms for as many of the words in the Word List as you can.

40 Fridge, trash can, suitcase Look at the word lists. Decide if they are words you would use regularly, never, or in the future. List them in your notebook.

Megacities

→ relative clauses and contact clauses
→ cities and aspects of urban life
→ describing a sequence of events

Speaking: city life

The must-haves of a modern city

1 A million people
83 cities with this many people in 1950; now there are nearly 500

2 Skyscrapers
6,000 in central São Paulo, more than 650 under construction, another 250 waiting for approval

3 Gated communities
600 in Johannesburg; also popular in the U.S., Mexico, Argentina, and Brazil

4 Blockbuster events
Olympic Games, World Cups, Grand Slam tennis, rock concerts—they take place only in big cities

5 Security cameras
500,000 in London; 5,000 installed in Mexico City in 2007

6 Young people
40% of the population of Long Beach, California, are aged 24 or younger

7 Nightlife
1,000 clubs in Shanghai; a new one opens every week

8 Ethnic diversity
65% of New Yorkers belong to an ethnic minority; more than 50% of new London residents are foreign born

1 In pairs

STUDENT A: Read and memorize the information for pictures 1–4. Then ask Student B questions about the information for pictures 5–8.
STUDENT B: Read and memorize the information for pictures 5–8, then close your book.

Change roles and repeat the activity.

2 In groups of three Discuss these statement starters. Then choose one each and prepare a three-minute talk to the class beginning with the words:

The one thing that really excites me about big cities is …

The one thing that really terrifies me about big cities is …

If I were in charge of a megacity, I would …

Vocabulary: cities and city life

A Skyscrapers and shantytowns, São Paulo, Brazil

B Traffic in Delhi, India

C Museum of Modern Art, New York

3 **Look at the three photos and answer these questions.**

   a What urban problem does picture A illustrate? What do you know about this problem?
   b What is the problem in picture B? Describe the situation in your area.
   c What aspect of city life does picture C illustrate? Give examples of similar things.

4 **In groups** Add words and expressions to the "cities" mind map.

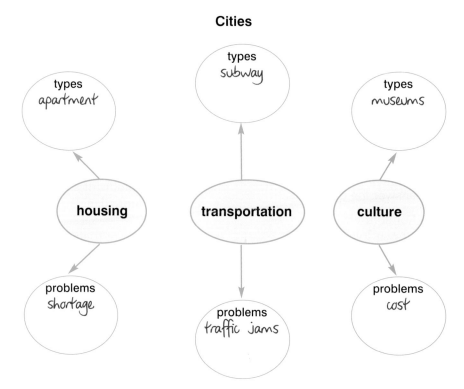

Cities

types
subway

types
apartment

types
museums

housing

transportation

culture

problems
shortage

problems
traffic jams

problems
cost

5 Compare the problems you have identified and discuss solutions.

6 Read these extracts from articles, letters, etc. What aspects of city life do they describe? Are they positive or negative?

   a The ambulance failed to get there in time because the downtown area was gridlocked.
   b We couldn't get tickets for the concert because they sold out in the first two hours.
   c Since I arrived here, I've met the most amazing people. One of the people I met actually works for the President.
   d Because of his low starting salary, he was forced to rent an apartment more than 60 miles from where he worked.
   e Two days after they started their vacation they were mugged in the street outside their hotel.
   f I couldn't believe that there was a Picasso exhibition in the gallery across the street from the college, and it was free.
   g The apartment is nice, but the people above me play loud music until the early hours of the morning.
   h The park in the downtown area is huge, and there's an exquisite Japanese garden in the middle.

Listening: Are you frightened of the city?

Tom Jacobs is a musician who lives in London, England.

Alice Carey is a hypnotherapist living in Johannesburg, South Africa.

Wilma Redding is a cleaner who lives in Chicago, Illinois.

Daniel Mason, who is an exterminator, lives in Sydney, Australia.

Vesna Lulic is a student from Bosnia whose family now lives in Stockholm, Sweden.

Wang Shen is a journalist and lives with her parents in Shanghai, China.

7   Read the biographical information above.

a   What do you know about the cities where they live?
b   Which of the people do you think may be frightened of living in a city and why?

8   You are going to hear personal statements from the six people. Before you listen, check the meaning of these expressions.

I had done a gig at a place in north London.
I just thank my lucky stars.
How can you live down there in the ghetto?
We're a tight-knit community.
He pulled a knife on the store owner.
People don't pay any attention to you.

9   Listen to Track 19, look at the photos, and write down the names of the people in the order they speak. Then answer the questions.

a   What event changed Tom's attitude to London?
b   How did Alice feel about living in downtown Johannesburg?
c   What does Wilma think about people who criticize her part of town?
d   What does Daniel think is the main reason why his part of town is safe?
e   What event made Vesna's family move to Stockholm?
f   How does Wang Shen feel about being on a bus at night?

10   Listen again and decide if these statements are true or false, or partly true.

a   Tom's trouble started because he had to change his late-night routine.
b   Alice should feel safer in her new home but she doesn't.
c   Wilma feels much happier when she's downtown.
d   Daniel feels safe in his community because he used to be a boxer.
e   Vesna thinks the people in Stockholm are very friendly.
f   Wang Shen feels frustrated at the lack of space in her apartment.

11   Tom, Daniel, and Vesna don't give all the details of the incidents they describe. Invent some details of your own and say what happened to them in each case.

a   Tom finished his gig in north London ... He was lying on the ground.
b   Someone pulled a knife on the store owner ... He won't be coming back.
c   Vesna's brother's friend was shot ... The family moved to Stockholm.

12   Discussion What conclusions can you draw from the experiences of the six people? Use these ideas to help, and say if you agree or disagree with them.

*   People feel safer if they know their neighbors.
*   You are in more danger if you live in the middle of a city.
*   Cities are more dangerous at night.
*   People are more frightened of places that they don't know.
*   If you have been in a war zone, then any city will feel safe.

Grammar: relative clauses

13 Study these examples of defining relative clauses:

*a musician **who lives** in London*
*a student **whose family** lives in Stockholm*
*a gated community **that has** guards*
*a movie **that we saw** in New York*

Now connect the two parts of these sentences.

a Denise is an architect
b She rented the apartment from a man
c I wanted a house
d It was in the suitcase
e We were able to talk to a film director
f There are many people
g They employed some guards
h This is the suburb

1 that had 24–7 surveillance.
2 that was stolen at the airport.
3 who prefer to live right in the middle of the city.
4 who had no experience of security work at all.
5 whose inhabitants were protesting.
6 who specializes in renovating old houses.
7 whose work I really admire.
8 whose brother she had met on holiday.

Read 9A in the Mini-grammar to help you.

14 Study these examples of non-defining relative clauses:

Daniel, who is an exterminator, lives in Sydney.
My neighbors, about whom I know very little, are from Bosnia.
The film, which was a worldwide success, cost very little to make.

Now complete these sentences in your own words and include a non-defining relative clause.

a My best friend, ...
b My classmates, ...
c Our English teacher, ...
d My uncle, ...
e The mayor of our town/city, ...
f The President of the United States, ...
g Shanghai, ...
h Hollywood, ...
i Brad Pitt, ...
j Shantytowns, ...

Read 9B in the Mini-grammar to help you.

15 Study these examples of contact clauses and participle clauses.

In all of them you can leave out the words in brackets:

One of the people (that) I met actually works for the President.
She's a hypnotherapist (who is) living in Johannesburg.
The people (that you ought) to ask are the folks who live here.
There was a man (who was) caught shoplifting.

Now read these sentences. Can the words in bold be omitted?

a I bought it from a man **that** I met on a train.
b We saw a lot of people **who were** waiting for someone to help them.
c The musicians **who** performed were all from Spain.
d There were some amazing photos **that were** taken from the plane.
e The person **that you should try** to talk to is the police inspector.
f Isn't that the woman **who** hosts that great music show on TV?
g Shanghai is a city **that** I really want to visit.
h We visited a town **that** has hardly changed since the nineteenth century.
i She works in a restaurant **that** received a Michelin gold star last year.
j We saw someone famous **who was** getting out of a taxi.

Read 9D–9E in the Mini-grammar to help you.

Functional language: describing a sequence of events

16 Replace the words in bold with a word or expression from the examples. Change the sentences where necessary.

*I'd been walking for about ten minutes **when suddenly** I noticed a bunch of young guys walking along on the other side of the road.*

***As soon as** I saw them, they crossed the road and began walking behind me.*

***The next thing I knew**, I was lying on the ground.*

*I **recently** moved into a gated community.*

***Before I** moved here, I was living in an apartment downtown.*

***After moving** into the gated community, I suddenly felt a sense of danger.*

*I was passing the store with a friend **as this was happening**.*

a I read an article about the problems of overcrowding **a few days ago.**

b The telephone rang **at exactly the moment** I walked through the door.

c I live in New York now. **I moved here from** Philadelphia.

d The factory fire was on the TV news, but I saw it **in real life** because I was looking out of my window when it started.

e My sister rented a car from him on Monday. **On Tuesday,** she realized that it wasn't working properly.

Reading: life in an African megacity

17 Before you read *Staying Alive in Lagos*, discuss the following questions.

a What do you know about the work of UNICEF (The United Nations Children's Fund)?

b The boy in the picture has no home. Where do you think he sleeps at night?

c How do you think he makes a living?

Staying alive in Lagos

Isaiah has spent five of his 15 years living on the streets of Lagos, Nigeria, the second largest city in Africa. Like hundreds of other children, he spends his days and nights in this **sprawling metropolis** trying to **fend for himself**. He was interviewed by the UNICEF-supported Child-to-Child Network. The resulting series, *Voices from the Street*, was broadcast to more than 60 million listeners.

"It is not easy living on the street but what can I do?" he asks. "I have two sisters that I have not seen in five years, I have smoked Indian hemp like other boys of my age, got beaten by bigger boys and been robbed of my money. I've taken a bath in the canal and slept under the bridge," Isaiah says in one broadcast. "The good thing is that I am alive!"

Isaiah works as a bus conductor—collecting fares from passengers who **squeeze on to** the yellow commercial buses of Lagos. He earns $5 to $6 a day. At the age of ten, Isaiah left his home in Ogun State. A friend, who **turned out to be** a child-labor recruiter, invited him to Lagos along with 11 other boys. "We left home without telling any of our parents," Isaiah says. The recruiter paid the boys' bus fare to Lagos. Then he took them to the city's biggest market "to sell them," according to Isaiah. "The more people he brings, the higher his 'rank' goes and the more money he gets paid," Isaiah adds. "I was eventually sold to a man for a fee of 5,000 naira (about $40). The man took me to a place I do not know; my duty there was to be a housekeeper."

After a few days, Isaiah **had had enough** and decided to run away. He met up with other street children who showed him how to survive on his own. "I started to sleep under the bridge or inside any of the buses parked under the bridge," he says. "If there are too many mosquitoes, I sleep inside the boot of the vehicles."

Isaiah hopes his family can hear his story on the radio. "I pray that the people of my place will listen," he says. "They will hear that I am still alive and that I am a big man now."

18 Read the text and decide if the following sentences are true or false, or partly true.

   a Isaiah has spent more than half his life living apart from his family.

   b The friend who invited Isaiah to go to Lagos wasn't what he seemed.

   c The yellow Lagos buses are usually full to overflowing.

   d The recruiter gets the same amount of money for all the people he finds.

   e Isaiah didn't like working as a housekeeper, so he told his employer he wanted to leave.

   f He needed help to work out how to live on the streets.

   g Mosquitoes make it difficult for him to sleep, but Isaiah has a solution.

   h Isaiah is anxious in case his family finds out what he's doing.

19 Which of these are accurate statements?

   a Isaiah hasn't seen his sisters since he was ten.

   b He's the only boy who has smoked hemp.

   c He has fought with boys who are bigger.

   d He has to wash himself in a river.

   e He ran away from home because he didn't want to be a housekeeper.

   f He always sleeps in the open air.

20 Discussion **Discuss the following questions.**

   a What can the city of Lagos realistically do to help children like Isaiah?

   b Should the government of Nigeria ask for international help?

Language in chunks

21 **The expressions highlighted in the text are used inappropriately in these sentences. Think of an alternative sentence.**

   a Oxford, England, is a sprawling metropolis of a hundred thousand people.

   b He knew lots of people when he arrived in the city and realized he would have to fend for himself.

   c The three of us were able to squeeze into the huge limousine.

   d The woman I didn't recognize, who was working in the store, turned out to be the girl I live with.

   e After working in the factory for three minutes, Dan decided he had had enough.

Writing: interpreting ideas

22 Read the ideas about city life.

   a What does Plato mean by "at war with each other"?

   b What does Michelangelo mean by "salvation"?

   c What does the city do to new arrivals according to Toni Morrison?

   d What is Andrés Duany's main message?

Any city, however small, is in fact divided into two, one the city of the poor, the other of the rich. They are at war with each other.
        Plato, 427 BC–344 BC, Greek philosopher

I have never felt salvation in nature. I love cities above all.
        Michelangelo, 1475–1564, Italian Renaissance artist

How soon country people forget. When they fall in love with a city it is forever, and it is like forever. As though there never was a time when they didn't love it. The minute they arrive at the train station or get off the ferry and glimpse the wide streets and the wasteful lamps lighting them, they know they are born for it. There, in a city, they are not so much new, as themselves: their stronger, riskier selves.
        from *Jazz*, a novel by Toni Morrison, born 1931, American author

In 1860, the capital city of Washington, with a population of 60,000, had unlighted streets, open sewers, and pigs roaming about its principal avenues. This condition was worse than the worst of our current cities. There is hope.
        Andrés Duany, born 1949, American architect and urban planner

23 Write two or three paragraphs, interpreting and comparing what the writers are saying.

Plato's comment suggests that cities are hostile places, whereas Michelangelo seems to find them inspiring.

> **Interpreting and comparing**
> X's meaning is clear/not clear in this sentence.
> What I think Y means is …
> X thinks … , whereas Y thinks …
> On the one hand, X seems to imply …
> On the other hand, Y thinks …
> As far as I understand it, X is suggesting …

Pronunciation: sounds and spellings

24 **Which of the other words in the lists rhyme with the first word?**

a **home:** come roam poem dome some

b **paid:** laid said stayed made weighed

c **enough:** tough stuff bough cough rough

d **show:** allow vow row bow (*lower your head*) bow (*and arrow*)

e **fought:** bought ought caught thought taught

Listen to Track 20 and check your answers.

25 **In pairs**

STUDENT A: Turn to Activity Bank 12 on page 131.
STUDENT B: Read the sentences on this page to your partner. Ask your partner to spell the word in bold.

a There was a lot of pink **foam** on the surface of the river.

b We watched the sunlight **fade** over the sea.

c He applied for the job even **though** he had no qualifications.

d Some of my friends **grow** their own vegetables at home.

e My uncle went to Brazil and **brought** me back a cool T-shirt.

Review: grammar

26 **Rewrite the two sentences in one sentence, using different kinds of relative clauses.**

a 1 The Brazilian architect is named Jaime Lerner.
   2 I spoke to him at a conference.

b 1 The wife of the man is called Michelle.
   2 He's the President of the United States.

c 1 There's a city less than 60 miles from here.
   2 Its population is more than ten million.

d 1 There's a man with a large file full of photos of planet Earth.
   2 He's sitting at the computer next to me.

e 1 The map of the world is on the wall above my desk.
   2 You gave it to me for my birthday.

f 1 One of the women is now the Minister of the Interior.
   2 She was arrested at the Earth Summit in 1992.

27 **Complete the text with the relative clauses (1–8).**

1 which means about three billion people
2 which is made worse by the increasing number of buses
3 some of which are still under construction
4 which is a particular problem in Latin American megacities like Mexico City and São Paulo
5 which means a city with more than ten million people
6 which puts great pressure on the road system
7 which took place in Barcelona
8 which greatly reduce the number of buses on the roads

Giving the opening speech at a meeting of world leaders and city mayors, **a** _____ , the Prime Minister of Canada warned that rapid urbanization is set to become one of the biggest challenges facing humanity in the twenty-first century. Already half of the world's population, **b** _____ , live in cities, and that could grow to two-thirds by 2050, the World Urban Forum was told.

The Canadian premier focused primarily on the problems of transportation, **c** _____ . Each Latin American megacity, **d** _____ , has distinct transportation problems. The number of private cars is rising in practically every Latin American city, **e** _____ , and everywhere buses are the main means of public transportation.

Traffic congestion, **f** _____ , is only the tip of the iceberg. The reliance on road transportation also increases air pollution, the number of accidents, and travel time.

Metro systems, **g** _____ , are in operation in all five Latin American megacities, and also in many smaller cities, including Caracas, Medellín, Pôrto Alegre, and Santiago. It is hoped that metros, **h** _____ , will be the first step in the long process of getting these major cities on the move again.

28 Choose the most likely explanation of these sentences.

a If we don't do something soon, global warming will **eventually** cause a rise in sea levels.
1 It will happen very soon.
2 It will never happen.
3 It will happen after an unspecified amount of time has passed.

b She **recently** attended a protest meeting about the new airport.
1 She attended it in the last few days.
2 The meeting was a long time ago.
3 The meeting is taking place now.

c The subway system is being **gradually** improved.
1 It is happening little by little.
2 It will happen soon.
3 The improvements are taking place all at once.

d The minister walked out of the building and was **instantly** stopped by a TV news reporter.
1 The news reporter stopped him after several minutes.
2 The reporter didn't stop him.
3 The reporter stopped him as soon as he came out of the building.

e Mexico City is **currently** the largest city in Latin America, but that could change.
1 Mexico City is the largest city at the moment.
2 Mexico City is usually the largest city.
3 Mexico City will soon be the largest city.

29 Explain these words and phrases from the Word List and Word Plus.

a Business is **booming** in the megacities of southeast Asia.
b When both parents have to work, children have to **fend for themselves**.
c The problem is the **infrastructure** of the city, which has been neglected for too long.
d The increase in taxes has led to **turmoil** among the middle classes.
e There is a real sense of **ethnic diversity** in Vancouver.
f The neighborhood was much more of a **tight-knit community** before it became just another suburb of the capital.
g You really **take your life in your hands** if you go to the port area at night.
h The brochure promised **24–7** surveillance and protection.
i Attempts to rescue them **were hampered** by rain and strong winds.
j The baby cried for hours but **eventually** it fell asleep.

30 Fridge, trash can, suitcase Look at the word lists. Decide if they are words you would use regularly, never, or in the future. List them in the appropriate part of your notebook.

Review: vocabulary

Word List

booming	paradise
bunch	recently
cab	sanitation
currently	security camera
downtown	sewer
due to	skyscraper
eventually	suddenly
ghetto	to broadcast
gig	to expand
gridlocked	to hamper
immediately	to overflow
infrastructure	to renovate
inhabitants	to squeeze into
militia	turmoil
mugged	wound (injury)
overcrowding	

Word Plus

24–7
to glimpse
bunch of (guys)
driving rain
ethnic diversity
gated community
pay attention to
shantytown
sprawling metropolis
tight-knit community
to fend for oneself
to go global
to hook up with
to pull a knife on someone
to take your life in your hands
to thank your lucky stars
under construction

UNIT 8

Spooks and sleuths

→ using a thesaurus
→ disappointment and disapproval
→ the subjunctive

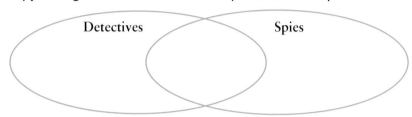

Vocabulary 1

1 Label the pictures with the names. Then match the authors and the fictional characters. Which character is the odd one out?

> Agatha Christie
> Ian Fleming
> Sir Arthur Conan Doyle
> Hercule Poirot
> James Bond
> Sherlock Holmes

2 Copy this figure. Write the words and phrases in the spaces.

Detectives   Spies

(secret) agent	interrogation	spook
counterterrorism	investigation	stake out
espionage	private investigator	surveillance
informer	security service	undercover operation
intelligence	sleuth	

Vocabulary 2

3 A *thesaurus* is a reference book that groups words of similar meaning. It helps you find the most appropriate words. Look at these thesaurus entries. Choose words from each to add to your lists in Activity 2.

detective *noun* investigator, private investigator, private eye (inf.), sleuth (inf.), gumshoe (inf.), dick (inf.), private dick (inf.), plain-clothes officer, policeman, policewoman, police officer, cop (inf.), flatfoot (inf.)

espionage *noun* spying, intelligence, counterintelligence, counterespionage, secret service, undercover work, infiltration, reconnaissance, snooping (inf.), surveillance, bugging (inf.)

spy *noun* agent, secret agent, double agent, fifth columnist, snooper, mole (inf.), informer, scout, operative

spy on *verb* observe, watch, keep under surveillance, shadow, tail (inf.), follow, keep an eye on, keep tabs on

4 Rewrite this passage using words and phrases from the entries.

Megan looked nervously into the rear mirror. There was no doubt about it: <u>she was being followed</u>. For days now she had had the distinct feeling that <u>someone was watching her.</u> <u>Playing spies</u> was obviously not to be taken lightly. She should tell someone. But who could she trust? The shabby <u>private investigator</u> seemed shifty and untrustworthy. Perhaps she should contact MI5 and let <u>real spooks</u> do the job. What she knew, or thought she knew, was too big a thing for her to handle. It was a matter <u>of national security</u>.

5 **In pairs** Think of a way to complete the story.
What does Megan know or think she knows?
Why does she think it may be a security threat?
What does she decide to do?

Speaking

6 Groups of five Prepare a simulation. An important British scientist has disappeared. Is he dead? If so, was there foul play? Has he been kidnapped? Who can help solve this mystery?

STUDENTS A AND B: You work for MI5. You need to find the right investigator to solve the case. Read the details below. Decide what kind of person you think is best for the job. Think about character, detection methods, contacts, experience, etc.

Britain's most important nuclear physicist, Sir Isaac Furlong, has disappeared and with him his technical drawings for a mega nuclear weapon. The scientist was attending a top secret conference in a secret location. The meeting was attended by internationally renowned scientists. Among them, the beautiful Olga Berkoff, a Russian expert in environmental science; Sam Austin of the World Oil Organization; Sir Cecil Carr of MI5 Service; and Sir Isaac's trusted secretary, Julia Rohan (with whom Sir Isaac was rumored to have a long-standing relationship). Security at the conference was high—no one could have entered or left the premises without the knowledge of the security personnel.

STUDENT C: Turn to Activity Bank 13 on page 132.
STUDENT D: Turn to Activity Bank 23 on page 137.
STUDENT E: Turn to Activity Bank 25 on page 138.

7 Now Students A and B explain the situation and describe the kind of person they are looking for. C, D, and E listen and make notes.

> **TIPS**
> **Presenting information**
> • Choose the most relevant information.
> • Give the information precisely and in a logical order.
> • List your requirements clearly.
> • Don't talk too fast and stress the important words.

8 In turn, Students C, D, and E introduce themselves and present arguments to persuade the panel to choose them. A and B listen and make notes.

> **TIPS**
> **Making a persuasive argument**
> • Stress the personal strengths you think will impress the panel.
> • Use rhetorical devices:
>   – hyperbole (exaggeration): *the very best, totally committed, entirely convinced*
>   – three-part statements (lists of three related things): *It's simple, it's fast, and it's (certainly) efficient.*
>   – rhetorical questions (a question for which you do not expect an answer): *Is there any doubt that I am the logical choice?*

9 Students A and B announce their decision and give reasons.

Reading: a mystery novel

10 Read the information about P. D. James. Answer the questions.

P. D. James was born in Oxford, England, in 1920. She worked in Britain's National Health Service and in the Home Office, first in the Police Department and later in the Criminal Policy Department. All that experience has been used in her novels. She's a Fellow of the Royal Society of Arts and has served as a Governor of the BBC, a member of the Arts Council, and a magistrate in Middlesex and London. She has won many awards for mystery writing in many countries, including the Mystery Writers of America Grandmaster award. She was awarded an OBE (Order of the British Empire) in 1983 and was created a life peer in 1991.

a Why is James well qualified to write crime fiction?

b What has been her greatest public recognition?

11 **In pairs** Read the blurb for P. D. James' *The Lighthouse*. What might the book be about? Make a list of ideas. Then read the excerpt from the prologue and check your ideas.

Combe Island off the Cornish coast has a bloodstained history of piracy and cruelty, but now, privately owned, it offers respite to overstressed men and women in positions of high authority who require privacy and guaranteed security. But the peace of Combe is violated when one of the distinguished visitors is bizarrely murdered.

12 **In pairs** Read the beginning of the prologue of *The Lighthouse*. Check your ideas in Activity 11.

Commander Adam Dalgliesh was not unused to being urgently summoned to nonscheduled meetings with unspecified people at inconvenient times, but usually with one purpose in common: he could be confident that somewhere there lay a dead body awaiting his attention. There were other urgent calls, other meetings, sometimes at the highest level. Dalgliesh, as a permanent ADC to the Commissioner, had a number of functions which, as they grew in number and importance, had become so ill-defined that most of his colleagues had given up trying to define them. But this meeting, called in Assistant Commissioner Harkness's office on the seventh floor of New Scotland Yard at ten fifty-five on the morning of Saturday, 23 October, had, from his first entry into the room, the unmistakable presaging of murder. This had nothing to do with a certain serious tension on the faces turned towards him; a departmental debacle would have caused greater concern. It was rather that unnatural death always provoked a peculiar unease, an uncomfortable realization that there were still some things that might not be susceptible to bureaucratic control.

There were only three men awaiting him and Dalgliesh was surprised to see Alexander Conistone of the Foreign and Commonwealth Office. He liked Conistone, who was one of the few eccentrics remaining in an increasingly conformist and politicized service. Conistone had acquired a reputation for crisis management. This was partly founded on his belief that there was no emergency that was not amenable to precedent or departmental regulations but, when these orthodoxies failed, he could reveal a dangerous capacity for imaginative initiatives which, by any bureaucratic logic, deserved to end in disaster but never did. Dalgliesh, for whom few of the labyrinths of Westminster bureaucracy were wholly unfamiliar, had earlier decided that this dichotomy of character was inherited. Generations of Conistones had been soldiers. The foreign fields of Britain's imperialistic past were enriched by the bodies of unmemorialized victims of previous Conistones' crisis management. Even his eccentric appearance reflected a personality ambiguity. Alone among his colleagues he dressed with the careful pinstriped conformity of a civil servant of the thirties while, with his strong bony face, mottled cheeks and hair with the resilient waywardness of straw, he looked like a farmer.

He was seated next to Dalgliesh opposite one of the wide windows. Having sat through the first ten minutes of the present meeting with an unusual economy of words, he sat, his chair a little tilted, complacently surveying the panorama of towers and spires, lit by a transitory unseasonable morning sun. Of the four men in the room—Conistone, Adam Dalgliesh, Assistant Commissioner Harkness and a fresh-faced boy from MI5 who had been introduced as Colin Reeves— Conistone, the one most concerned with the matter in hand, had so far said the least, while Reeves, preoccupied with the effort of remembering what was being said without the humiliating expedient of being seen to take notes, hadn't yet spoken. Now Conistone stirred himself for a summing up.

"Murder would be the most embarrassing for us, suicide hardly less so in the circumstances. Accidental death we could probably live with. Given the victim, there's bound to be publicity whichever it is, but it should be manageable unless this is murder. The problem is that we haven't much time. No date has been fixed yet but the PM would like to arrange this top-secret international get-together in early January. A good time. Parliament not sitting, nothing much happens just after Christmas, nothing is expected to happen. The PM seems to have set his mind on Combe. So you'll take on the case, Adam? Good."

Before Dalgliesh could reply, Harkness broke in, "The security rating, if it comes off, couldn't be higher."

Dalgliesh thought, "And even if you're in the know, which I doubt, you have no intention of telling me who will be meeting at this top-secret conference, or why. Security was always on a need-to-know basis."

The Lighthouse, P. D. James, Alfred A. Knopf, 2005

13 Fact check

a What kind of job does Adam Dalgliesh do?
b Why does Dalgliesh think that this particular meeting is about a murder?
c Who is present at the meeting?
d What does Dalgliesh think of Alexander Conistone?
e What kind of person may the victim be?
f Why does Dalgliesh need to solve the case quickly?

14 Vocabulary Replace the words underlined with the highlighted words in the text.

a Their inefficiency resulted in <u>complete and utter failure</u>.
b The Foreign Office <u>officially ordered</u> her to attend a meeting.
c His boss always came up with <u>new plans and processes</u> to solve problems.
d The new statistics <u>are a warning sign</u> that the company is in financial trouble.
e Harry is an <u>original</u> (some say even weird), unlike his father, who was <u>very conventional</u> and did everything by the book.

15 From the text, what kind of man do you think Dalgliesh is? Can you suggest an actor to play him in a movie?

Grammar: the subjunctive

16 Read these Internet conversations. Write the numbered sentences in a table like this.

Advice/suggestions	Explanations

female avatar 1
They had this program on the radio about MI5. How do you go about getting a job there? I want to be a secret agent for the British government! Any suggestions?

avatar 2
1 Civil Service, I guess.

avatar 1
What's Civil Service? Do you just turn up and say I want a job?

avatar 2
2 It's like, if you work for the Foreign Office or the Ministry of Defence then you're in the Civil Service. 3 Try the employment section of newspapers. 4 Or how about the MI5 website?

avatar 3
Are you actually serious? 5 Then you'd better delete this. They tend to prefer discretion!

avatar 4
So you think it's like James Bond. Better think again. 6 Most MI5 staff are chained to a desk somewhere. 7 Only a few operate without any diplomatic cover and they are probably military/police trained.

avatar 5
The pay isn't that good btw. Do you want glamour? 8 Try becoming a Bond girl in one of the movies instead.

avatar 6
9 Don't tell anyone that you're applying. I know some people who applied; they weren't even allowed to say they had put in an application.

avatar 7
Are you looking for a challenging job? 10 Why don't you do something where you help people instead of all this cloak and dagger stuff?

17 Complete the sentences in the box below with these verbs. Then answer the questions.

recommend   suggest   explain

> **Reporting verbs + *subjunctive***
> **a** "Stop reading all that spy stuff."
> She .... **that she stop reading** spy stuff.
> **b** "It's called the Civil Service because you work for the government."
> He .... **that it was called** the Civil Service because you worked for the government.
> **c** "It may be desirable to choose different reading materials."
> The tutor .... **that she choose** different books to read.
> **d** "Should you need some assistance, contact my PA."
> He .... **that I contact** his PA.
>
> 1 Sentence **b** is different from the others. Why?
> 2 What is being reported in sentences **a**, **c**, and **d**?
> 3 What difference does formality make in reporting the 5 sentences?

Read 10A in the Mini-grammar to help you.

18 Report the sentences in Activity 16 in the same way.

19 Underline the differences in the pairs of sentences.

a He looked as if he were going to explode.
  He looked like he was going to explode.
b I feel as though I were floating on air.
  I feel like I'm floating on air.
c He'd probably be killed if he were found.
  He would be killed if he was found.

Rewrite these sentences using the past subjunctive *were*. Write three similar sentences.

a He looks like he's going to cry.
b It smells like someone's burning papers.
c If I was a crime writer I'd have a female detective.

Read 10B in the Mini-grammar to help you.

Pronunciation: expressing attitude

Move away from the edge and drop the gun.

20 Listen to Track 21. Choose an adjective from the following to describe the attitude of each speaker.
aggressive   calm   unemotional   pleading   casual

21 **In pairs** Read out sentences to your partner. Your partner guesses the attitude.

22 Read out what the people are saying in these situations. Think about the stress and intonation.

I'll take that file thankyou

Easy now, Give me the bag, Ok?

EXPLOSIVE

Give me the bag, right now!

Listening: solving a crime

23 Listen to Track 22. Choose the correct synopsis.

A The son of Jonas Rushmore has been kidnapped. He agrees to pay a ransom and not to involve the police. His younger son goes to meet the kidnapper with the money. He is hit on the head. He catches a glimpse of the kidnapper and is able to give the police a vague description. The police have two suspects.

B The son of Lawrence Rushmore has been kidnapped. The kidnapper wants the younger son, Jonas, to take a ransom of half a million dollars to a drop site in a park. He is attacked. He had a good look at the assailant and is able to give the police a detailed description. The police have two suspects.

24 Listen again. True or false?

a	The Rushmores thought it would be risky to call the police.	T	F
b	Josh Rushmore was last seen on Wednesday.	T	F
c	It is unusual for Jonas Rushmore to want to spend money.	T	F
d	The police arrived on the scene quickly.	T	F
e	Bob Logan is a petty criminal, known to the police.	T	F
f	Jack Bury found the cardigan in the dumpster.	T	F
g	The police fear for Josh's safety.	T	F

25 Complete Lawrence's description of the events. Then listen again and check your answers.

"As soon as I parked the car I had the feeling I was being watched," Lawrence testified, and "I was .... through the .... when I became .... of footsteps .... fast. Before I could turn .... a heavy object .... against the back of my head. I fell down. But I didn't lose .... completely. The .... didn't quite .... me out. I managed to .... my head and saw a man's back by the light of a street lamp. Never got to see his front. He was running away with the .... bag. A tall guy with white .... He was wearing blue jeans … a dark .... with buttons. Then I .... out. Sorry I can't be more ...."

26 Can you solve the case? Explain the clue that helped you.

Functional language: expressing disappointment and disapproval

27 In pairs Look at these objects from an exhibition. What do you think the exhibition is about?

JAMES BOND IS BACK!

HARRY SALTZMAN & BROCCOLI present

FROM RUSSIA WITH LOVE

28 Listen to Track 23. Collect the expressions you hear. Copy and complete the table.

> **Expressing disappointment**
> I wish there were more posters.
> *I am rather disappointed that* you have chosen not to show this.
> *I would/wouldn't have expected* you to focus more on Fleming's books.

> **Expressing disapproval**
> I don't go in for that sort of thing.
> *I was rather dismayed to* see that particular item.
> I *(strongly/wholly) disapprove of* the display.
> It is *(quite/totally) inappropriate to* show such items.

29 In pairs You are at an exhibition called *For Your Eyes Only: Ian Fleming and James Bond*. Comment on the exhibits. Use the pictures in Activity 27 and expressions from the table.

Writing: newspaper reviews

30 Read the two reviews. How do you think they each rate *Spooks*?

0–4 bad   5–7 fair   8–9 very good   10 superb

Spooks (MI-5 in the U.S.) is a popular British TV drama. The name is a colloquialism for spies, and refers to MI5, the British Security Service.

Last night saw the finale of the ever-fantastical BBC spy series *Spooks*. It is about a group of egotistical clerical officers who take themselves far too seriously, and snoop on baddies from largely non-Christian countries.

The teams in *Spooks* frequently engage in surveillance, undercover operations, armed assaults, and more. But the show is plagued by woefully implausible plots. As long as the heroes look glamorous, the villains look evil and there's plenty of technology and split-screen fun to keep us all on the edge of our seats.

Spooks is a gripping spy show that exploded on to British screens with one of the most violent murder scenes ever shown on UK television. *Spooks* never allows its audience the luxury of knowing that the good guys will win in the end. They often don't, and since the good guys can be killed off unexpectedly, *Spooks* will have you hiding behind a cushion at least once every episode. And it will often churn your stomach, and quite possibly make you stop breathing.

The Spooks are the counterterrorist team of MI5. Led by charismatic Tom Quinn, they risk their lives each week for queen and country, fighting terrorists, neo-Nazi groups, and more. Intrigue and betrayal are par for the course. TV and movie promoters like to tell audiences that they've "never seen anything like this before" —but in this case it happens to be true. *Spooks* is one of a kind.

31 Complete the table with words and phrases from the reviews. Note whether they refer to the series, the acting, the plot, or the characters.

Positive opinion
Gripping (plot)

Negative opinion
ever-fantastical (series)

32 Write a review of a TV program or movie.

WRITING TIPS
Writing a review
- Make notes on the positive and negative aspects of the program or movie.
- Group your notes according to topic (acting, etc.).
- Think of different ways to express your views. Use a thesaurus or a dictionary.
- Get comments on your draft: are your views clear and logical?

33 **In pairs** Rate your partner's review.

Review: grammar

34 Match statements a–i with the categories in the box.

advice	order	request
agreement	proposal	suggestion
demand	recommendation	
insistence		

a   "Why don't you apply for the job?" she said to me. ....

b   "Yes, like you, I also think Jones should go," the Assistant Commissioner said. ....

c   "I know you are reluctant to do so but I repeat: you simply must attend this meeting, Lewis," the inspector said. ....

d   "How about this—you bring Bond to us and we take over from there," Goldfinger said to the double agent. ....

e   "If I were you, I'd leave immediately," Tessa said to Oscar.

f   "You ought to send your excellent manuscript to a publisher," I said to the student. ....

g   "Please come to my office at 10 o'clock promptly," her boss said to Susan. ....

h   The protesters said: "We ask the government, in the strongest possible terms, to release the prisoners." ....

i   "You will pay a $5,000 fine and all legal costs," said the judge. ....

35 Report the sentences in Activity 35 using the corresponding verb.

Example: a) *She suggested that I should apply for the job.*
She suggested that I apply for the job.

Review: vocabulary

Word List

(counter)espionage	reconnaissance
(secret) agent	renowned
acclaimed	security service
cardigan	sleuth
counterintelligence	spying
counterterrorism	surveillance
debacle	to presage
eccentric	to shadow
informer	to spy on
initiative	to stake out
interrogation	to summon
investigation/investigator	villain
private investigator/eye	

Word Plus

assailant	to be susceptible to
cop	to bug
implausible	to catch a glimpse
petty criminal	to keep an eye on/tabs on
plain-clothes officer	to keep under surveillance
spook	to set one's mind on
the matter in hand	to snoop
to acquire a reputation for	to tail
to be amenable to	undercover operation

36 **In pairs** Write a mystery story. Use as many words from the Word List and Word Plus as you can.

Jake Chapman is a secret agent who works for MI5…

37 **Fridge, trash can, suitcase** Look at the word lists. Decide if they are words you would use regularly, never, or in the future. List them in the appropriate part of your notebook.

The sky's the limit

→ determiners and partitives
→ extreme sports and activities
→ describing ambitions

Reading: two news items

1 Look first at the photo and the headline of the first news item. What do you think it is about?

2 Read the first news item and answer the questions.

a What did Yves Rossy use to do?
b How exactly did he make history?
c What was the first thing that happened when Rossy jumped out of the plane?
d What did he do to stop his fall?
e What extraordinary tricks did he perform during his flight?
f How did he manage to reduce speed enough to land?
g What are his future ambitions?
h What problem does he have to solve before he can achieve his second ambition?

Rocket Man Soars over the Alps

On May 15th, 2008, former fighter pilot Yves Rossy sat in a tiny plane 7,500 feet over the Swiss Alps and strapped on a pair of 7.3-foot-wide wings, attached to which were four jet engines. He was about to become the first person ever to make a solo jet-propelled flight.

Tension was high on the plane as Rossy prepared for his leap into history. Moments before he was scheduled to jump, a member of his technical support team spotted a problem with one of the engines. With seconds to spare, they fixed it, the door opened, and Rossy threw himself out and began to unfurl his metal wings.

After plummeting toward the Earth for an alarmingly long time, Rossy triggered the four engines, accelerated to 185 mph and soared back up toward the mountains. Steering only by using his body, he looped the loop, performed figure eights, and flipped over on his back in a 360-degree roll that even an eagle would find impossible. Eventually, he opened his parachute and landed safely on an airfield near the eastern shore of Lake Geneva.

Rossy has several new challenges in his sights. First of all, he plans to fly across the English Channel and eventually he hopes to fly along the Grand Canyon in Arizona. He admits that he has a few problems to solve before he can do this, the main one being how to carry even more powerful engines on his back and still be able to fly. "I may struggle a bit to stay airborne," he admitted, "but I'm sure we can sort it out."

3 Match the words in blue with these definitions.

a go faster
b switch on
c turn quickly
d go down fast
e go up high
f guide, usually by means of a device
g solve
h attach
i have difficulty with
j unroll or spread out
k notice

4 Use the words in blue to complete these sentences.

a Before the plane took off, one of the passengers had .... some liquid dripping from the engine.
b We managed to .... the problem with my passport when we reached Immigration.
c When there was a break in the traffic, Jean put her foot down and .... past the truck in front of her.
d The police .... to control the demonstrators who were trying to get into the building.
e Shortly after blastoff, the captain of the spaceship .... the automatic controls.
f He .... the skis to the top of his car before they set off for the mountains.
g The eagle swooped down to the river, caught a fish, and .... into the sky again.
h You .... a hang-glider by moving from side to side.

5 In groups Discuss these questions.

   a How do you think Rossy felt in the few minutes before he jumped out of the plane?
   b How do you think his technical support team felt?
   c What do you think was the main emotion felt by all of them when Rossy landed?
   d Why do you think people do things like this?
   e Would you do something like this; or something a little less daring? Describe it.

6 Look at the photo and the headline of the second news item below and predict the content.

7 In pairs Both of you read the article. Then:

STUDENT A: Close your book. Tell Bethany's story to your partner.
STUDENT B: Listen and ask Student A questions to elicit any information he/she has forgotten. Give clues to help, if necessary.

The Courage of the One-armed Surfer

Before she had even reached her teens, Bethany Hamilton was already a surfing champion. She came first in a competition for girls aged 15 and under when she was only 10, and had already won a medal the year before. Living in Hawaii and with lots of opportunities for practice, it seemed certain that she would go right to the top of her chosen sport.

All that changed dramatically on October 31st, 2003. Thirteen-year-old Bethany went for an early morning surf with some friends on Tunnels Beach, Kauai. As she was lying on her surfboard waiting for a wave, she had her left arm dangling in the water. Suddenly, a ten-foot tiger shark attacked her, ripping off the arm just below the shoulder. Showing incredible bravery, Bethany managed to get back to the shore, where one of her father's friends made a tourniquet out of a surfboard rope. She was then rushed to hospital for emergency surgery. By an astonishing coincidence, the person whose surgery had to be postponed to accommodate her was her father, who was about to have an operation on his knee. Despite losing 70 percent of her blood in the attack, she survived.

Three weeks later, surfers were astonished to see Bethany back on the beach and surfing again. Within a year, she was surfing competitively. In 2005, she came first in the U.S. National Scholastic Surfing Association National Championships. In 2008, competing against the world's best women surfers in an Association of Surfing Professionals tournament, she was awarded third prize.

8 Complete these sentences.

   a Bethany won her first surfing competition
      1 when she was a teenager.
      2 before she was a teenager.
      3 when she was 13.
   b She was able to practice a lot because
      1 she was a champion.
      2 she lived in a place where there were surfing opportunities.
      3 she enjoyed surfing.
   c The incident happened
      1 before she had started to surf.
      2 while she was surfing.
      3 after she had finished surfing.
   d She survived because
      1 she didn't lose much blood.
      2 she lost a lot of blood.
      3 someone helped her to stop losing blood.
   e By coincidence, her father
      1 was waiting for her at the hospital.
      2 had an accident the same day and was rushed to hospital.
      3 was about to be operated on when she arrived at the hospital.
   f Bethany started surfing again
      1 within a week.
      2 within a month.
      3 within a year.
   g She took part in an international competition and
      1 came first.
      2 won a prize.
      3 didn't win a prize.

9 Discussion Discuss the questions.

   a In different ways both Yves Rossy and Bethany Hamilton are brave people. What adjectives would you use to describe them?
   b Are they role models for other people? What kind of people?
   c Would you tell these stories to a class of primary school children? Why or why not?
   d If you could ask Yves and/or Bethany just one question, what would it be?

Vocabulary: extreme sports and activities

10 Match the pictures with six of the extreme sports on the right.

BMX biking	rock climbing	snowboarding
bungee jumping	scuba diving	surfing
hang-gliding	skateboarding	water-skiing
kiteboarding	skydiving	white-water rafting

11 Now complete these definitions.

a .... is a form of competition cycling on bicycles with special wheels, which originated in California in the 1970s. It is now an Olympic sport.

b .... is swimming underwater, carrying your own source of breathing gas (usually compressed air). You can stay underwater longer than you can if you are snorkeling.

c .... is an activity in which you jump from a high place (often a bridge over a river) with one end of an elastic cord attached to your ankles and the other end to the jumping-off point. When you jump, the cord stretches to take up the energy of the fall, then you fly upwards as the cord snaps back. You go up and down until the energy created by the jump has finished.

d .... is a sport that involves going down a snow-covered slope on a board attached to your feet using a special boot. It was inspired by surfing and skateboarding, and the sport shares superficial similarities with skiing. It became a winter Olympic sport in 1998.

e .... is an air sport in which you hang by flexible straps from a machine made of a fabric wing in an aluminum frame. The machine is controlled by shifting your body weight, although some have aircraft flight control systems.

f .... involves jumping out of an aircraft and then freefalling, before releasing a parachute.

12 Answer these questions.

a Which of the illustrated sports isn't defined?
b Which sport isn't illustrated but is defined?
c Can you define the sports that are not defined? Use the words and expressions in the box to help you.

rappel	inflatable boat	rough water
balance	kite	tied to
boots	paddle	wave (in the sea)
crampon	rope	wind power

13 **In groups** Answer these questions about the sports on this page. Then share your answers with other groups.

a Has anyone in the group or anyone you know tried any of these activities? If so, share any stories with the rest of the group.
b Which of the activities appeal to you and why?
c Which of them don't appeal to you? Why not?
d If you had the chance to do one of them this weekend, which one would you choose?
e Are there any other extreme sports you would like to try (if money were no object)?

Listing: turning dreams into reality

Amy and Adam

Emily and Harry

Natalie (left) and Helen

14 Listen to Track 24. You will hear three generations of the same family talking about the extreme sports they have done. Find out the following:

a What prompted Emily to book a vacation in New Zealand?
b What was her initial reaction when she was finally able to realize her ambition?
c Why did Natalie want to give her mother a nice present?
d What kind of surprise did she have in mind?
e What surprise did Natalie herself get?
f How would you describe Amy and Adam's relationship with each other?
g What is their general attitude to extreme sports?
h What happened to help them with their ambitions?

15 Listen again. Who said the following and what were they referring to?

a "See? It's always both of us, or neither of us!"
b "Yeah, I mean, he jumped at the chance!"
c "Totally! You can say that again!"
d "She often gets like this."
e "So I said: 'You're not going to catch me doing that!'"
f "I wouldn't have missed it for the world."
g "My mum scraped the money together from somewhere."
h "So I was in a quandary."
i "Both of us were completely turned on by it!"
j "She took to it like a duck to water."

16 Read these extracts from the listening text. Which one is correct?

a 1 My heart was set on doing something that involved flying.
   2 My heart was set to do something that involved flying.
b 1 I have this burning ambition being an airline pilot.
   2 I have this burning ambition to be an airline pilot.

c 1 I'm determined of doing something different.
   2 I'm determined to do something different.
d 1 I desperately wanted to go skiing.
   2 I was desperately to go skiing.
e 1 I must admit, it's always been a secret ambition of mine.
   2 I must admit, it's always been a secret ambition to me.

17 Phrasal verbs Complete these sentences from the listening text. Which is closer in meaning to the original, 1 or 2?

a "It turned .... that there were ten winners."
   1 We discovered there were ten winners.
   2 Ten winners arrived at the place.
b "A few of the people hadn't turned ...."
   1 A few of the people didn't want to do it.
   2 A few of the people hadn't arrived.
c "So I turned .... the TV and went online to find out more about it."
   1 When we stopped watching TV, I went online.
   2 I went online on my TV set.
d "Both of us were completely turned .... by it!"
   1 We both loved it.
   2 We both hated it.

Language in chunks

18 Study the examples. Then use them to complete the sentences. Make any changes necessary.

*Extreme sports are **way too expensive**.*
*I **jumped at the chance** to go skydiving.*
*You're not going to **catch me doing that**!*
*She **worked her socks off**.*
*They thought I was **out of my mind**.*
*She **took to it like a duck to water**.*
*My mom **scraped the money together** from somewhere.*

a At first I thought we couldn't afford it, but we .... by selling some CDs.
b I can't believe she failed the exam. She's been .... for months now.
c My grandmother has just started horseback riding, and it's amazing because ....
d When my sister told us that she wanted to stop studying and travel around the world, we thought ....
e When they said they had a spare ticket for the concert, I ....

19 Now use the expressions to talk about something in your personal experience, or a story that you know.

Grammar: determiners and partitives

20 Determiners: all, a lot of ...

Make ten sentences from the table that are true about you, your family, or people you know.

> **Example:** Most of the people in this class have a mobile phone. None of us has been to Japan.

All A lot Lots Several Some Enough A few Both	of	you us them the people the buildings …	are … were … can … do … did … have done …
Neither None One	of	you us them the people the buildings …	is … was … can … does … did … has done ...
All A lot Enough A little None	of	the water the air the land the wine …	is … was …

Read 11A in the Mini-grammar to help you.

21 Determiners: *Neither … nor …*

Study the examples and then make one sentence from the two sentences in a–h.

Neither Amy nor Adam has been hang-gliding before.
Either Emily or Harry will tell you.
You can call either Emily or Harry.
Both Natalie and Helen enjoyed the trip.

a   Bob can help you with your homework. Or you can ask Jim.
b   Sandra went to the concert. Alan did, too.
c   My mother has never been to Europe. My father hasn't, either.
d   France has a border with Belgium. So does Holland.
e   I don't eat meat. I don't eat fish, either.
f   You can get there by plane. You can get there by boat, too.
g   I haven't the slightest interest in visiting New York. My sister feels the same way.
h   Natalie enjoyed the vacation a lot. Her mother did, too.

Read 11B in the Mini-grammar to help you.

22 Partitives

Make common expressions with these words. You can use some of the words more than once. How many more things can you think of?

a bottle		beans
a glass		cards
a carton		chewing gum
a pair		jeans
a piece		meat
a slice	of	glasses
a bunch		wine
a can		jam
a pack		cake
a deck		milk
a scrap		paper
a jar		scissors
a set		roses

23 Find the correct expression to complete these sentences.

a   He has .... of different colored pens.
b   Did you see .... paint I was using?
c   She had the most delicious looking .... grapes and didn't offer one to anyone else.
d   After the concert, the singer was given a beautiful .... flowers.
e   I need to buy .... chewing gum before we get on the plane.
f   I think my mother would like me to get her .... marmalade.
g   Can you lend me .... paper, please?
h   You have to understand that this society has .... rules that must be obeyed.

Read 11C in the Mini-grammar to help you.

Speaking: talking about your ambitions

24 Discussion Look at the photos on this page and discuss these questions.

a What kind of ambitions do the photos represent?
b Which of the images most appeals to you and why?

The Forbidden City, Beijing, China

wildlife sanctuary

airline pilots

mansion with swimming pool

rock climbing

25 In groups Each person describes his or her greatest ambition to the group. Make notes of the ambitions of the rest of the group. Choose someone in the group who will describe them to the class.

26 Take a vote Listen to the ambitions of the groups and vote for the best ones. If you like, vote for the best in the different categories.

Writing: writing an advertisement

27 You are going to write an advertisement for the Virgin Galactic Spaceliner, the first commercial space vehicle designed for paying customers. Before you start, think about the following:

a What is new or unusual about the experience of flying in space?
b What kind of people should you aim your advertisement at?

28 Read the news article about the Virgin Galactic Spaceliner and discuss these questions.

a What information from the article can you use in your advertisement?
b What information is it best not to mention to potential customers?
c What can you say to make the ride seem worth the cost?

If you have $200,000 burning a hole in your pocket, you may want to use it to book a seat on board the new Virgin Galactic Spaceliner and spend a few minutes in space. If it seems like a lot of money to experience weightlessness for about two minutes, at least you don't have to go through all that tedious training at NASA in the U.S. or Star City near Moscow.

The Spaceliner can carry five passengers. The advertising promises "luxurious seats and spectacular views." It still seems like a lot of money when most people who go into space start to feel sick rather than ecstatic.

It takes off from the Mojave Desert near Los Angeles, connected to a carrier craft. At a height of almost 50,000 feet, the Spaceliner fires its rockets and climbs to a height of 60 miles before it falls back into the atmosphere and glides back to Earth.

However, not everyone is convinced that space tourism can become a fully fledged part of the travel industry. "Traveling in space isn't comfortable," said Alan Henderson, a travel industry consultant. "A lot of people have a problem dealing with zero gravity, and you may not enjoy the experience of visiting a vacuum toilet. It could all put the average well-heeled traveler off the idea, particularly with the large price tag which is attached."

"It's not a volume market," he added. "'Tourism' is the wrong word—it's like an extreme sport."

29 Decide on the following:

a where your advertisement will appear: newspaper, magazine, billboard, TV, radio, etc.
b whether it will be mainly text, mainly image, film, or sound only
c who your target market is
d what your unique selling points are

30 Plan your advertisement. Present it to the class.

Review: grammar and functional language

31 Choose the correct answer to complete this conversation.

SANDRA: Are **a either / some** of you going to Connie's birthday party in Mexico City?

BETTY: I'm not.

ELAINE: Neither am I.

BETTY: You aren't either? OK then **b neither / both** of us is / are going.

SANDRA: Why not? I thought **c all / enough** of her classmates wanted to go.

BETTY: We do. But going to Mexico is expensive. **d All / Some** of Connie's friends aren't as well off as she is, and I have to work.

ELAINE: So do I. Plus, I don't have a passport.

BETTY: Neither do I.

SANDRA: **e None / Neither** of you has a passport?! Really?

BETTY: Sandra, **f some / one** of us don't / doesn't actually need a passport for our everyday life.

SANDRA: That's a real shame. Connie wants to hire a driver to take us around the sights of Mexico City. But if **g none / not enough** of us go, she won't be able to afford it.

BETTY: Sandra, will you listen? **h Both / Neither** of us are / is working that weekend and **i some / neither** of us have / has a passport. So we can't go.

SANDRA: Well, I think she'll be disappointed. Can't at least **j one of you / all of you** be sick and not go to work?

32 Read the text and decide if the sentences are true or false.

Six Degrees of Separation
(1993 film version of an original play)

There is a theory that if you make a list of all of the people you know, and they make a list of all of the people they know, and this continues and continues, the sixth set of lists will reach everyone on Earth. This theory is known as Six Degrees of Separation.

Although the theory was first suggested in 1929 by a Hungarian short story writer, it took nearly 40 years for someone to find a way to test the theory scientifically. In 1967, American sociologist Stanley Milgram chose a group of people at random in the American Midwest. They all had to send packages to different strangers who lived in Massachusetts (in other words, a long way from where they lived). The senders knew the recipient's name, occupation, and general location but not his address. The people who were going to receive the packages were chosen because none of their friends and relations lived in the Midwest.

They were instructed to send the package to one of their friends or acquaintances who they thought might know the target personally. That person would do the same, and so on, until the package was delivered to the right person.

Milgram had no idea how many people it would take. Some of his colleagues expected the chain to include at least a hundred intermediaries. In fact, 90 percent of the packages were delivered after between five and seven intermediaries were involved. Milgram revived the name "Six Degrees of Separation" to describe his findings.

The idea became even more popular when, in 1990, playwright John Guare wrote a play by that name, which was eventually made into a movie.

In 2001, Duncan Watts, a professor at Columbia University, updated the idea by recreating Milgram's experiment on the Internet. Watts used an email message as the "package" that needed to be delivered, and, surprisingly, after reviewing the data collected by 48,000 senders and 19 targets in 157 countries, Watts found that the average number of intermediaries was ... six!

a The theory suggests that the people you know actually know all the people in the world.

b Professor Milgram knew all the people chosen.

c None of the recipients of the packages lived in the Midwest.

d Some of the people in Massachusetts knew people in the Midwest.

e It took five to seven people to deliver most of the packages.

f The 2001 experiment used a different method to test the theory.

g Fewer people were involved in this experiment than in 1967.

h This time, most of the email packages were delivered by the same number of people.

33 Look at the photos. What do you know about Rihanna and Jay-Z?

Rihanna

Jay-Z

Now read the text.

Rihanna was born in the Caribbean island of Barbados and attended a top high school, where she shone at several subjects and showed considerable academic prowess. She also won a beauty contest and sang a Mariah Carey song in a school talent show. At the time, she had no particular ambition to be a professional singer, but her life was turned upside down after a chance meeting with a man named Evan Rodgers, a New York music producer who was on vacation on the island with his Bajan wife.

Rihanna sang a song for Rodgers and also told him that her favorite singer was Beyoncé Knowles. Rodgers felt that Rihanna had star quality and arranged for her to go to New York to meet Jay-Z, one of the world's top rap artists and CEO of Def Jam Records (and also Beyoncé's husband).

Jay-Z is a famous, successful star-spotter. He decided that she had what it takes as soon as he heard her sing and signed her up to a recording deal with the company. She was 16 years old when she signed the contract with Def Jam. Within four years, she had released four albums and racked up eleven Top 40 hit singles in the U.S.

What would have happened to Rihanna if she hadn't had that chance meeting with Rodgers?

34 Are the sentences true or false?

a Rihanna always wanted to be a singer.
b She was one of the best students at her school.
c She didn't arrange to meet the New York record producer.
d She told the man her favorite singer was Beyoncé Knowles, and he arranged for her to meet Beyoncé's husband.
e Jay-Z is good at spotting talent.
f Since signing for Def Jam Records, Rihanna has had only limited success.

35 Discussion Do you know any stories of someone with no particular ambition being successful?

Review: vocabulary

Word List		
airborne	snowboarding	to steer
airfield	sports	to strap
BMX biking	surfing	to stretch
bungee jumping	to accelerate	to struggle
coincidence	to activate	to trigger
freefalling	to attach	tourniquet
hang-gliding	to dangle	waterskiing
kiteboarding	to flip	weightlessness
rock climbing	to plummet	whitewater
scuba diving	to postpone	rafting
skateboarding	to rip off	
skydiving	to snap back	

36 In groups Choose five words from the Word List and start a conversation. Continue until everyone in the group has used all five words at least once.

Word Plus	
by an astonishing coincidence	to loop the loop
emergency surgery	to scrape the money together
flight control systems	to set your heart on doing something
I wouldn't have missed it for the world	to shift your body weight
in a quandary	to take to something like a duck to water
in his sights	to work your socks off
spectacular view	way too expensive
tension was high	with seconds to spare
the star of the show	you're not going to catch me doing that
to burn a hole in your pocket	

37 In pairs Extend and complete this conversation, using as many of the expressions in the Word Plus box as you can.

A: Something really strange happened to me last week.
B: Really? What was that?
A: Well, I was at the bus stop, and suddenly ...
B: No way! Doesn't she go everywhere in a limo?
A: That's what I thought! I asked her ...
B: And what did she say?
A: She said: ...
B: Really? Wow! That must have been exciting for you!
A: You're right! ...

UNIT 10

The world's your oyster

→ multiculturalism
→ expressing anger
→ passive constructions

Vocabulary 1: multiculturalism

1 Look at the photographs. In what countries would you find these things?

2 **In pairs** Write a list of words and ideas suggested by the photos.

Words: immigration, ...
Ideas: different cultures living together

Compare your lists with others.

3 **In pairs** Discuss the advantages and disadvantages of living in these places. Give reasons.

4 Definitions Match the word with the definition.

melting pot	refugee	multicultural
to assimilate	asylum seeker	ethnic minority
to integrate		

a .... To join or cause a social group to join in society as a whole.
b .... To become like the people of a country in ways of behaving and thinking.
c .... A group of people of a different race from the main group of a country.
d .... A person without papers who gets protection from another country because they are persecuted in their own country.
e .... A person from a foreign country who may stay and work in a country for their personal safety.
f .... A word to describe a society of people from different cultures and races where all the cultures are respected.
g .... A society of people from different cultures and races that merge into a homogeneous society.

5 How much does the man or woman in the street actually know about cultural diversity? Listen to the street survey on Track 25 and check your answers to Activity 4.

Vocabulary 2: attitudes to minorities

6 Look up these nouns in the dictionary. Find the corresponding adjectives and any prepositions that go with them. Then copy and complete the table.

assimilation	integration	sympathy
discrimination	open-mindedness	tolerance
ignorance	prejudice	
inequality	racism	

Living in a multicultural society			
Threats		Positive characteristics	
		tolerance	tolerant of/toward

7 **In pairs** Are you an immigrant? Or perhaps you would like to emigrate to another country? Tell your partner what you find, or would find, easiest and most difficult as an immigrant.

Speaking: expressing your point of view

8 **Preparing a discussion** You are the manager of a small factory that employs many immigrants. Times are hard and you have to lay off two staff members. You have to be fair to everyone. Read the descriptions of the staff and make notes.

	Points in favor	Points against	Likely consequence of being laid off
Ali Mahood	loyal, hard working knows business well	bad health	may affect his pension
Pete McCarthy			
Rhonda Miller			
Sajitha Patel			
Hassan Hussein			
Goysha Kopec			

Ali Mahood has been in the company for 30 years. He is a loyal, hard-working employee and he knows the business better than anyone else. But his health is not very good and he often has to miss work. He is two years from retirement.

Pete McCarthy has been in the company for ten years. His performance is somewhat erratic. The 60-year-old is well liked by the others and is their union representative.

Rhonda Miller is a single mother of two children whom she is putting through college on her salary and savings. She is a serious worker, but the others don't like her because they feel she is a bit racist. She is 49.

Sajitha Patel is 32. She has a university degree and may be over-qualified for the job. She is an invaluable member of staff but she has a terrible temper, which occasionally causes arguments. The others think she looks down on them.

Hassan Hussein has recently arrived from Somalia. He is eager to please and is happy to take on jobs the others don't like. He doesn't have his green card yet, so legally he shouldn't be working. You sympathize with him and would really like to help him. He is 23.

Goysha Kopec has recently come over from Poland. She has problems communicating because her English is poor, and she shows no interest in learning it. On the other hand, she is very good at her job and puts in overtime to get things done. She is 21.

9 Decide which two staff members you would lay off. Justify your choices.

Expressing your point of view
I am certain/convinced/sure that is the right choice because ...
I have no doubt that ... can find another job easily.
You shouldn't employ people illegally, therefore ... is unquestionably/undoubtedly/certainly the first choice.

10 **In groups of four** Try to persuade the group that you have made the best choices. At the end of your discussion you must reach consensus.

Reading: tales of immigration

11 Look at the photos and read the quotes below.

a What do you think happened in Chávez Ravine?

b What do you think is the relation between Chávez Ravine and Dodger Stadium?

c What was Frank Wilkinson's involvement?

d What do you think is the relation between immigration and Chávez Ravine?

"They didn't want to move. They didn't want to lose their friends. They didn't want to lose their homes."

Carol Jacques, former Chávez Ravine resident

"It's the tragedy of my life, absolutely. I was responsible for uprooting I don't know how many hundreds of people from their own little valley and having the whole thing destroyed."

Frank Wilkinson, former assistant director, Los Angeles City Housing Authority

12 Read the article and check your answers.

Chávez Ravine: the lost neighborhood beneath Dodger Stadium

The story of Chávez Ravine begins with the **influx** of Mexican families who migrated to southern California during the Mexican Revolution. By 1960, it was home to two to three generations of Mexican Americans as well as a smaller number of Chinese American families. It was an exclusively immigrant community. Most of the houses were **makeshift** or badly constructed. Overcrowding was common. The *barrio* (neighborhood) grew **haphazardly**. But the families took great pride in their homes and there was a strong sense of community. It had a high school, a Catholic church, and local shopkeepers.

With the rapid expansion of urban Los Angeles, Chávez Ravine became a prime location, ripe for redevelopment. The Housing Authority of the City of Los Angeles, with federal funds from the Housing Act of 1949, launched an ambitious housing project, Elysian Park Heights. The project was conceived to alleviate the housing shortage of post-war America. It included housing, new playgrounds, and schools. In 1950 the residents were notified of the plan in a memorandum:

"This letter is to inform you that a public housing development will be built in this location for low income families ... The house you are living in is included ... You will be visited by representatives of the Housing Authority who will inspect your home in order to estimate its value. It will be several months at least until your property is purchased. Later you will have the first chance to move back into the Elysian Park Heights development."

The residents viewed the project with suspicion at first: the older generations in the *barrio* could hardly speak English, let alone read it and understand the legal jargon. In the end they **succumbed** to the hard-sell techniques and false promises of the buyers. The vibrant *barrio* was reduced to a few houses as families sold their land, with the exception of a few who stubbornly refused eviction from their homes.

Before construction could begin, however, the project ground to a halt as the political climate changed. The housing project smacked of socialism in the eyes of the conservative government and the business community. The Los Angeles City Council buckled under the pressure and **rescinded** the public housing contract with the Housing Authority.

In those days, American cities were eager to subsidize sports stadiums in a bid to bring prestige to their cities. Los Angeles was no exception. The land that had always been intended for public housing was sold to the baseball team Brooklyn Dodgers from New York for the construction of their new stadium. Legal challenges to the controversial decision were to no avail and on May 8th, 1959, the bulldozers arrived. What was left of the *barrio* was razed to the ground and more than 30 people were forcibly evicted from their homes.

The former residents of Chávez Ravine are determined to keep the story of the community alive as a symbol of the **plight** of many immigrant communities. Judy Baca's famous mural *The Great Wall of Los Angeles* depicts the destruction of Chávez Ravine, with the Dodgers represented as aliens from outer space. In 1949, photographer Don Normark recorded the daily life in the *barrio*. Fifty years later he published his photos with comments from former residents in his book *Chávez Ravine—A Los Angeles Story*. In 2005, Ry Cooder made *Chávez Ravine*, a CD of songs about the *barrio*, its colorful residents, and the **demise** of the neighborhood.

13 Fact check Read the text quickly. Which paragraphs give the following information?

a How the immigrants came to sell their property.

b A description of the neighborhood.

c Arts projects about Chávez Ravine.

d How the Dodgers' stadium came to be built.

e The origins of the neighborhood.

14 Which of statements a–g are correct according to the article? Quote from the text to support your answers.

a The first residents of Chávez Ravine came from Mexico.
The story of Chávez Ravine begins with the influx of Mexican families who migrated to southern California during the Mexican Revolution.

b People who used to live in Chávez Ravine don't want people to forget what happened.

c Like many American cities, Los Angeles City Council felt that big stadiums brought status to the city.

d Developers thought it would be easy to fool the residents because they couldn't speak English.

e The residents of the *barrio* didn't want to sell up but were tempted by the offers.

f As soon as the residents sold their properties, construction work began.

g When Don Normark took his photos he never imagined what would happen later.

15 Vocabulary Rewrite the sentences using the words highlighted red in the text.

a He planted his garden <u>in an unplanned, disorderly manner</u>.

b We sympathize with the <u>terrible situation</u> of those people.

c The council <u>annulled</u> the permission to build the center.

d The sudden <u>arrival of large numbers</u> of refugees put their resources under stress.

e We were saddened by the <u>death</u> of our favorite sportsperson.

f They <u>used whatever we could find</u> to build a temporary shelter.

g The residents eventually <u>gave in</u> to the demands of the Council.

Language in chunks

16 Read the expressions from the text. Tick the alternative that can best replace the expressions.

a "Chávez Ravine became a prime location **ripe for redevelopment**." (*paragraph 2*)
1 It was old enough to be redeveloped. ☐
2 It was the ideal time for redevelopment. ☐
3 It was prepared for redevelopment. ☐

b "The project **ground to a halt** as the political climate changed." (*paragraph 5*)
1 The project's end came slowly. ☐
2 The project was suddenly dropped. ☐
3 The project was postponed. ☐

c "The housing project **smacked of** socialism." (*paragraph 5*)
People thought the project was ...
1 a socialist policy, which they disapproved of ☐
2 a socialist policy, which they approved of ☐
3 sounded illegal ☐

d "The Los Angeles City Council **buckled under the pressure**." (*paragraph 5*)
The Council ...
1 gave in ☐
2 heated up ☐
3 fought under pressure ☐

e "Legal challenges to the controversial decision were **to no avail**." (*paragraph 6*)
1 Legal challenges were unavailable. ☐
2 No legal challenges were made. ☐
3 The challenges were useless. ☐

f "What was left of the *barrio* was **razed to the ground**." (*paragraph 6*)
The houses were ...
1 badly damaged ☐
2 completely destroyed ☐
3 redeveloped ☐

17 Using the chunks, write sentences about:

a two things that can be razed to the ground.

b two places in your town you think are ripe for redevelopment.

c something politicians are doing, or have done, which smacks of dishonesty.

d an example of someone who buckled under the pressure.

e something in your city or country that has ground to a halt.

18 In pairs What is your reaction to the story of Chávez Ravine?

Grammar: passive constructions

19 Read the text. Answer the questions.

a Why did Joe leave his country?
b What is going to happen to Joe?
c What can you do to help?

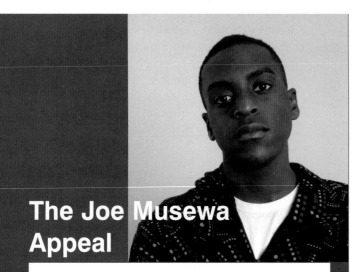

The Joe Musewa Appeal

Joe is 15. He is from a country where terror and lawlessness reign. Having been persecuted and tortured, Joe was left for dead until he was found by farmers who looked after him. This was Joe's only lucky break. But he couldn't risk being found, and he embarked on a harrowing journey to safety. He arrived in this country with the clothes on his back and no papers, traumatized by his experiences. But he had hope: he had heard this country had a long tradition of helping people in his situation. He wasn't afraid of being arrested and gave himself up to the authorities on arrival. He was detained and taken to a detention center where all asylum seekers seem to be taken, regardless of their age and circumstances. At the center, and through no fault of his own, Joe was involved in an incident. Having been seriously hurt in the incident, Joe's health, both mental and physical, appears to be deteriorating rapidly. A deportation order has been issued: Joe is to be returned to the horrors back home. Help Joe in his plight. Sign the petition and send it to friends and family. All it takes is two clicks to save someone's life.

20 Match these sentences with sentences with similar meaning in the passage.

a After Joe was tortured he was left for dead.
b Joe left because he was in danger.
c Joe wasn't worried about being arrested.
d Joe's health is getting worse because he was hurt in the incident.

21 Rewrite using a passive -ing construction.

Example: I don't mind people asking me for directions.
I don't mind being asked for directions.

a Sarah hates it when people call her an "alien."
b Some immigrants resent it when people refer to them as "ethnic minorities."
c He was awarded a prize for his services to the community and felt very honored.
d Do you mind when people ask you where you are from?
e Peter has been stopped by the police so many times he doesn't care anymore.

Read 12A in the Mini-grammar **to help you.**

22 In pairs Read the pairs of sentences. Identify the tense (e.g. present, past) and say whether it is active or passive.

a Joe's health is getting worse.
   Joe's health appears to be getting worse.
b Joe lost his papers.
   Joe seems to have lost his papers.
c All asylum seekers are detained.
   All asylum seekers seem to be detained.
d His papers were stolen.
   His papers seem to have been stolen.

23 Complete the information in the box with reference to Activity 22.

- The verbs *appear* and *seem* are followed by .... in the present. They are followed by .... in the past.
- In the passive, *appear* and *seem* are followed by .... in the present. They are followed by .... in the past.

Read 12B in the Mini-grammar **to help you.**

24 Rewrite these sentences using *appear* or *seem to*.

a Many people are welcome in this country.
b Thousands of people are waiting for their papers.
c Their appeal was answered by thousands of people, I think.
d This appeal was published only on the Internet.
e Few deportation orders are issued in this country.

Listening

25 What do the pictures all have in common?

26 Listen to the program on Track 26 about the immigrant communities. Label the pictures with words from the box. Number them in the order you hear them.

Bhangra	salwar kameez	tikka masala
Bollywood	*Bombay Dreams*	V.S. Naipaul

27 Listen again. Find:

a a reason why Namita went on the radio program
b a reason why, culturally, countries can benefit from immigration
c one example of Indian culture going mainstream
d one example of an important immigrant writer
e a reason why younger Asian Canadians remain attached to the country of their parents
f one example of the influence of Asian clothing on fashion

28 In pairs Discuss these questions
a Are there any immigrant communities in your country?
b Have they influenced your culture? How?
c Do you belong to an immigrant community? Do you preserve your ancestors' culture?

Functional language: expressing emotions

29 Look up these expressions to describe anger in a dictionary. Mark them *neutral* (*N*) or *informal* (*INF*).

to lose your temper	to get in a huff
to get angry	to see red
to fly off the handle	to fly into a temper
to lose one's cool	to get annoyed

Now rank the expressions in order of strength (1= mildest; 8= strongest).

30 Listen to Track 27. Match the conversations with the pictures.

31 Listen again. Complete the sentences with words from the conversations.

Conversation 1
Oh, for goodness' .... !
I'm so .... them.
Hey, ... down!
Don't take it .... me!
You need to ....

Conversation 2
Give me a .... !
You can be .... idiot!
Take .... !

Conversation 3
I wish you .... our plans.
.... is ....
.... I'm upset.

32 Copy and complete the table with the expressions in Activity 31.

Expressing anger
Calming people down

33 In pairs Choose one of the situations in Activity 31. Act out the conversations.

34 In pairs Make up a conversation for this picture.

Pronunciation: expressing anger

35 Read the exclamations. They are all said angrily. Underline the main stress.

a That's so inconsiderate!
b You're such an idiot!
c I wish you'd listen!
d You're always complaining!
e Don't take it out on me!
f Oh, for goodness' sake!
g I'm so fed up!

36 Listen to Track 28. Check your answers and add the intonation.

37 In pairs Choose one of the sentences. Read it to your partner. Your partner reacts using one of the exclamations in Activity 35.

"You never told me that, did you?"
"Sorry I woke you up. I forgot my keys."
"This soup's too salty and the bread is stale."
"Answer the phone. It's getting on my nerves!"
"Sorry to interrupt you again. I need help with this."
"I broke your favorite mug. Sorry!"

Writing: an opinion essay

38 Read the people's opinions and write them in the table on the next page. Add at least two opinions of your own.

Can countries benefit from immigration?

"I've been out of work for 18 months. I blame immigration. Immigrants come here and take our jobs. They want to stay in the country so they take really low wages. Employers prefer them to Aussies because we know our rights and we won't work for peanuts. I'm sick and tired of immigrants living off our taxes while families like mine have nothing. Immigration is a hell of a problem."

Jake Adams, factory worker, unemployed, Adelaide, Australia

"I am thankful that I grew up in this country. I got a decent education and have made a nice life for myself and my family. But I've worked really hard to get where I am today. Immigration is important for the UK economy. Immigrants take jobs that other people won't take and they increase productivity. They also enrich the culture of the country. Without them we would all be the poorer."

Leonie Richards runs her own clothing factory in Bristol, England

Immigration
Advantages
Disadvantages

39 Read Jake Adams' opinion.
a What sentence(s) express his opening point?
b What sentence(s) support his main point?
c How does he conclude his opinion?

40 Write an essay on the question: *Can countries benefit from immigration?*

WRITING TIPS
Expressing an opinion
Make notes:
* **Introduction:** What is the subject matter? What is your opinion?
* **Main body:** Choose the two or three most important points from Activity 38. Give examples to support each reason.
* **Conclusion:** Restate your opinion.
Write a first draft.

Review: grammar and functional language

41 Complete the sentences about the situations. Use passive constructions.

Example: You can't find your wallet. Maybe it was stolen.
My wallet seems to have been stolen.

a You get a letter. It has no stamp. Maybe someone delivered it by hand. The letter seems ....
b Mary got home to find it in a mess. Perhaps someone broke into it. The house appeared ....
c Ahmed was brought to this country as a child. He is now fully integrated. Having ....
d The officer interviewed the family. They didn't mind.
The family didn't mind ....
e Elena's firm has promoted her. She can now afford to buy a condo. Having ....

42 Complete the sentences with true information about yourself. Use a passive *-ing* construction (*being* + *past participle*).

Example: I'm afraid of being mugged.

a I'm afraid of ...   d I can't stand ...
b I hate ...   e I object to ...
c I don't mind ...   f I remember ...

43 Write four sentences about things that anger or annoy you.

Example: I wish you wouldn't speak Mandarin in front of me.
It's so rude!

Review: vocabulary

Word List		
asylum seekers	integration	racism
cuisine	mainstream	refugees
demise	makeshift	succumb
discrimination	melting pot	sympathy
ethnic minority	multicultural	to alleviate
haphazardly	open-mindedness	to assimilate
ignorance	plight	to rescind
inequality	prejudice	tolerance
influx	prestige	vibrant

Word Plus	
ripe for (redevelopment)	to grind to a halt
smack of (+ something negative)	to lose one's cool
to buckle under the pressure	to no avail
to fly into a temper	to raze to the ground
to fly off the handle	to see red
to get in a huff	

44 Write a letter to the newspaper about your opinions on immigration in your country. Use words from the Word List and Word Plus.

UNIT 11

Performing arts

→ spoken tags
→ extending word use (*act, conduct, dance, play*
→ presenting (*suggesting courses of action*)

Speaking

1 List the following school subjects in order of importance.
Which is the most important for children to study?
Which is the least important?

Art

Drama and dance

Home economics

Economics and business studi

Foreign language(s)

Geography

History

IT training

Language and literature

Mathematics

Music

Science

2 **In groups** What percentage of school time would you give to the
different subjects on the curriculum and why?

3 Compare your conclusions with other groups.

Functional language and pronunciation: presenting suggestions

4 Listen to Track 29. The speaker is explaining to a committee why she thinks home economics should be the most important subject in the school curriculum. Put the parts of her talk in order.

a The speaker asks for questions. □
b The speaker emphasizes her argument by restating it. □
c The speaker explains what she is going to say. □
d The speaker explains why she holds her opinions. □
e The speaker makes dire predictions about inaction. □
f The speaker restates her point of view to finish her presentation. □
g The speaker starts to present her case. □
h The speaker talks about contrary opinions and dismisses them. □

5 Put these phrases that the speaker uses into the correct place in the chart. (Write the letters in.)

a After that, if it's all right with you, …
b But secondly …
c Does anyone have any questions?
d First of all let me say that I think that …
e Firstly, …
f I have two main reasons for saying this.
g I'll move on to …
h I'll start by …
i I'll take questions, …
j I'm going to say why I think …
k If we want to … my contention is that …
l Let's just suppose that such people are right; well, then …
m We'd better take that chance now, because if we don't …
n So that's it.
o To those who say that … I would just say that …
p We must act now, before it is too late.

1	Describing the structure of the presentation	
2	Getting going with the main argument	
3	Structuring the order of arguments	
4	Introducing counterarguments in order to show that they are wrong	
5	Suggesting what should be done	
6	Warning about future consequences	
7	Concluding the presentation	
8	Offering question time	

What other language items can you add to the chart?

6 **Pronunciation** Look at Activity Bank 27 on page 139 and listen again.

a Which sentences and phrases are "language in chunks" (that is, common fixed or nearly fixed phrases)?
b Practice saying the language chunks as fast as you can.

7 **In pairs** Choose a paragraph of the talk and practice saying it so that you sound as fluent as possible.

8 **In groups** Prepare a presentation. Explain why another subject in Activity 1 should be the most important part of the curriculum. Design your presentation using the same kind of structure as the speaker in Activity 4.

9 **Role play** You are attending a meeting of the school curriculum board, which has to decide on a new school curriculum. This is the procedure for the meeting:

a Different speakers present their school subjects. (You can toss a coin to see who makes the presentation.)
b When they have finished, the listeners ask questions.
c At the end of the meeting, participants vote on the best presentation.

Reading

10 Your reactions
Look at the two pictures and give each a score from 0 (= it doesn't interest me at all) to 10 (= I am really, really interested in this). Compare your scores with your classmates.

11 Discussion in groups
Consider the following questions.

a What, if any, is your favorite kind of music? Where do you like listening to it?
b Who normally goes to (a) the ballet and (b) classical music?
c If you went to the ballet or a classical music concert, who would you go with and why?

12
Read the text on the next page. In as few words as possible, contrast what happened in Paris in 1913 and in Berlin in 2003.

13 Detail check

a What can you find out about Enrique Sanchez Lansch, Igor Stravinsky, *Le Sacre du Printemps*, Njinksy, Royston Maldoom, Simon Rattle, Thomas Grube?
b What is the importance of these numbers: 16, 25, 30, 45, 250, 3,000?

14 Wordsearch
Find words beginning with the letters.

a c.................. : a word that means planned the dance moves.
b b.................. j.................. : two words that mean to shout rudely, mostly without words.
c d.................. : a word that means unpleasant, because the notes do not go together.
d s.................. : a word that means an event that shocks people.
e d.................. : a word that means not having any rights (or power) in society.
f c.................. : a word that means having a natural ability to be interesting and attractive.
g i.................. : a word that means not paying attention.
h r.................. : a word that means upset because you think something is unfair.
i m.................. : a word that means something wonderful (and unexpected) that happens.
j s.................. : two words that together mean continuing to do something even when it is very difficult.
k t.................. : a word that means changing—in a good and wonderful way.

Language in chunks

15
Complete the sentences with the exact words from the text, or your own words if the sentence is not part of the text.

a A ballet really starts when the dancers come ....
b People are about to go crazy. Let's get out of here before all ....
c Before the orchestra starts playing the conductor raises his ....
d Everyone got so angry at the meeting that fighting .... all over the hall.
e Everyone's going to the new show at the theater. It's one of the ....
f People are overexcited. We need to calm ....
g The arrival of Columbus in the New World in 1492 changed the ....
h When I saw her she was in .... I've never seen anyone so sad.

16 Your opinion
Comment on the following:

"You can change your life in a dance class."
"Music is not a luxury, but a need, like the air we breathe and the water we drink."

Do you think the young people's lives were changed by their experiences in Berlin? Why?

"Music is not a luxury, but a need, like the air we breathe and the water we drink."

Ballet and classical music are for wimps and snobs? Think again, says journalist Peter Hedley

Paris, France, 1913. The lights go down and the crowd waits expectantly. This is the first night of a new show by the dance company Ballet Russes, and it's one of the hottest tickets in town. Like the opening of a new rock musical today, only bigger!

The theater is crowded because the new show has been choreographed by the famous dancer Njinsky, one of the real celebrities of his day. The ballet is called *Le Sacre du Printemps* (*The Rite of Spring*).

The conductor raises his baton and a solo bassoon starts to play. And almost immediately all hell breaks loose. The audience starts to boo, then jeer, then shout insults at the stage. When the dancers come on they don't look like classical ballet dancers at all. They are in peasant costumes and their movements are modern, angular, spiky. The people in the theater hate it!

And the music! Discordant, harsh, crashing rhythms, and thumping drums. No one has ever heard anything quite like it. And still they jeer, and when some other people in the audience try to stop them, fighting breaks out all over the theater and the police have to be called to calm things down. The composer of the music, Igor Stravinsky, runs from the theater in tears. The performance is a disaster.

The next day Njinsky and Stravinsky are depressed, but the owner of the ballet company says that the scandal is "just what I wanted." And he is right. *Le Sacre du Printemps* rapidly becomes one of the most performed works both on stage and in the concert hall—a position it still occupies today. Stravinsky's composition changed the course of music—classical, rock, pop—forever, and no one could think of ballet in quite the same way ever again.

Berlin, Germany, 2003. In an old bus depot in front of an audience of 3,000, 250 young people from poor and disenfranchised neighborhoods of the city are dancing *The Rite of Spring*, with the music provided by the Berlin Philharmonic Orchestra, one of the greatest musical bands in the world. Conducting them is the charismatic British musician Simon Rattle, and watching the youthful dancers is Royston Maldoom, a Londoner who has spent the last 30 years traveling around the world in an old red postoffice van, undertaking dance projects, mostly with street children. "You can change your life in a dance class," Maldoom says, and Rattle is no less enthusiastic about what he does. In his words "Music is not a luxury, but a need, like the air we breathe and the water we drink."

The project which ended in the bus depot started when Rattle, newly appointed as conductor of the orchestra in Berlin, became aware of Maldoom's work. The musician had always wanted to get young people dancing to Stravinsky's masterpiece because the music "is full of energy, one of the most powerful pieces that have ever been written. This piece of music immediately takes hold of your whole body and it feels as if you are emerging from the depths of the earth."

And so they started. Maldoom got hold of 250 young people, representing 25 different ethnicities. At first the kids were inattentative, resentful, and truculent. Just getting them to quiet down and overcome their fears and insecurities was a miracle. Sixteen-year-old Olayinka, for example, was a war orphan from Nigeria, recently arrived in Germany but without a word of German. Martin was a loner who hated being touched, and Marie confessed to a lack of attention and laziness at school. But as the 45 days of rehearsal unfolded a remarkable change took place. The young people, struggling with new concepts of discipline and bodily control, started to work with stubborn determination, overcoming their fears and phobias until, when they finally performed in the bus depot, their brilliance, energy, and commitment overwhelmed and moved everyone who saw it. There were cheers and many tears.

And throughout the whole project, filmmakers Thomas Grube and Enrique Sanchez Lansch were there to record what was going on. The result was a documentary called *Rhythm Is It*, described in a Chicago Film Festival brochure as a "truly delightful ode to the transformative power of art," and by critic John Green as "a musical declaration of love to the dancing teenagers, a film about the fascination of music, a visual and aural experience full of passion, humility and a zest for life."

The Paris theater-goers of 1913 would not have been able to believe their eyes!

Vocabulary: extending word use (act, conduct, dance, play)

17 Read the text. Fill in the blanks with the correct form of the words *act*, *conduct*, *dance*, *play* (as nouns or verbs).

Open air

It was a beautiful summer's day. Flags were **a** .... *in the breeze.* Up on the open-air stage the orchestra was tuning up, ready for the first **b** .... The director of music walked on to the stage, but instead of starting the music his first **c** .... was to turn to the people in the crowd. "Some of you," he said (and as I watched him I thought he was **d** .... *strangely*), "have accused members of my orchestra of *disorderly* **e** .... on their last visit to this town when they attended the dance at the town hall. But nothing could be further from the truth. It was *just part of an* **f** .... to publicize the concert that evening. I can't see why anyone would want to *make a song and* **g** .... *about it.*" Then he turned back to his musicians and the music started and a couple **h** .... the tango up there in front of us. Then a young ballerina came on to the stage to dance a solo, but she was very nervous because she knew that the tango dancers were a *hard* **i** .... *to follow.*

In the special seating area the mayor was **j** .... *attendance* on the conductor's wife, a woman of great beauty. Simon was looking over at them, pointing and giggling. "*Get your* **k** .... *together,*" I hissed, but he was jumping up and down, **l** .... *like a baby.* That's when I knew I had to leave because nothing, apart from an **m** .... *of God*, could possibly be worse than what I was experiencing.

18 Find phrases in italics in Activity 17 that mean:

a a natural event (flood, hurricane, etc.) that you cannot control
b bad behavior
c Behave! Get more organized!
d behaving childishly
e behaving in a peculiar way
f doing absolutely everything possible to please someone
g exaggerate and act excessively about something
h It is difficult to do as well as the person or people before.
i moving in a light wind
j They were only pretending.

19 What do these phrases mean?

a to dance to someone else's tune
b to lead someone a merry dance
c to act as if you are better than someone else
d to get in on the act

20 **Language research** Use a dictionary or any other source to look up the word "play" and complete the following tasks.

a How many different main meanings does the verb have?
b How many different main meanings does "play" have as a noun?
c How many phrasal verbs (often called phr. v. in dictionaries) include the word play?
d How many idiomatic phrases (e.g. "play hard to get") does the verb occur in?

21 Choose two phrasal verbs and two idiomatic expressions with the words *act*, *dance*, or *play*. Use them in sentences and ask your colleagues to say your sentences with the same meaning, but without using the words *act*, *dance*, or *play*.

Grammar: spoken tags

22 Noticing language Read the following conversation and underline all the tags. The first one is done for you.

LILY: You're free this evening, <u>aren't you</u>?

ANDY: Sure. Why?

LILY: There's a new show on at the Arts Theater, isn't there?

ANDY: Yeah. It's called something like *O Go My Man*. By that writer Stella Feehily. Somebody said, didn't they, that it was a really good piece of work.

CATHERINE: Is it? I haven't heard anything about it.

MARTIN: Hey, Chris, open the window, would you?

CHRIS: Sure. That better?

MARTIN: Yeah. Thanks. So let's get tickets for it, shall we?

CATHERINE: Oh, come on. No one wants to go to the theater, do they?

MICHELLE: Well, I do.

CATHERINE: No, you don't! You told me that you hated the theater.

MICHELLE: When was that?

CATHERINE: About six months ago.

MICHELLE: Yeah, well, people can change their minds, right?

ANDY: So you like theater now, do you?

MICHELLE: Dunno. I'd like to give it another try, and who knows, I may enjoy it. I used to like ballet when I was a kid, didn't I?

MARTIN: What's that got to do with it?

MICHELLE: Well, that's something, itsn't it?

CATHERINE: Oh, all right. You win. I'll call, shall I, and see if they've got any tickets for tonight.

LILY: Why not go to the theater website?

CATHERINE: I can buy them there, can I?

LILY: Yep. Sure.

23 In pairs Study the dialogue again and say whether the following phrases are true or false.

a If a sentence is negative the tag is always positive (or vice versa).

b Tags always come after the sentence or phrase they refer to.

c We can use tags to make a request more polite.

d With *let's* we use *shall* in the tag.

e With verbs like *used to* and *ought to* the verb is repeated in the tag.

Read 13A–13G in the Mini-grammar to help you.

24 Add tags to the following sentences. Where possible put the tags in the middle of the sentence.

a Call me after the show.

b Get me some coffee.

c He ought to try an evening at the ballet.

d Let's put on a play for the school.

e She used to act in theater shows at the university.

f You can get tickets for the show.

g You like going to the theater.

h You told her about our arrangement to meet outside the theater at nine.

i You would like to be an actor.

j I reminded you that she wanted to join us in the restaurant after the theater.

Listening

25 TV commercial Look at the following script for a TV ad. It is for a breakfast cereal called "All-Brown." Practice reading it with a partner.

Scene. A young mother or father is walking the dog. Two children are running behind. The mother/father speaks to camera.

Mother/father:
I work hard. I play hard. Sometimes I just need a regular* day. That's when I reach for the "All-Brown." And some ice-cold milk—then I'm ready for anything life throws at me.

* Regular means the digestive system is working well!

26 Choose an actor Different students act out the scene in front of the class. Who should get the job?

27 Listen to Track 30 and complete the chart

Name of the program

Name of the play (and author)

Description of the play

Description of Sarah

Description of the scene you are going to hear

28 Listen to the scene from the play on Track 31. Think of adjectives to describe:

a the scene
b Sarah
c the director

29 Explain the following lines. Who says them: Sarah or the director?

a Acting is a vocation.
b Do you have the sheet with the lines, yes?
c Get a job at Kroger's.
d I did burn. I still burn.
e I made an awful mess of that.
f I want you to deliver the monologue with that exact sense of discovery and passion.
g I'd really like to have another go.
h I've come this close to being in a film with Kevin Spacey.
i If you could just stay on the blue mark, please.
j Once was more than enough.
k Principles need finance.
l That does it for me every time.

30 In groups of three Two students take the parts of Sarah and the director. The third is the real director and helps the two actors. Read the scene from *O Go My Man* in the Activity Bank 28 on page 140. Rehearse one of the following scenes:

Extract 1: from the beginning of the scene **to** SARAH That does it for me every time.
Extract 2: from DIRECTOR Talk to me a bit about a pash **to** SARAH Does it matter? Do I?
Extract 3: from DIRECTOR Do you have the sheet with the lines, yes? **to** DIRECTOR Once was more than enough. Goodbye.

The real director helps the actors say the lines correctly, and use gestures and facial expressions correctly.

31 Look at the Audioscript again and answer the following questions.

a Do the characters interrupt each other? If so, why and when?
b Do the characters speak in the same way as people write? What, if any, are the differences?
c What is the function of the words and phrases in italics?
d When do the speakers use question tags? How many different types do they use?

Writing: write (a scene from) a play

32 Choose one of these situations (or a different situation if you prefer). Use the Writing Tips to help you write a short scene for the situation you have chosen.

• An actor goes for an audition for a part in a commercial.
• Someone goes for an interview for a job—but doesn't know anything about the job and has to pretend that he or she does.
• Someone is trying to teach two teenagers to dance, but they aren't interested and make fun of the teacher.
• Someone wants to go to the movies, but a friend or friends aren't very enthusiastic.

Practice your scene with classmates and act it out. If possible, film the scene.

WRITING TIPS
• Try to make your scene sound like spoken rather than written English. For example, someone offering a cup of coffee might just say "*Coffee?*" instead of "*Would you like some coffee?*"
• Include interruptions (if you think it is necessary).
• Use spoken features of English (like tags, etc.).
• Put in stage directions to say how someone feels (*wearily*).
• Put in stage directions to say where a character goes (*going over to the window*) or what he or she does (*taking a sip of coffee*).

Review: grammar and functional language

33 Tag confusion Read the conversation. The tags are all mixed up. Can you unscramble the conversation and put them in the right place?

A: There's a new movie on at the Picturehouse, have you?

B: Yeah. It's a German one by that Turkish director. You said, shouldn't we, that you'd seen his first film.

A: I told you that, haven't I?

B: Yes, and you said we should see whatever he did next, can you?

A: Yeah. I remember. So let's go tonight, will you?

B: Well, we ought to call Keith and ask him, won't I?

A: I suppose so. Call him up, shall we?

B: Why can't you?

A: I have things to do, did I?

B: Like what? You haven't missed another deadline, isn't there?

A: Afraid so.

B: You just can't finish your work on time, didn't you?

A: You're right.

B: And if it goes on like this you'll lose your job, shall we?

A: Guess so.

B: So let's not go to the movies, won't you?

A: OK. I suppose I'll just have to stay in and work, didn't you?

B: You suppose right.

34 The tag-tag chain Student A asks Student B a question. Student B makes a sentence with a tag on the same topic. Student C makes a new sentence with a tag (but must not say the same sentence or tag). Now it's Student D's turn. How long can the class keep going?

A: Would you like to go to the movies?

B: The movies are a great art form, aren't they?

C: You like the movies, do you?

D: People ought to go to the movies more often, shouldn't they?

35 Fridge, trash can, suitcase
Look at the word lists. Decide if they are words you would use regularly, never, or in the future. List them in the appropriate part of your notebook.

36 Act, draw or explain Make teams. A member of team A is given a word from the Word List, or a phrase from Word Plus. They act it out, draw it, or explain it (without using the word or phrase). Their teammates have to guess the word or phrase.

Review: vocabulary

Word List

act (noun)	home economics
boo	miracle
charismatic	resentful
choreographed	scandal
classical music	stubborn
determination	to jeer
discordant	transform
disenfranchised	transformative

Word Plus

act of God
all hell broke loose
calm someone down
change the course of history
come on to the stage
disorderly conduct
fighting broke out
flags dancing in the breeze
hard act to follow
hottest ticket in town
inattentive
just part of an act
raise his or her baton
the (first) act/someone's first act
to act as if ...
to act like a ...
to act strangely
to dance attendance on someone
to dance to someone else's tune
to get (your) act together
to get in on the act
to lead someone a merry dance
to make a song and dance of something

UNIT 12

Telling stories, telling jokes

→ phrasal verbs
→ story words and phrases
→ ghostwriting

Speaking: making a story

1 **In groups** Look at the pictures. Find as many words as you can to describe them (and what's in them). Say what they remind you of and how they make you feel (positive or negative).

a

b

c

f

e

g

h

i

Reading: the arrival

4 **Read the following introduction and complete the task that follows.**

You are going to read a passage from a novel called *The Ghost* by the British author Robert Harris.

In *The Ghost* the narrator has been asked, in somewhat suspicious circumstances, to help the fictional ex-Prime Minister of Britain (Adam Lang) write his memoirs. Lang is staying in Martha's Vineyard, an island off the east coast of the United States.

When the narrator-ghostwriter arrives at Martha's Vineyard it is night. It is winter.

Imagine that you are the narrator of *The Ghost*. Describe your arrival.

a How do you get there?
b Who meets you?
c What is the place like at this time of year?
d How do you feel?

2 **In pairs** Try to think of a fictional story which uses as many of the ideas/items in the pictures as possible. You can use one of these titles or come up with your own.

It Could Have Been Worse!
That's the Problem with Love!
The Arrival
Two Ways to Get what You Want

3 **Competition** Tell your story to the class. Who tells the best story?

5   Now read the extract. Were there any similarities to your description?

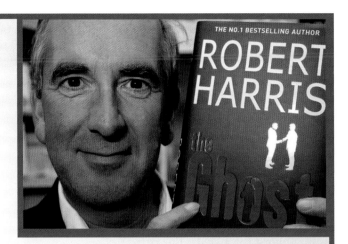

THE NO.1 BESTSELLING AUTHOR
ROBERT HARRIS
the Ghost

We rounded the West Chop lighthouse and came into the ferry terminal at Vineyard Haven just before seven, docking with a rattle of chains and a thump which almost sent me flying down the stairs. I hadn't been expecting a welcoming committee, which was fine, because I didn't get one, just an elderly taxi driver holding a torn-out page from a notebook on which my name was misspelled. As he heaved my suitcase into the back, the wind lifted a big sheet of clear plastic and sent it twisting and flapping over the ice in the car park. The sky was packed white with stars.

I'd bought a guide book to the island, so I had a vague idea of what I was in for. In summer the population is a hundred thousand, but when the vacationers have closed up their holiday homes and migrated west for the winter, it drops to fifteen. There are a couple of highways, one set of traffic lights, and dozens of long dandy tracks leading to places with names like Squibnocket Pond and Job's Neck Cove. My driver didn't utter a word the whole journey, just scrutinized me in the mirror. As my eyes met his rheumy glance for the twentieth time I wondered if there was a reason why he resented picking me up. Perhaps I was keeping him from something. It was hard to imagine what. The streets around the ferry terminal were mostly deserted, and once we were out of Vineyard Haven and on to the main highway there was nothing to see but darkness.

By then I'd been traveling for seventeen hours. I didn't know where I was, or what landscape I was passing through, or even where I was going. All attempts at conversation had failed, I could see nothing except my reflection in the cold darkness of my window. I felt as though I'd come to the edge of the earth, like some seventeenth-century English explorer who was about to have his first encounter with the native Wampanoags. I gave a noisy yawn and quickly clamped the back of my hand to my mouth.

"Sorry," I explained to the disembodied eyes in the rear-view mirror. "Where I come from it's after midnight."

He shook his head. At first I couldn't make out whether he was sympathetic or disapproving: then I realized that he was trying to tell me it was no use talking to him: he was deaf. I went back to staring out of the window.

After a while we came to a crossroads and turned left into what I guessed must be Edgartown, a settlement of white clapboard houses with white picket fences, small gardens, and verandas, lit by ornate Victorian streetlamps. Nine out of ten were dark but in the few windows which shone with yellow light I glimpsed oil paintings of sailing ships and whiskered ancestors. At the bottom of the hill, past the old whaling church, a big misty moon cast a silvery light over shingled roofs and silhouetted masts in the harbor. Curls of wood smoke rose from a couple of chimneys. The headlights picked out a sign to Chappaquiddick ferry, and not long after that we pulled up outside the Lighthouse View Hotel.

Again, I can picture the scene in summer: buckets and spades and fishing nets piled on the veranda, rope sandals left by the door, a dusting of white sand trailed up from the beach—that kind of thing. But out of season the big old wooden hotel creaked and banged in the wind like a sailing boat stuck on a reef. The sea was pounding away nearby in the darkness. I stood with my suitcase on the wooden deck and watched the lights of the taxi disappear around the corner with something close to nostalgia.

6   In your own words how would you describe:

   a   the taxi driver
   b   the narrator's "mistake"
   c   the narrator's state of mind
   d   the houses he saw
   e   the hotel

Did you like reading this extract? Do you think you would like to read the book?

7 Vocabulary Find in the text:

a a place where ferries leave and arrive.

b a verb that means "looked carefully, in detail."

c a verb that means "traveled annually to a different place" (as birds do, for example).

d the name of a native American people.

e a type of boundary around a lawn, very typical of American houses.

f things that children play with on beaches.

g a word for a sharp line of rocks.

h a feeling of sadness for what has passed.

i a wooden platform outside a house.

Language in chunks

8 Match a–d with 1–4 to make phrases from the text. How would you explain their meaning to a learner of English?

a I had a vague idea of what I

b My driver didn't

c out of

d Perhaps I was keeping him from

1 season

2 something

3 utter a word

4 was in for

9 Complete the following sentences with phrases from Activity 8.

a Don't let me .... your work. I just wanted to ask you a question.

b How can one be expected to know how you are feeling if you .... ?

c .... the whole town is deserted.

d As I went into the principal's office my mind was racing with questions and nervousness. I had no idea ....

Grammar: phrasal verbs

10 Look at the text by Robert Harris again. Find phrasal verbs with *make, pick, pull* that mean:

a to collect   b to discover/decide   c illuminated   d stopped

11 Finding phrasal verbs Which of the phrases in italics are phrasal verbs?

Happy ending

It all started when a taxi driver *backed into* her car. Luckily she was stationary at the time, so no one was hurt. But despite that she *blew up* instantly and *got out* of her car shouting angrily. The taxi driver was apologetic. He watched her as she *walked up* to him and you could tell that he was not *looking forward to sticking up for* himself. The woman *stuck* her head *into* the window and started yelling, but then suddenly she *broke off* and *looked at* the taxi driver, and *ran back to* her car. The taxi driver *got out* of his cab and *went over to* her. He asked her if she was all right and, to his surprise, she *broke down*. She said that she had recently *broken up with* her boyfriend, and as she spoke she was *tearing* a cardboard cigarette pack *into* little pieces. At that moment he knew that he wanted to *look after* her and now, a few months later, they are both *looking forward to* their wedding. The moral of the story? Well, even the worst events can *bring about* good results!

Read 14A in the Mini-grammar to help you.

12 Meanings Which of the verbs in the text in Activity 11 mean:

a became angry

b care for

c cause to happen

d defending

e finished a relationship

f started to cry

g stopped

h thinking of the future with eager anticipation

13 Look at the dictionary entries for these two phrasal verbs. What are the grammatical differences between them?

go into sth. *phr. v.*
1 JOB [not in passive] to start to do a particular type of job: *I always wanted to go into nursing.* | *She's thinking of* **going into business** (=starting a business).

come up with sth. *phr. v.*
1 to think of an idea, answer, etc. *Is that the best excuse you can come up with?* | *We've been asked to come up with some new ideas.*
2 informal to produce an amount of money: *We wanted to buy the house but we couldn't come up with the cash.* | *How am I supposed to come up with $10,000?*

Read 14 B–D in the Mini-grammar to help you.

14 Rewrite the following sentences using the phrasal verbs in brackets. Where possible, put the object between the verb and the particle (*on*, *in*, *up*, etc.).

The not-so-happy ending

a (head toward) We were going in the direction of his parents' house.

b (double back) But we had to change direction 180 degrees because we had taken a wrong turn.

c (put up) I wished they hadn't agreed to have us stay with them.

d (stand out from) It was easy to see their house. It was very prominent among the houses around it.

e (turn off) I stopped the engine.

f (bring up) After dinner he started to talk about the difficulty between us.

g (go through with) Finally, he said that he couldn't do it after all.

h (turn up) He arrived late for breakfast.

i (play back) Since then I have repeated the conversation in my mind many times.

j (get back to) I have called him many times, but he hasn't replied to me.

15 **Language research** Use a dictionary to find five different phrasal verbs. Write a grammar exercise like Activity 14 and give it to the class. Can they do it correctly?

Listening: a poetry podcast

16 **In groups** Rewrite this sentence so that it accurately reflects the opinion of the group (e.g., you can change *like* to *dislike*, *love*, or *don't really like*, and you can write your own reasons).

I like poetry because you can hear a whole story in just a few lines.

Compare your sentence with other pairs. Can you remember any poem by heart in English or in any other language? Tell the class.

17 **In pairs** You are going to hear four poems. Look at the titles below and answer the questions.

TITLES
"Two Cures for Love"
"Bloody Men"
"The Road not Taken"
"In Two Minds"

a Have you seen or heard them before?
b What do you think they will be about?
c What words do you expect to hear in each poem?

18 Listen to Track 32. Get as much meaning as you can from the sound of the poems. Which do you like best so far?

19 Listen to the poems again. You can read them in Activity Bank 14 on page 132 while you listen. Which poem:

a   says that no one has walked on the leaves that lie on the ground?
b   says that something is grassy and has not been walked on yet?
c   talks about standing and looking?
d   uses a metaphor to talk about men trying to get a woman's attention?
e   uses different (and somewhat literary) word order so that the poem sounds better?
f   uses a phrase that describes someone or something that always boringly does the same thing as everyone else?
g   uses a phrase that means "to know more about someone because you spend more time in his or her company"?
h   uses a phrase that means "showing off-ness"?
i   uses a phrase that means when two or more people join together against another person?

Which poem is the class favorite? Which one is *the class horror*?

20 Be group poets Write your own "In Two Minds" poem.

a   Choose a topic to write a poem about.
b   Read "In Two Minds" again and think of the structure of the poem:

What I <u>like</u> about *A* is *B*
What I <u>hate</u> about *B* is *C*
What I <u>love</u> about *C* is *D*
What I <u>hate</u> about *D* is *E*, etc.

c   Write your poem in groups.

Pronunciation: reading aloud (stress and pausing)

21 In pairs Read this poem. With a partner decide:

a   which words rhyme
b   which words or parts of words you would stress
c   where you would pause

Fire and Ice *by Robert Frost*

Some say the world will end in fire,
Some say in ice.
From what I've tasted of desire
I hold with those who favor fire.
But if it had to perish twice,
I think I know enough of hate
To say that for destruction ice
Is also great
And would suffice.

22 Practice reading the poem. Don't speak too fast.

Then listen to Track 33. Is it read in the same way that you read it? Speak along with the reader on the audiotrack.

23 Look again at the poems in Activity Bank 14. Practice reading them in the same way.

24 Competition Choose one of the poems and read it to the class. Vote on the best reader.

Vocabulary: story words and phrases

25 Dictionary definitions Match the words with their dictionary definitions.

a anecdote	1	a description of something that happened which may or may not be true, but which people tell to impress or entertain others with
b fantasy	2	a question (often in story form) that confuses you and tries to hide its humorous or clever answer—something that is difficult to understand
c legend	3	a short story that people tell about their own personal experiences
d myth	4	a story about exciting imaginary events—for example, a story for children
e riddle	5	an exciting or wonderful event or experience that you imagine happening to you—even though it probably never will
f story	6	an old, well-known story, often about bravery, adventures, or magical events (and so not often really true)
g tale	7	a story or idea which many people believe, but which is almost certainly not true

a ☐   b ☐   c ☐   d ☐   e ☐   f ☐   g ☐

26 In groups Do you know any good stories, fairy tales, riddles, or legends? Can you think of any myths?

27 Read the dialogue and answer the questions.

HELEN: Hi, Clare, how are you?
CLARE: I feel great. I'm single again.
HELEN: Single?
CLARE: I mean in the business sense. I don't work with Herbert any more.
HELEN: Why not?
CLARE: Well, *contrary to myth*, Herbert isn't clever or organized like people think. In fact, he *lives in a fantasy world* where everything just resolves itself without any effort.
HELEN: Oh dear.
CLARE: But *that's not the whole story*. He says he's a very careful person, but when he started spending the company's money—buying ridiculous things for our offices, for example— *it was a different story*.
HELEN: Oh dear!
CLARE: Yes, oh dear. But anyway, *to cut a long story short*, I sort of divorced him.
HELEN: What, just like that?
CLARE: Yep. I just walked out and left. *End of story*.

Which of the phrases in italics means

a he was not the same in that situation?
b I'm going to finish now?
c he thinks his life is different from what it is?
d there is more that I should tell you?
e unlike what people believe … ?
f in order not to go on and on … ?

28 In pairs Make a dialogue in which two people talk about something that happened to them yesterday. Use as many of the words and expressions from Activity 27 as you can.

29 Team game Team A takes one of the words or phrases below and writes one correct dictionary definition and two false ones. Can Team B guess which is the correct one? Then it is Team B's turn.

cock-and-bull story	shaggy dog story
cover story	sob story
lead story	urban myth

Now play the game with other words.

Functional language: telling jokes

30 Listen to Track 34. Which is the funniest joke? Can you guess the missing punchline?

Now look at Activity Bank 30 on page 142. Were you right? Is it funny?

31 Copy and complete the chart with the appropriate language:

Do you know the joke about …
Have you heard the one about …
Hey, hey, listen to this …
I don't get it.
I've forgotten the punchline.
It doesn't make sense.
Stop me if you've heard it before.
That's the unfunniest joke I've ever heard.
What's funny about that?
… wait for it …

Starting jokes
Reacting to jokes
(Trying to) finish jokes

32 Read the following joke. Is it funny? Practice saying it using the language from Activity 31.

One day the President went out jogging by himself. Suddenly a man wearing a ski mask jumped out from behind a tree. He was carrying a gun. He pointed the gun at the President and said, "Give me your money!"
The President was outraged. "You can't do that," he said, "I'm the President!"
The gunman thought for a bit and then said, "You're the President? OK, then, give me MY money!"

33 Guess the punchline Student A look at Activity Bank 15 on page 134. Student B look at Activity Bank 21 on page 136. Student C look at Activity Bank 29 on page 141. Student D look at Activity Bank 32 on page 142. Follow the instructions you find there.

34 Competition Who can tell the funniest joke?

Writing: be a ghostwriter

In the novel *The Ghost* by Robert Harris (see page 95), the narrator is a ghostwriter—that is, a writer who helps someone (a celebrity, politician, sportsperson, etc.) write his or her autobiography, for example. Ghostwriters don't usually get their names on the cover, but without them celebrities wouldn't know how to put their own thoughts into words.

35 Listen to Track 35. A ghostwriter is interviewing soccer star Jimmy Miller about an overseas trip he took. Answer these questions.

a Was Jimmy Miller alone or with someone else?
b Where had he just been?
c Who took what from him?
d What did Jimmy Miller do?
e What happened next?
f How did Jimmy Miller feel about the incident?

36 The ghostwriter wrote two versions of the story.

a Which version is more fun to read? Why?
b What are the exaggerations and inventions that the ghostwriter uses in one of her versions?

A

I have a problem with anger and sometimes it can land me in trouble. It nearly happened to me one night in Barcelona when I was on vacation. We had been to a restaurant called La Barceloneta, and had a romantic candlelit dinner for two. As we walked back through the city streets the air of romance was all around us, and perhaps we were too relaxed. So when a couple of guys came up and offered us tickets for a dance club (Brazilian music, he said, and we like that), I was really interested. Well, the guy seemed friendly. And then he tripped me. Only slightly.

I knew at once, of course. I reached into my back pocket, just to check, and it was true. My wallet was gone. And that was when it hit me, that feeling of rage, pure uncontrolled rage. It frightens me, you know. And I turned on my heel and shouted something rude and charged after those guys. I'm a fast runner, and I was really mad so I was catching up with them—and I would have caught them, too. But at that moment one of them threw the wallet down in the street at my feet. A really smart thing to do. Of course, I bent down to pick it up and by the time I realized that it was empty and all my money was gone—the thieves had disappeared.

But I was lucky that time. If I had caught them, who knows what might have happened? They might have had a knife or I might have beaten them senseless. It's something I need to control, that temper of mine.

B

We were walking home after an enjoyable but expensive meal at La Barceloneta restaurant. It was about eleven o'clock and we were feeling relaxed. Two or three men—they were very friendly—came up to us and offered us tickets for a dance club, and then one of them tripped me and took my wallet.

I felt my back pocket and I realized what he had done, so I turned and ran after him. I was angry, you see. And I nearly caught him. But he threw my wallet down in the street in front of me. It was empty and I lost two hundred euros. I suppose it was a good thing I didn't catch him because he might have had a knife.

37 In pairs Student A interviews Student B about one of the topics below. Try to get as much information from B as you can. Use the interview language below.

Topics
- Arriving in a new country
- First day at school
- Victim of a crime
- The best present I have ever received
- The time I narrowly avoided injury
- One of my finest achievements
- The worst/best journey I can remember

Ghostwriter interview language
Can we go back to the bit where you ... ?
How did you feel when this happened?
I'd just like to establish the sequence of events / I want to get the sequence of events clear in my head.
So what you are saying is that you ... .

Then change. Student B interviews Student A.

38 Write the interview as a first person narrative. Make it sound good and interesting, just as real ghostwriters do.

WRITING TIPS
- Try to find a theme for the extract (like the ghostwriter in Activity 36, who focused on the "anger" theme).
- You can add some of your own ideas—but not too many.
- Work out a good sequence for your extract.
- Find a dramatic way of saying simple things ("pure unconditional rage" rather than anger).
- Think of a good concluding sentence or thought.

Review: grammar

39 Look at the list of phrasal verbs. Choose five and write sentences that have the same meaning but do NOT use your verbs. Can your classmates guess the phrasal verbs?

act something out	bring up	put somebody up
act up	double back	run up
blow up	get back to	stand out from
break down	go through with it	turn off
break off	head toward	turn up
break up with	looking forward to	
bring about	play back	

Example: She suddenly got very angry. (= blow up)

40 Put the following words in order to make sentences. Add the correct punctuation (including capital letters).

a between / broke / countries / out / the / two / war
b a / after / children / could / couple / for / hours / look / of / please / the / you
c don't / for / I'll / if / it / it / off / off / turn / turn / you / you
d could / for / I / if / night / put / the / up / want / you / you
e agreement / back / don't / now / of / our / out / please
f a / because / dictionary / didn't / I / I / in / it / know / looked / the / up / word

Complete these sentences with the lines a–f. Write in the correct letter.

1 .... and many people lost their lives.
2 .... and now I can use it with confidence!
3 I can't stand the noise of that wretched radio ....
4 I need to go out and get some things at the store so ....
5 If you really don't have anywhere to stay ....
6 Listen, I've already spent money on our plan so ....

Review: vocabulary

Word List	
anecdote	nostalgia
bucket and spade	picket fence
cock-and-bull	reef
conformity	riddle
cover story	scrutinize
deck	shaggy dog story
fantasy	sob story
gang up on	tale
lead story	unseemly
legend	swank
migrate	urban myth

Word Plus
a (very) different story
contrary to myth
cut a long story short
end of story
keep someone from something
live in a fantasy world
not utter a word
out of season
that's not the whole story
a vague idea (about/of)

41 Complete the sentences with a phrase from Word Plus.

a .... the place is really depressing because there's no one around.
b .... the President is not ill, as everyone seems to think.
c Don't let me .... I'll just wait till you're finished.
d He .... if he thinks he's ever going to win the lottery.
e I could go on and on, but .... there was no one there to meet me when I arrived.
f I have .... about quantam physics, but I can't say I know much about it.
g In public she's all sweetness and light, but at home it's ....

42 Fridge, trash can, suitcase
Look at the word lists. Decide if they are words you would use regularly, never, or in the future. List them in the appropriate part of your notebook.

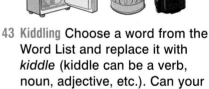

43 Kiddling Choose a word from the Word List and replace it with *kiddle* (kiddle can be a verb, noun, adjective, etc.). Can your classmates guess what word it is?

Example: According to kiddle, Brendan, an Irishman, discovered America before Columbus! (= legend)

Extra activities

Unit 1

Reading

1 Find places for sentences a–f in the text. There is one sentence that does not fit into any of the spaces.

a Although most advertising is directed toward our consumer desires, a lot of it is directed toward our fears.

b For example, people fear flying because they think they might crash, or heights because they think they might fall.

c He thought that advertising was brainwashing and called advertisements "the poison of mass suggestion."

d There are several other words of Greek origin relating to fears and phobias.

e At one extreme, there is mild caution, which manifests itself, for example, in the care one takes when walking down a darkened staircase.

f If you are frightened of flying, this is a phobia, a common one that, incidentally, has two names—aviophobia or aviatophobia.

"Fear is not the natural state of civilized people."

The quotation above is from Aung San Suu Kyi, the Burmese pro-democracy activist, one of the bravest people of her generation, and someone who has faced frightening circumstances in her life and has dealt with them well. But many people, whether in "civilized" countries or not, live in a permanent or regular state of fear, even if their lives are not in any particular danger. Why should this be?

Fear is an emotional response to threats and danger, often connected to pain. [1_____]

Fear is a survival mechanism, and usually occurs in response to a specific negative stimulus.

There is a wide spectrum of fear responses. [2_____]

At the other, there is extreme phobia or paranoia, which is a disturbed thought process where the fears and anxieties felt are excessive and out of all proportion to the situation.

The difference between a phobia and paranoia can best be explained by the following example. [3_____]

However, if you are on a plane and get a panic attack because you are convinced that the pilot is untrained or didn't sleep the night before, or is an alcoholic, or even worse that he/she has some secret reason for wanting to crash the plane—this is paranoia.

The original Greek word παράνοια (paranoia) simply means "madness" (**para**—outside, **nous**—mind). While it would seem sensible for society to find ways to reduce the overwhelming sense of fear that some people have, there is one area of modern life where our fears are emphasized—in advertising. [4_____]—the fear of growing old, the fear of becoming poor and—possibly the strongest—the fear of not being as affluent as our neighbors, sometimes referred to as "keeping up with the Joneses."

More than 30 years ago, social philosopher Erich Fromm was one of the first to criticize the advertising industry and the type of person it appealed to. "A healthy economy is only possible at the expense of unhealthy human beings," he said. [5_____]

Unsurprisingly, the advertising industry spent millions of dollars trying to undermine Dr. Fromm's message, calling it biased and unfair.

Wordplay

2 These are four well-known phobias. Do you know anyone who suffers from them? Describe the feelings.

arachnophobia: fear of spiders
claustrophobia: fear of enclosed spaces
agoraphobia: fear of open spaces
acrophobia: fear of heights (normally called vertigo)

3 Read the list of less well-known phobias. One of them is made up. Can you spot which one? Why do you think so?

The ABC of phobias

arachibutyrophobia: the fear of peanut butter sticking to the roof of the mouth
bibliophobia: the fear of books
caligynephobia: the fear of beautiful women
decidophobia: the fear of making decisions
ephebiphobia: the fear of teenagers
foodophobia: the fear of eating
genuphobia: the fear of knees
hippopotomonstrosesquippedali-ophobia: the fear of long words
ichthyophobia: the fear of fish
kathisophobia: the fear of sitting down

Decisions

4 What would you say in the following circumstances?

a Someone has invited you and your friend for a helicopter ride over a famous city. You want to do it but your friend is frightened of the idea of flying in a helicopter. What would you say?

b You are in a small harbor and you see a group of people about to depart on a whale-watching trip. One of the people decides not to go. You would love to go but you don't know the people. What would you say to them?

c You and three other people on a beach have just rescued a child who was in danger of drowning. The other three don't speak English and a TV news company wants to interview you. What would you say?

And finally …

5 The following groups of three words are in alphabetical order. Each time the middle word only is defined. What are the middle words? All the missing words are in the Word List on page 13.

Example: dangerous
be prepared to do something dangerous = dare
dark

a fraud
to preserve by making very cold = ...
frequent

b nothing
famous for doing something bad or dangerous = ...
nourishing

c precious
a creature that kills and eats other creatures = ...
prediction

d subtext
indirect, so that people hardly notice = ...
success

e tennis
not definite, not certain = ...
terrace

Unit 2

Reading

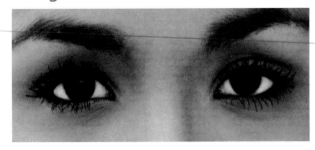

1 Read the following passage and choose the best answers.

Keep an eye on it!

One of the best things you can do for your eyes is to have them checked by your doctor whenever you have a physical examination.

An ophthalmologist is a medical doctor who **specializes in examining, diagnosing, and treating eyes and eye diseases.** An optometrist is not a medical doctor, **but has been trained to diagnose and treat many of the same eye conditions as ophthalmologists,** except for treatments involving surgery.

It's a good idea to have your eyes checked at least every two years or even more frequently if you have a family history of eye problems, such as glaucoma or early cataracts.

Dealing with common eye problems and injuries:

• If you have a red eye, pain in an eye that doesn't go away within a short period of time, or at any time have had changes in your vision, **then it's time to have your eyes checked.**

• If you get any small foreign objects in your eye, such as sand or sawdust or metal shavings, **don't rub it. Flush your eye** for several minutes with lukewarm water (it may be easiest to do this in the shower). If it still feels as though there is something in your eye, then **be sure to see an eye specialist.**

• If you've been hit in the eye and it looks strange or appears to be bleeding, or if you have changes in or lose your vision, go to a hospital emergency department right away to be checked out.

The best rule of thumb for when to see an eye specialist if you injure your eyes is: "When in doubt, check it out!"

1 An ophthalmologist …
  a is not a medical doctor.
  b can perform eye surgery.
  c is the same as an optometrist.
  d has not specialized in eyes.

2 It is recommended that …
  a everyone should have their eyes checked twice a year.
  b families who have eye problems check their eyes more often.
  c you should check your eyes every two years if you have a cataract.
  d you don't need to check your eyes if your family has good eyes.

3 You should see an eye specialist if …
  a you had a pain in your eye that went away.
  b you removed something recently from your eye.
  c you have cleaned your eyes with water.
  d you can feel something strange in your eye.

4 You should go to the hospital emergency room if you were hit in the eye …
  a but your eye looks normal.
  b but your vision remains constant.
  c and your eye seems different.
  d and you haven't had a checkup.

Grammar

2 Now rewrite these sentences from the text using the word given. Use between three and six words.

a One of the best things you can do for your eyes is to have them checked by your optician. (ought)
  → You _____ by your optician.

b An ophthalmologist is a doctor who specializes in examining, diagnosing, and treating eyes and eye diseases. (can)
  → An ophthalmologist is a doctor who _____ and eye diseases.

c An optometrist is not a medical doctor, but has been trained to diagnose and treat many of the same eye conditions as ophthalmologists. (can)
  → An optometrist is not a medical doctor, but _____ many of the same eye conditions as ophthalmologists.

d It's time to have your eyes checked. (should)
  → You _____ .

e If you get any small foreign objects in your eye, don't rub it. (must)
  → You _____ if you get any small foreign objects in it.

f If it feels as if there is something in your eye, be sure to see an eye specialist. (must)
  → You _____ if it still feels as though there is something in it.

3 Read this passage and complete it with one word for each blank.

How eye color develops

The colored part of the eye is called the iris, which has pigmentation **a** .... determines our eye color. Human eye color originates with three genes, two **b** .... which are well understood. These genes account for **c** .... most common colors—brown, blue, and green. Other colors, such as gray, hazel, and multiple combinations, are not fully understood or explicable **d** .... this time.

We used **e** .... think of brown being "dominant" and blue being "recessive." But modern science has shown that eye color is **f** .... at all that simple. Also, eye colors don't come out **g** .... a blend of the parents' colors. Each parent has two pairs **h** .... genes on each chromosome. So multiple possibilities exist, depending **i** .... how the "wheel of fortune" spins.

Most babies **j** .... born with blue eyes that can darken in **k** .... first three years. Darkening occurs if melanin, a brown pigment usually not present **l** .... birth, develops with age. Children can have completely different eye colors **m** .... either of their parents. But if both parents **n** .... brown eyes, it's most likely that their children **o** .... also have brown eyes.

Vocabulary

4 Say which of these eye colors these sentences refer to according to the text in Activity 3.

> brown blue green hazel gray

a It was originally thought to be the dominant eye color. ....
b Parents with eyes this color will probably have children with the same color eyes.
   ....
c Most babies are born with eyes this color.
   ....
d It was originally thought to be the recessive eye color. ....
e Scientists do not completely understand how these colors occur ....
f These are the most common eye colors:
   ....

5 Think of one word that can be used in all three sentences. The words are all in the Word List on page 21.

a • Her .... really hurt and she thought it might be broken.
   • Do you think it's a good idea to .... the police? Do they need guns?
   • He was not carrying a weapon. He had left his .... at home.
b • The little girl liked to .... around as quickly as she could.
   • It's a simple game. You have to throw this .... at that board.
   • He let his eyes .... over the photo, trying to find her face.
c • She's very unusual looking. You really notice her eyes; they're very ....
   • The workers were .... again for higher wages.
   • As she arrived, Big Ben was .... two o'clock.
d • I can't make .... of this article. It's so badly written.
   • Rob has a great .... of smell.
   • I can usually .... when there is something wrong with my mother.
e • Jake was very .... of people watching him.
   • When they took my tooth out I was .... the whole time.
   • Was it a .... decision to change jobs or were you fired?

Unit 3

Reading

1 Read the text and answer the multiple-choice questions.

The Exonerated is a play that tells the stories of six Americans who were sentenced to death for crimes they did not commit, and who were later freed after spending time—in some cases many years—on Death Row. The information is taken from the letters, case files, and personal statements of the six people.

Although they were all freed, they endured harsh and brutal treatment, often from other prisoners, while they were in prison. And, of course, they woke up every morning knowing that they might be executed for a crime they had not committed.

The six include a man from Texas named Kerry, who spent 22 years in jail before being freed on DNA evidence. Another man, Gary, was actually convicted of murdering his own parents, and only freed when two motorcycle gang members confessed to the crime.

Some of the stories are unbelievable. Robert, an African-American, spent seven years on Death Row in Florida for the murder of a white woman, despite evidence that the victim had grabbed the hair of her attacker, and the hair was from a white person. Or David, a shy young man who wanted to become a priest, who was forced to confess to a robbery and murder he had nothing to do with.

At the center of these stories is Sunny, a bright and cheerful woman who spent 17 years in prison after she and her husband Jesse were convicted of the murder of two police officers. They had been framed by another suspect, who put the blame firmly on Sunny and Jesse, who were hitchhikers he had given a ride to. Eventually, the man confessed to having committed the crimes himself, but not before Jesse had been sent to the electric chair.

The Exonerated was performed in New York more than 600 times and toured for 27 weeks across the country. Productions of the play were staged in several other countries, too. In 2002, it was watched by Governor George Ryan of Illinois. At the time, he was considering whether to commute the sentences of over 140 Illinois Death Row inmates. It was also made into a film in 2005, starring Susan Sarandon as Sunny and Danny Glover as David.

1 *The Exonerated* is a play about six people who
  a committed serious crimes.
  b confessed to serious crimes.
  c were convicted of serious crimes.
  d were guilty of serious crimes.

2 Despite the fact that the six people were all freed,
  a terrible things happened to them in prison.
  b they might have committed the crimes.
  c they were imprisoned again.
  d people continued to think they were guilty.

3 One of the reasons why they were freed was that
  a the crimes didn't take place.
  b there was no evidence.
  c someone else confessed to the crime.
  d the police believed them.

4 Sunny and her husband were convicted of a crime
  a that was committed by someone they didn't know.
  b that took place in a car.
  c after they were accused of it by another suspect.
  d that involved the killing of two hitchhikers.

5 The play was seen by a state governor
  a after he had agreed to the execution of a lot of prisoners.
  b after he had freed a lot of prisoners.
  c while he was thinking about changing the sentences of Death Row prisoners.
  d who didn't know if he could release prisoners on Death Row.

6 *The Exonerated*
  a is a stage play that was performed only in New York.
  b is a stage play and also a film.
  c has never been seen outside the United States.
  d was performed on stage by a cast including Susan Sarandon.

Discussion

2 Read the descriptions and decide if a crime or misdemeanor has been committed. Find its name and agree what the punishment should be.

a A young man goes to a bar, gets drunk, and has an argument with another customer. At a certain point, the young man threatens to kill the other customer. The owner of the bar calls the police.

b Some people are taking part in a street demonstration against the expansion of an airport. The organizers of the demonstration have been given police permission to hold the demonstration. One demonstrator runs forward and accidentally knocks a policeman over. The result is an ugly argument involving seven demonstrators and four policemen.

c An employee of a bank "borrows" $100,000 from the bank and invests it in some shares which he is sure will make an instant profit. They do, and he plans to put the money back in the bank, but his action is discovered before he can do this.

d A man is walking past a jewelry store at two o'clock in the morning. He is carrying a brick.

e A man plants some trees, which grow quickly and cast a shadow over his neighbor's garden. The neighbor complains to the police.

f When a young man's computer is searched for stolen files, police discover that he has downloaded several hundred music tracks from the Internet.

And finally...

3 The following are genuine excuses given to police officers for speeding. Which do you think is the best?

1 "When the car eventually stopped, the man told me he was rushing to the hospital because he had been stung by a bee and was allergic."

2 "The driver told me that she was speeding because she was late for her appearance in court for traffic violations. She didn't want to upset the judge."

3 "I discovered the gentleman was 89 years old. He was driving at 100 mph. When I told him I had to give him a ticket, he said that his wife had a heart condition, and he thought that telling her he had received a ticket might give her a heart attack. He also asked if there was a senior citizens' discount on the speeding fine."

4 "The driver told me that her fish had just died and she couldn't focus on her driving."

5 "When I asked him why he had just parked in a no-parking zone, the driver told me that he had no control over his actions because someone had hypnotized him to park illegally."

Reading

1 In this newspaper article about how people are attracted to each other two paragraphs have been removed. Which are the missing paragraphs?

Sexual attraction: the magic formula

Finding your perfect match really is about the right chemistry, but it's a complex equation, says the American scientist Martie G. Haselton.

As a scientist studying human behavior, I am not too surprised by the mysterious nature of how we go about choosing a partner. Mate selection is a highly complex process. We are consciously aware of only part of it; the rest is either inherently unpredictable or operates outside our awareness, which leads us to the perception that love is about ineffable chemistry. [1]

Of course, we don't fall in love with supermates like these. The average person who did would be headed nowhere, because supermates are inaccessible to all but a few. This is likely to be part of the reason why love evolved: to bond us for cooperative child-rearing, but also to assist us in choosing, so that we don't waste time and energy falling for someone who is unattainable. Instead, people tend to fall for others who, on attractiveness, intelligence, and status, are of a similar ranking to themselves. [2]

How do people who differ in their MHC find each other? This isn't fully understood, but we know that smell is an important cue. People appear to literally sniff out their mates. In studies, people tend to rate the scent of T-shirts worn by others with dissimilar MHC as most attractive. This is what sexual "chemistry" is all about.

A So much for outward appearances. What about the less obvious cues of attraction? Fascinating work on genetics and mate preferences has shown that each of us will be attracted to people who possess a particular set of genes, known as the major histocompatibility complex (MHC), which plays a critical role in the ability to fight pathogens. Mates with dissimilar MHC genes produce healthier offspring with broad immune systems. And the evidence shows that we are inclined to choose people who suit us in this way: couples tend to be less similar in their MHC than if they had been paired randomly.

B Physical attraction seems to be the most straightforward, but it can sometimes surprise us the most. Despite the notion that physical attraction is simply about who is "good-looking," it goes far beyond what our eyes see. Physical attraction is influenced by everything from the chemicals our bodies produce to the images we're exposed to in the media. Luckily, physical attraction can be also shaped by personal experiences, which means that even if you aren't physically drawn to someone immediately, you can become more so over time.

C Let's start with the conscious part. There are some things we all find attractive. Men tend to desire women with features that suggest youth and fertility, including a low waist-to-hip ratio, full lips, and soft facial features. Recent studies confirm that women have strong preferences for virile male beauty—taut bodies, broad shoulders, clear skin, and defined, masculine facial features, all of which may indicate sexual potency and good genes. We also know that women are attracted to men who look as if they have wealth or the ability to acquire it, and that men and women strongly value intelligence in a mate. Preferences for these qualities—beauty, brains, and resources—are universal. The George Clooneys and Angelina Jolies of the world are sex symbols for predictable biological reasons.

2 Now read the whole text and choose the best answer.

1 The author says
 a it's easier to find a partner nowadays.
 b we are fully aware of how we choose a partner.
 c that part of attraction has to do with chemistry.

2 Both men and women are attracted to
 a a person who seems young and able to have children.
 b a person who has skin without blemishes.
 c a person who seems to be clever.

3 Humans tend to fall in love with a person who
 a is a celebrity of some kind.
 b is similar in many ways.
 c will already have children.

4 Couples tend to produce healthier children if their MHC genes are
 a different.
 b the same.
 c similar.

Grammar

3 Read this description and the comments on the book *The Time Traveler's Wife*. Would you like to read the book? Why or why not?

The Time Traveler's Wife is the story of Henry DeTamble, a librarian who involuntarily travels through time, and Clare Abshire, an artist who lives life in chronological order. Henry and Clare's passionate romance lasts and tests both the bonds of love and the strength of fate.

As Clare and Henry take turns telling the story, a sci-fi premise becomes a powerfully original love story.
People

A singular tale of a charming man with a funny condition (he slips in and out of time) and the woman who loves him.
San Francisco Chronicle

To those who say there are no new love stories, I heartily recommend *The Time Traveler's Wife*, an enchanting novel, which is beautifully crafted and as dazzlingly imaginative as it is dizzyingly romantic.
Scott Turow (author)

Haunting, original and so smart it took my breath away … in short the rare kind of book that I finish and jealously wish that I'd written.
Jodi Picoult

Audrey Niffenegger imagines this story of an accidental time traveler and the love of his life with grace and humanity. Fiercely inventive, slyly ambitious and, lovingly told, *The Time Traveler's Wife* sparkles as it fearlessly explores the delicate interplay of love and time.
Anne Ursu

Niffenegger compassionately develops her unique characters with the grace to accept their difficult circumstances as well as their blessings. Don't be deceived by the easy charm of Henry and Clare's relationship … . They will break your heart.
Curledup.com

4 Underline all the adverbial phrases in the comments above.

Example: … <u>powerfully original</u> love story

5 Change the parts in bold in these sentences to include adverbial phrases.

a **The writer wrote the story with great passion and** it is one of the most popular novels of the year.

  Example: Passionately written, this story is one of the most popular novels of the year.

b Because the story **is written very well, the director can direct the movie in an intelligent way.**

c She **is also able to tell the story with love** because it is **written in a passionate way.**

d **The woman was stirring the beans very fast** as she sang her favorite song.

e **He hit the ball with great skill** to win the game.

f **The movie develops in a very slow way,** but I recommend this movie very highly.

g The **writer is very funny in a charming way** and makes the reader feel **involved in a very intimate way.**

Unit 5

Vocabulary

1 **Complete the text with the correct words.**

	1	2	3	4
a	hundreds	one	great many	several
b	recorded	discovered	written	played
c	extremely	nearly	already	usually
d	ban	banned	bans	banning
e	more notorious	least-liked	best-ever	best-selling
f	previous	following	same	different
g	classic	classical	classically	classics
h	world	world's	worldly	worldwide
i	featuring	starring	inclusive	reminiscent
j	awarded	nominated	won	given
k	title	unique	latest	solo
l	childhood	vacation	career	recording

The Power of Love

"When the power of love overcomes the love of power, the world will know peace." *Jimi Hendrix, rock star (1942–1970)*

Over the years, there have been **a** .... pop songs with the word "power" in the title. The earliest (and possibly still the most famous) is the 1971 song "Power to the People," written and recorded by former Beatle John Lennon and the Plastic Ono Band. The album, *John Lennon/Plastic Ono Band*, was Lennon's first solo album and was released in 1970. The album was **b** .... at the Abbey Road Studios, the place where most of the Beatles' albums were made, and is generally considered one of Lennon's finest solo albums and a landmark recording.

The years between 1984 and 1991 saw the release of not one but FOUR different songs, all with the same title — "The Power of Love."

The first band to release a song with this title was Frankie Goes to Hollywood, a Liverpool group fronted by the outrageous and **c** .... provocative Holly Johnson. Johnson was determined to disturb what he considered to be the dull and bland world of pop. The group's debut single, "Relax" (1984), was famously **d** .... by the BBC while at number six in the charts, which immediately led to massive demand for it. The song subsequently topped the UK singles chart for five consecutive weeks. "Relax" went on to become the seventh **e** .... UK single of all time. The band's next two singles, "Two Tribes" and "The Power of Love," also topped the charts, making Frankie Goes to Hollywood only the second act in the history of the UK charts to reach number one with their first three singles.

The **f** .... year, 1985, saw the release of two more songs called "The Power of Love." American Jennifer Rush's song is now a **g** .... pop ballad (it's the one with the line "I am your lady, and you are my man"). Interestingly, the song was not a hit in her native country, but it became a **h** .... megahit, was translated into several languages, and was covered by several artists, including Céline Dion.

In Spanish the song was translated as "Si Tu Eres Mi Hombre" ("If You Are My Man") and has been recorded by many Latin artists including Amanda Miguel, Angela Carrasco, and Los Melódicos. Some versions of the song have been made in a Latin style i .... salsa and merengue rhythms. Brazilian singer Rosana recorded a Portuguese version, "O Amor e o Poder," in the 1980s. Dominican singer Anaís sang a "Spanglish" version of the song in her Así Soy Yo tour concerts.

"The Power of Love" is also the title of a 1985 single by Huey Lewis and the News written for the film *Back to the Future*. It gave the band their first number one hit on the U.S. Billboard Hot 100 and was j .... for an Academy Award. The song appears in the film when Marty McFly (Michael J. Fox) and his band play the song for a Battle of the Bands audition. Interestingly, Huey Lewis himself plays the part of one of the judges.

The fourth and last song called "Power of Love" was the k .... track of the seventh album by Luther Vandross and was released in April 1991. Vandross, who died in 2005, was an American rhythm-and-blues and soul singer-songwriter and record producer. During his l .... , he sold over twenty-five million albums and won eight Grammy Awards, including Best Male R&B Vocal Performance four times.

So "The Power of Love" seems to have been quite a powerful thing in the lives of all the people who wrote and recorded it.

2 Watch the four songs on YouTube™. Write a short review of each one, indicating whether you like it or not.

3 Here are three different types of words connected with the word *pleasure*. Choose other words from the Word List on page 45 or use a dictionary and make similar lists.

pleasure

Same word:

pleasant pleasing pleased

Same meaning:

enjoyment happiness delight joy contentment satisfaction

Opposite meaning:

displeasure dissatisfaction pain unhappiness

Unit 6

Vocabulary

1 Choose the correct word to complete this biography of Estée Lauder.

The early part of the Estée Lauder biography is a mystery. Voting records say her birth date is July 1st, 1908, whereas her family says she was born in 1906. She was born Josephine Esther Mentzer, the youngest of nine kids to a .... Max and Rose Schotz Mentzer. Her family called her "Esty," which became "Estée" after a school official **b** .... it as such. They lived in the apartment above her father's hardware store in Queens, New York.

Estée Lauder started her **c** .... in selling when she agreed to help out her uncle, Dr. Schotz, a chemist. She helped him sell some of the creams he made for the company, New Way Laboratories, that he **d** .... in 1924. She sold creams with names like Six-In-One Cold Cream and Dr. Schotz Viennese Cream to beauty shops, beach clubs, and resorts.

In 1930 she married Joseph Lauter (which later became Lauder). They separated in 1939, only to **e** .... in 1942. Estée Lauder said of this, "I was married very young. You think you missed something out of life. But I found that I had the sweetest husband in the world."

She and her husband continued to make their creams in their factory—a **f** .... restaurant—and Estée Lauder Inc. was formed in 1947. Their initial **g** .... came after they won a concession from Saks Fifth Avenue in 1948 to sell their cream. After the initial products sold out in only two days, their path was set.

The event that put Estée Lauder firmly on the map was the **h** .... of Youth Dew in 1953. It was both a bath oil and a perfume (retailing at $8.50) and sold over 50,000 units in the first year.

Explaining her success, she said, "I have never worked a day in my life without selling. If I believe in something, I sell it, and I sell it hard." This attitude, together with an uncompromising **i** .... in her product and the beauty in all women, made Estée Lauder a **j** .... household name.

Over the years, numerous lines were added to the Estée Lauder companies. Estée Lauder continued to be **k** .... involved in the company—always attending new launches—until she broke a hip in 1994. In 1995, the company **l** .... $335 million when Estée Lauder finally went public.

Estée Lauder died on April 26th, 2004, but her contribution is remembered. Today, Estée Lauder is a recognized **m** .... name in over 118 countries with $3.6 billion in annual sales and her family's shares are worth $6 billion. Her company might never have set a **n** ...., but they were never left behind.

a	1 immigrants	2 foreigners	3 strangers	4 fathers
b	1 rewrote	2 described	3 put	4 misspelled
c	1 job	2 career	3 profession	4 life
d	1 made	2 produced	3 formed	4 built
e	1 remarry	2 marry	3 commit	4 return
f	1 changed	2 converted	3 reconstructed	4 rebuilt
g	1 advance	2 plan	3 breakthrough	4 progress
h	1 announcement	2 presentation	3 entrance	4 introduction
i	1 belief	2 feeling	3 opinion	4 idea
j	1 respected	2 cherished	3 beloved	4 admired
k	1 dynamically	2 actively	3 completely	4 boldly
l	1 earned	2 won	3 raised	4 gained
m	1 company	2 business	3 brand	4 enterprise
n	1 direction	2 mode	3 vogue	4 trend

Reading

2   They were unlikely friends, **Arthur Conan Doyle** (1859–1930), the Scottish-born creator of the detective Sherlock Holmes, and Harry Houdini (1874–1926), America's most important magician of the day. On closer examination they appear to have plenty in common: both men were famous around the globe, and while their career paths were different, they were both extremely athletic and strong. But what brought them together was what, ironically, eventually drove them apart—spiritualism, the belief that one could communicate with the dead.

Conan Doyle had come to believe in spiritualism after his son was killed in World War I. Conan Doyle became an expert in the field and even wrote a two-volume *History of Spiritualism* in 1926. Houdini, on the other hand, was deeply sceptical of spiritualism and took every opportunity to use his understanding of magical illusion to expose mediums and psychics he thought were fakes.

Soon after their correspondence had turned into a friendship, introductions from Conan Doyle allowed Houdini access to dozens of mediums during an extended tour of Great Britain. Unknown to Doyle, however, Houdini was far from becoming a believer: "The more I investigate the subject," he wrote, "the less I can make myself believe." Inevitably, despite a growing personal friendship, the two great men moved towards a confrontation.

Their dispute began when Houdini joined the Doyles for a seance, in which Lady Doyle suggested contacting Houdini's beloved mother. Houdini did believe in an afterlife, so he agreed, but by the time Lady Doyle had filled 15 sheets with automatic writing she claimed had come from his mother, Houdini had only become further convinced that he was witnessing a fraud. Although he left without saying anything, Houdini knew that he had not heard from his mother. Houdini's mother had been a rabbi's wife, and Houdini knew she never would have used the Christian sign of the cross as Lady Doyle said she had; and, more convincingly, she had barely spoken any English when alive and it now seemed that after death she had become totally fluent! It simply did not sound like his dear mother, and Houdini resented it. It was the beginning of the end of the friendship between Doyle and Houdini.

Choose the best answer according to the text.

a   Arthur Conan Doyle and Houdini became friends because
   1 of a mutual interest in sports and athletics.
   2 their careers were similar in some ways.
   3 they were both interested in spiritualism.

b   Houdini used his knowledge of magic and illusions to
   1 communicate directly with dead people as a psychic.
   2 show people when someone else was not telling the truth.
   3 write books about talking to people who were dead.

c   When Houdini was on a tour of Great Britain
   1 he visited many different psychics who knew Conan Doyle.
   2 he met Arthur Conan Doyle for the very first time.
   3 he became a firm believer in psychics and mediums.

d   Houdini agreed to try to contact his dead mother because
   1 he believed that it was possible to contact people after death.
   2 he was no longer a friend of Arthur Conan Doyle and his wife.
   3 his mother and Lady Doyle had had a friend in common.

e   Houdini knew the communication did not come from his mother because
   1 his mother spoke much better English than the writing.
   2 his mother's faith was misrepresented by the communication.
   3 his father would not allow her to communicate with him.

Grammar

3   **Complete these paragraphs about the end of Houdini's life by writing the verb in the correct form.**

Houdini a .... (lie) on his couch after a performance in Canada in 1926, while an art student b ....(draw) him. A student named Gordon Whitehead c .... (come) in and d ....(ask) if it was true that Houdini e .... (be able to) take any blow to the stomach. Houdini f .... (repeat) what he g ....(say) on many previous occasions—that, yes, this h ....(be) true. At that moment, Whitehead i .... (hit) him three times, before Houdini j .... (have) time to prepare himself. Although he k .... (be) in serious pain, Houdini, nevertheless, l .... (continue) to travel without seeking medical attention. He m ....(suffer) from appendicitis for several days and n ....(refuse) medical treatment.

When Houdini o .... (arrive) at the Garrick Theater in Detroit, Michigan, on October 24th, 1926, for what p .... (be) his last performance, he q ....(have) a fever of 104°F (40°C). Despite a diagnosis of acute appendicitis, Houdini r .... (go) on stage. Afterwards, he s ....(take) to hospital and t .... (die) on October 31st, 1926, at the age of 52.

Unit 7

Reading

1 Read Text 1 and answer multiple-choice questions a–c.

Text 1

FACTFILE: What is a megacity?

In 1800, only 3 per cent of the world's population lived in cities. By the end of the twentieth century, nearly 50 per cent did so. In 1950, there were 83 cities with populations exceeding one million. By 2007, this number had risen to 468 **agglomerations** of more than one million people.

A **megacity** is a **metropolitan area** with a population of more than 10 million people, usually with a **population density** of 2,000+ people per square kilometer. A key feature of a megacity is **rapid economic growth**, often combined with high levels of poverty, crime, and **social fragmentation**. Often, megacities are formed when two or more metropolitan areas converge into one, usually called a **conurbation**.

In 2000, there were 18 megacities—conurbations such as Tokyo, New York City, Mexico City, São Paulo, and Karachi. Greater Tokyo already has a **dependent population** of 35 million people, which includes such areas as Yokohama and Kawasaki. This is more than the entire population of Canada.

These days, important cities with smaller populations, such as London or Paris, which are also important centers of the global economic system, are referred to as **global cities**. These cities attract foreign investment and are home to the **corporate headquarters** of **multinational companies**. In addition, they usually have large **expatriate communities**, a **thriving cultural scene**, and are host to **world sporting and cultural events**.

Although in most countries, employment prospects, accommodation, health care, and entertainment are better in cities than in rural areas, the fact is that one billion people, one-sixth of the world's population, now live in **shantytowns**. Crime, drug addiction, alcoholism, poverty, and unemployment are rife in these areas, and the situation is getting worse. It is estimated that by 2030, over two billion people in the world, nearly one quarter of the world's population at that time, will be living in **slums**.

a Which of the following is an example of "social fragmentation"?
   1 Lots of employment opportunities.
   2 The breakup of families.
   3 Families emigrating to new countries.
   4 People who like living alone.
b Which of the following is NOT one of the outward signs of a successful megacity?
   1 Offices of companies that are not necessarily owned by people from that city.
   2 A lot of foreigners living and working in the city.
   3 People emigrating to other countries.
   4 An event such as the Olympic Games.
c What is likely to happen worldwide to the population of the poorer areas of cities?
   1 It will rise to one-sixth of the population.
   2 It will stay the same.
   3 It will go down.
   4 It will rise to about 25 percent of the people in the world.

2 Now read Text 2 and answer multiple-choice questions d–f.

Text 2
The birth of a world city

The conglomeration that is now Mexico City was founded on March 18th, 1325, by the Nahua Aztec people, who called it Tenochititlán. It quickly became a thriving and prosperous metropolis. Built on a small island in the middle of Lake Texcoco, it was connected to the shoreline by a series of causeways, some of which were the origins of the various *calzadas* (roads) that are the main avenues of the city today.

The beautiful old Aztec city was mostly destroyed by Hernán Cortés and the Spanish conquistadores and the rebuilt city became the capital of the viceroyalty of New Spain. The Mexicans freed themselves from Spanish rule in 1821. Subsequently, Mexico City, in common with most world cities, was shaped and influenced by various different styles.

The three decades that Porfirio Diaz was in control of the country, toward the end of the nineteenth century and the beginning of the twentieth, led to a French influence on the architecture of the city. About this time, the stunning bronze Angel of Independence was built to celebrate the first centenary of the beginning of the War of Independence.

The expansion of the metropolitan area of Mexico City has been astonishing. In 1900, there were 344,000 residents. By 1940, the population had increased to 1,670,000 and by the year 2000 it had reached 18 million.

By any interpretation of the expression, Mexico is a global city. Quite apart from the size of its population and its cultural and economic importance in the Americas, Mexico has also hosted one summer Olympic Games (1968) and two soccer World Cups (1970 and 1986).

In the last twenty years, Mexico City has continued to grow as an economic and cultural center of international importance, which has in turn led to the construction of new skyscrapers in the downtown area. Mexico now boasts Latin America's tallest building, the Torre Mayor, and a rebuilt World Trade Center Mexico, originally the Hotel de México, which was built in the 1960s.

d What were the origins of Mexico City?
  1 It was built by the Spanish conquerors.
  2 The original influence on the city was French.
  3 The first inhabitants were Aztecs.
  4 It was built on the shores of a lake.

e How did the population of Mexico City grow?
  1 It increased by more than a million in the first 40 years of the twentieth century.
  2 It was already a million during the presidency of Porfirio Diaz.
  3 It increased slowly from 1940 to the end of the century.
  4 It remained the same during the second half of the twentieth century.

f Which of these indicates that Mexico is a global city?
  1 It has the tallest skyscraper in Latin America.
  2 It has continued to grow for 20 years.
  3 World sporting events have taken place there.
  4 It has a growing population.

Discussion

3 Read this list of problems in large urban areas. Decide which you think are the three most serious and give reasons.

  1 unemployment
  2 crime
  3 drug dealing and use
  4 inadequate water supplies
  5 poor public transportation
  6 traffic congestion
  7 poor health services
  8 inadequate education services
  9 air pollution
  10 social fragmentation

4 Discuss what the world community can or should do to help people who are suffering from these problems.

Reading

1 **Read the texts. The missing sentences on the right are in the texts below. Write the right letter in the space. There is one more sentence than you need.**

Queens of crime

Patricia Highsmith was born in Texas in 1921 but she spent much of her life in Switzerland and France. Her first novel, *Strangers on a Train*, was first published in 1950 and was an immediate success. 1 .... But despite this early commercial success Patricia Highsmith was never fully appreciated in her native country as long as she lived.

Her most popular literary creation was Tom Ripley. 2 .... He was a charismatic sociopath who made his first appearance in 1955 in *The Talented Mr. Ripley*. 3 .... After Highsmith's death, *The Talented Mr. Ripley* was made into a film. The success of the film renewed interest and appreciation in Highsmith's literary work in the U.S.

Patricia Highsmith wrote more than 20 novels, many of which have been translated into many languages. She won many awards, including the O'Henry Memorial Award, The Edgar Allan Poe Award, the *Grand Prix de Littérature Policière*, and the Award of the Crime Writers Association of Great Britain. She died in Switzerland in 1995, where her literary archive is kept.

Ruth Rendell is an acclaimed mystery and psychological crime writer. She was born in England and has also published under the pseudonym Barbara Vine. Rendell's most prominent creation is Chief Inspector Reginald Wexford, the protagonist of 21 of Rendell's novels. 4 .... He has made his latest appearance in the 2007 novel *Not in the Flesh*.

Apart from the Wexford novels, Rendell has written psychological crime novels whose protagonists are isolated and disadvantaged. Rendell explores themes such as the impact of chance and coincidence and the effects of miscommunication. 5 ....

Ruth Rendell has won many awards, including the Crime Writer's Association Gold Dagger for 1976's best crime novel; a second Edgar in 1984 from the Mystery Writers of America; and a Gold Dagger Award in 1986 for *Live Flesh*, later to be made into a film by acclaimed Spanish filmmaker Pedro Almodóvar. She was the winner of the 1990 *Sunday Times* Literary Award, as well as the Crime Writers' Association Cartier Diamond Dagger for outstanding contribution to the genre. In 1996 she was awarded the CBE (Commander of the British Empire). Her books have been translated into 22 languages. 6 ....

A They are also published to great acclaim in the United States.

B Unlike other crime fiction creations Tom Ripley was neither a detective nor a hero.

C He appears in Rendell's first novel *From Doon with Death* (1964).

D Four more novels with Ripley as the main character were to follow.

E She has made an outstanding contribution to the genre.

F It was made into a film by Alfred Hitchcock.

G Rendell further explores psychological themes, such as the effects of secrets kept hidden.

Grammar and vocabulary

2 Read the text and write in the letter next to the word that best fits each space.

How to become a mystery writer

Ever since childhood I have enjoyed stories, both making them up and reading them. I am particularly **1** .... to the excitement of a good mystery novel, whether it revolves around the trials and tribulations of secret agents or a good, old-fashioned detective.

But telling a good story is one thing; writing a good story is quite another. Having **2** .... becoming a mystery writer, I needed help to get started. I searched numerous websites for hard-and-fast rules to no avail. **3** ...., most "teach yourself" manuals seem to agree that the best place **4** .... is the library. They suggest **5** .... good examples of the genre. They recommend that **6** .... through the work twice. A good mystery novel will demand that you read it fast; after all, one of the attributes of good fiction is that the reader cannot put the book down. The second reading, though, should be slow and deliberate to allow you to analyze the qualities that keep the reader turning the pages: the way different authors describe scenes and link them to others, how they introduce and develop characters, and the **7** .... they build up suspense.

What about ideas? Where do they come from? A writer looks at the world in a slightly different way from other people and lets his or her imagination take flight. You may read a story in a newspaper that triggers your imagination. Or you may see someone on the bus who simply looks to you as if **8** .... a character in a book. Someone a little bit **9** .... perhaps or, on the contrary, a **10** .... whose conventional lifestyle may hide a host of dark secrets. As soon as you recognize the potential for a story it is advisable **11** .... them down while they are still fresh in your mind. For this purpose I have taken to carrying a little notebook with me. I have enjoyed going through my notes and writing the odd paragraph. I have yet to write the novel, but I feel I may have taken the first step towards the completion of my first blockbuster. Well, one has to start somewhere!

1 (a) susceptible	b keen	c interested	d into
2 a set my mind to	b made up my mind	c set my mind on	d decided to
3 a What is more	b Moreover	c Therefore	d However
4 a to get starting	b to get start	c to get started	d for start
5 a one to read	b that one reads	c that to read	d one reading
6 a the reader go	b the reader went	c the reader to go	d the reader going
7 a how	b method	c strategy	d way
8 a he is	b he were	c he had	d he would be
9 a boring	b conventional	c eccentric	d conformist
10 a boring	b conventional	c eccentric	d conformist
11 a you writing	b writing	c that you write	d to you to write

3 Read this passage and complete it with one word for each gap.

Philip Marlowe is a fictional character created by Raymond Chandler in a series of novels including *The Big Sleep* and *The Long Goodbye*. Marlowe **1** .... appeared in *The Big Sleep*, in 1939. Marlowe didn't appear in any of Chandler's early short stories, though many of **2** .... were republished years later with the name of the main **3** .... changed to Philip Marlowe. Marlowe is a tough, hard-drinking man **4** .... is not afraid of violence, **5** .... he would not be violent for the sake of violence. **6** .... the tough façade, though, the private eye is an educated, contemplative man. He is college-educated and has a **7** .... for classical music.

In his role as narrator, Marlowe moves through the criminal world and social elite of Los Angeles in the 1930s. He was **8** .... on the screen by several famous actors, notably Humphrey Bogart in the 1946 adaptation of *The Big Sleep*.

And finally...

4 Who do these sentences refer to? Write the names:
Humphrey Bogart
Raymond Chandler
Philip Marlowe

a This private eye is one of the best-known characters in crime fiction. ....

b He is best known for his tough but honest private investigator. ....

c Others have since played the role but his remains the best portrayal of the famous sleuth. ....

d Unlike other famous gumshoes, he is not susceptible to the charm of *femmes fatales*. ....

e As a master of the unsentimental school of crime fiction, he criticized other writers for their lack of realism. ....

Reading

1 Find a place in the text for these phrases:

a   but represented other countries
b   for the last 30 years
c   in both events
d   fewer than three million people
e   70 per cent of people on the island
f   the first time in the history of this event
g   there is no evidence
h   third largest island
i   this is a much higher percentage
j   two of the questions

Extreme talent—why are Jamaicans so good at sprinting?

Jamaica is the **1** .... in the Caribbean Sea, about 100 miles south of Cuba. It has a population of **2** .... and a reputation as a place where people like to hang loose and relax.

And yet this island exploded into prominence at the 2008 Beijing Olympics when sprinters Usain Bolt and Shelly-Ann Frazer won the men's and women's 100 meters gold medals. In the women's event, Sherone Simpson and Kerron Stewart, also from Jamaica, dead-heated in second place and were both awarded the silver medal. This is **3** .... that the same nation has provided all three medallists on the podium.

Jamaica also won gold in the men's and women's 200 meters finals, thanks to Veronica Campbell-Brown and Usain Bolt (again!). Bolt also broke the world record **4** .... Competitors from the island won several other sprint medals, including the men's 4 x 100 meters relay and the women's 400 meters hurdles.

So **5** .... everyone is asking are: Why are Jamaicans so good at sprinting, and why have they never won medals like this before?

To answer the second question first: although it is true that athletes representing Jamaica had never won sprint medals before, three men who won the Olympic gold medal for 100 meters— Lynford Christie, Ben Johnson, and Donovan Bailey—were born in Jamaica **6** .... Christie ran for Great Britain and Johnson and Bailey represented Canada in 1988 and 1996, respectively. Johnson was, however, stripped of his gold medal after testing positive for anabolic steroid use.

7 .... , sprint medals have almost always been won by runners of west African descent who were born in, or grew up in, other countries. In fact, by 2004, runners from these ethnic groups had 495 of the top 500 times at 100 meters—a phenomenal statistic.

Jamaicans have another natural advantage. Not long ago, it was discovered that **8** .... have the strong form of the ACTN3 gene, which produces a protein that helps "fast-twitch" muscle fibers, the kind that help you with short, explosive bursts of action. **9** .... than other nationalities. Sadly for athletes hoping to emulate their Caribbean rivals, **10** .... that slow-twitch muscles can turn into fast-twitch, even after extensive training!

Vocabulary

2 Identify these items using a partitive expression.

Example: a carton of milk

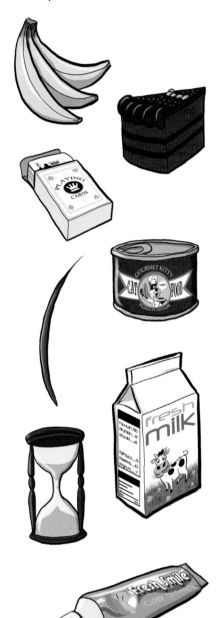

3 Complete these sentences using the expressions in Activity 2, and then explain what they mean.

a Wayne Rooney covered every .... of grass during the game.
b William Blake once said you can see the whole world in a .... of sand.
c That examination was a .... of cake!
d She's the kind of person who squeezes the last drop out of a .... of toothpaste.
e The man invited me on to the stage, showed me a .... of cards, and asked me to choose one.
f That car isn't worth a .... of bananas!

And finally …

4 The following verbs have (at least) two meanings. Use each one twice to complete the sentences.

turn away	turn on
turn back	turn out
turn down	turn up
turn in	

a Could you .... the music .... please? I'm trying to sleep.
b Can someone remember to .... the lights when you leave?
c Manchester United get such big crowds that thousands of fans are .... every week.
d I had just .... the TV .... when his face appeared in the news item.
e It's after midnight and I'm tired, so I'm going to ....
f After an unimpressive start, he .... to be a fine student.
g The weather was so bad I couldn't see through the windshield, so I decided to .... and go home.
h Have you noticed how he always .... at meal times?
i He was pleased that his shares managed to .... another good performance.
j Jazz really .... me .... and puts me in a good mood.
k As I walked toward him, he .... , as if he didn't want me to see his face.
l If they .... the sound .... any louder, we will all go deaf.
m He's asked her out at least five times, but she keeps .... him ....
n The Viking king Canute tried to stop the sea but he discovered it was impossible to .... the tide.

Unit 10

Grammar

1 Complete the passage with a correct form of the verbs in brackets.

My name is Tina N'Guyen. I come from Vietnam. We had a big house in Vietnam, and my family lived together. In 1975, my family moved to Malaysia in a small boat. The boat journey was very frightening but we were lucky and our boat didn't capsize like so many others had. Having a .... (take) turns rowing for 48 hours, we finally arrived in Malaysia. We'd been in Kuala Lumpur for two days then we were told we had to move. We **b** .... (send) to Bulaubidong Camp, where most illegal immigrants appeared **c** .... (detain). We couldn't leave the camp to find fire wood, vegetables, or any food for the children—we **d** .... (treat) like prisoners. Sometimes my husband went fishing to feed us but we didn't have enough rice to cook. The health of the family appeared **e** .... (deteriorate) fast. Eventually, one of the children died. Having **f** .... (deny) permission to bury her according to our customs, we simply buried her in the camp. That's why I say I left part of my heart in Malaysia. After two years, when all our hopes seemed **g** .... (dash), my husband's brother sponsored us. Having finally **h** .... (release) from the camp, we left for the Philippines where we learned English for six months. Then we finally came to the United States. We didn't mind **i** .... (interview) thoroughly, because we knew we had reached our destination and were determined to overcome all obstacles. When we first arrived, we had trouble because we didn't speak English very well. We weren't used to the customs and the way of life in the U.S. I couldn't use the oven, turn on the faucet and shower, nor vacuum the floor because I had never used these things in my homeland. But we seemed **j** .... (accept) by American society and to **k** .... (give) every opportunity to succeed. Eventually, we adapted to our new life through hard work and determination. We now have a very happy family, a nice house, and a successful business.

Reading

2 Read these pages from the website "Citizenship and Immigration Canada." Find the title for the whole text and for the sections (A–K). Add them to the text. There is only one possibility for each.

A Confirmation of permanent residence
B Skilled workers and their families
C Change of address
D Criminal and security checks
E Who can apply?
F Skilled workers and professionals
G The application assessment process
H Medical examinations
I The decision on your application
J Processing time
K Welcome to Canada
L What to do next

(title) ....

1 ....
Skilled workers are people who can become permanent residents because they are able to become economically established in Canada. Your application to come to Canada as a skilled worker will be assessed on six selection factors and a point system. The six selection factors are:
- your education
- your abilities in English and/or French, Canada's two official languages
- your experience
- your age
- whether you have arranged employment in Canada
- your adaptability

You must also show that you have enough money to support yourself and your dependants after you arrive in Canada, and pass a medical examination and security and criminal checks.

2 ....
There are two application processes for skilled worker applicants to Canada:
- the simplified application process and
- the regular application process.

You must use the regular process if:
- you have been lawfully admitted to Canada for a period of at least one year and you are submitting your application at the Canadian visa office in Buffalo, or:

- you have been lawfully admitted into the United States for a period of at least one year and you are submitting your application at the Canadian visa office in Buffalo
- you are a provincial nominee
- you have been selected by Quebec
- you are eligible for points for arranged employment.

If none of the situations described above applies to you, you must use the simplified application process.

3 ....

After you submit your application, a Citizenship and Immigration Canada (CIC) officer will verify that you have submitted all the required documentation with your application. The officer will make sure you have:
- completed your application form correctly and signed it
- paid your processing fee, and
- included the required supporting documentation if you used the regular application process.

If you applied using the simplified application process, the visa office will contact you and ask you to provide the required documentation about four months before your application is to be processed.

If your application is not complete, the visa office will return it to you without processing it.

The visa office where you applied will send you a letter when it receives your completed application and verifies that it is completed properly. The letter will tell you what you need to do and what happens next.

4 ....

The length of time it takes to process applications varies, depending on where you applied. You can check application processing times in the I Need To ... section on the right-hand side of this page. You may be able to avoid unnecessary delays by:
- making sure all the necessary information is included with your application
- notifying the visa office of any changes to personal information on your application, such as your address, phone and fax numbers or a change in the make-up of your family
- avoiding repeated inquiries to the visa office
- ensuring that the photocopies and documents you provide are clear and legible
- providing certified English or French translations of original documents that you submit in other languages and
- applying from a country where you are a citizen or permanent resident.

Your application will be delayed if the visa office has to take extra steps to assess your case. Your application will take longer if:
- there are criminal or security problems related to your application
- your family situation is not clear because of a situation such as a divorce or an adoption that is not yet complete or child custody issues that have not been resolved or
- the visa office that processes your application has to consult with other CIC offices in Canada or abroad.

You can check the status of your application online after the visa office has started to process your application. Select the *Check my application status* button in the I Need To... section on the right-hand side of this page.

5 ....

You must pass a medical examination before coming to Canada. Your dependants must also pass a medical examination even if they are not coming to Canada with you.

Applications for permanent residence will not be accepted if an applicant's health:
- is a danger to public health or safety, or
- would cause excessive demand on health or social services in Canada.

Instructions on how to take the medical examination will normally be sent to you after you submit your application to the visa office. I Need To... section on the right-hand side of this page.

6 ....

If you have a criminal record, you may not be allowed to enter Canada. People who pose a risk to Canada's security are not allowed to come to Canada either.

If you want to immigrate to Canada, you and any family members over the age of 18 who come to Canada with you must provide police certificates to the visa office.

If you apply using the regular application process, you must submit the police certificates with your application. If you apply using the simplified application process, the visa office will contact you and ask you to provide the required documentation at a later date.

You can find more information about criminal and security checks in the I Need To... section on the right-hand side of this page.

7 ....

A CIC officer will make a final decision on your application based on the current requirements for immigration to Canada. The decision will be based on several factors, including the results of your medical examination, and the criminal and security checks.

The officer will also assess the proof of funds you have provided, to ensure that you will be able to support yourself and your family when you arrive in Canada.

The visa office will contact you if it needs more documentation or if you are required to attend an interview.

If your application is approved, you will be asked to submit your passport to the Canadian visa office where you applied, in order to receive your permanent resident visa.

8 ....
If you move or change your address, telephone number, or any other contact information after you submit your application, you must contact the visa office where you submitted your application.

9 ....
If your application is approved, the visa office will issue a permanent resident visa to you. Your permanent resident visa includes your Confirmation of Permanent Residence (COPR) and your entry visa. Your COPR will include identification information as well as your photograph. Please check the information on your COPR to make sure it is correct. It should be the same as the information on your passport. If there is a mistake on your COPR, contact your visa office.

You must have your COPR and your visa with you when you arrive in Canada.

3 **Answer the questions by choosing answers from list A–K. All the questions have only one answer.**

1 Who must you notify of any change of contact information?

....

2 Where can you find information on criminal and security checks?

....

3 What must an applicant and any family member provide?

....

4 Who makes the final decision on your application?

....

5 What will disqualify you from entering Canada?

....

6 What application process must you use if your situation is not listed on this page?

....

7 What may cause your application to be returned unprocessed?

....

8 What documents must you have when you arrive in Canada?

....

A COPR and visa
B an immigration lawyer
C police certificates
D the visa office
E the Canadian consulate
F the I Need To... section
G a criminal record
H an incomplete application form
I a CIC officer
J the simplified application process
K the website

And finally ...

4 **The following people want to live in Canada. Will their application be successful? Say what problems they may have, according to the information on the website.**

a Pascal Leduc is French. He is a musician. He has committed several driving offenses.

b Sonya Studinka is Polish and in the process of divorcing her British husband, who is contesting custody of their only child.

c Pedro Gómez was evicted from his home and has no permanent address or contact number.

d Gino Pasquale wants to move to Canada with his family. He has no money, having lost it all after his business went bankrupt.

e You want to live in Canada permanently. Would you have any problems with your application?

Unit 11

Reading: music and youth

1 Match the pictures 1 or 2 with the texts on this and the next page.

Picture 1

Picture 2

2 Read Text A and fill in the blanks with one word for each space.

Text A:

Want to get rid of troublesome teenagers? Try Mozart.

If you have ever felt **a** .... when standing at a bus stop or a railway station because there are a lot of threatening **b** .... people standing around and causing trouble, then this will be music to your **c** .... The Tyne and Wear passenger transport authority have come up with a new way of **d** .... teenage troublemakers from making your life a misery. How do they do it? It's easy! Just ask Mozart, Rachmaninov, and Vivaldi!

In the past the authorities have used expensive **e** .... circuit TV systems, and heavy policing. But they have found that piping the **f** .... of classical and romantic composers has the same effect—and it costs far less. According to Tom Yeoman from the transit authority, "We had problems with youths hanging around, not getting up to criminal activities exactly, but involved in low-level anti- **g** .... behavior like swearing and harassing passengers. We were worried about what might **h** .... Passengers were complaining, so we introduced classical music at Tynemouth, Whistley Bay, and Cullercoats stations. It has completely **i** .... the problem. The young people seem to loathe it. It's pretty uncool to be seen hanging around somewhere when Mozart is **j** ...."

A woman who works locally says: "The music has made a huge **k** .... I used to feel intimidated by the children, but now you don't see them hanging around anymore."

3 Read Text B and complete it with five of the following sentences. The other sentences do not belong in the text.

a But the task didn't stop with making music more accessible.

b I played those four notes all day.

c It looked like Legner's life was heading in one direction only—and it wasn't a good one.

d Maestro Abreu sums it up perfectly.

e The orchestra has played to rapturous receptions all over the world.

f The maestro decided children from every walk of life should have access to a classical music education.

g Thousands of other underprivileged kids across Venezuela have made a similar journey.

Text B:

Want to help troublesome teenagers? Try *El sistema*.

At the age of 12, Legna Lacosta was on the streets. He left his home in Caracas, Venezuela, and started a life of crime. A year later he was carrying a gun and at the age of 15 he ended up in a young offenders' institution after a savage police beating. 1 .... "I was bored," he says, "and I didn't want to do anything."

But one day, a youth orchestra project turned up and he had his first contact with a clarinet. "When the instruments arrived, the director told me there was a clarinet left. I didn't know what it was. I was fascinated when I saw it. He taught me the first four notes. 2 ...."

By 17, Legner was back at the detention center, but this time in a smart polo shirt and trendy thick-rimmed glasses, to teach clarinet. "Music saved my life," he says. "It helped me let out a lot of the anger inside. If music had not arrived, I wouldn't be here today." He has now moved to Germany to continue his studies.

3 .... They have drifted off the smog-filled streets where car horns and salsa compete for maximum volume into one of the many teaching centers that are cropping up all over the country's *barrios*. They are part of *El sistema* (the System), and it's come a long way since it started in 1975. Its flagship, the Simon Bolivar Youth Orchestra, now has an international reputation as one of the world's most impressive musical groups.

The program is the brainchild of maestro José Antonio Abreu, a trained economist and classical musician, who rejected the elitism and economic exclusions inherent in Venezuela's classical music scene. Faced with the challenge of democratizing a music scene in a country whose oil wealth has not trickled down to the poor majority, Abreu designed an ambitious program tailored to Venezuela's social reality. 4 .... But the task didn't stop with making music more accessible. *El sistema*'s main objective was, and still is, to create a new musical culture as a way to make music a way of life. A walk through the rabbit-warren corridors of *El sistema*'s headquarters in downtown Caracas reveals countless photo collages of zillions of smiling children, each brandishing his or her instrument. From his office overlooking the urban sprawl of the center, Javier Moreno, general manager of *El sistema*, tells me: "We're interested in creating citizens with all the values they need to exist in society: responsibility, teamwork, respect, cooperation, and the work ethic." 5 .... He says an orchestra is the only group where people get together to reach agreement and they reach that agreement by producing something beautiful.

Vocabulary: collocations to do with "youth"

4 Which of the following collocations have good, negative, or neutral connotations? You can research the phrases in your dictionary or on the Internet to see what contexts they appear in.

childish behavior
childish excitement
childish laugh
childish name-calling
childish pleasure
childish sense of humor
juvenile crime
juvenile delinquent
young at heart
young for her age
youthful ambition
youthful appearance
youthful husband-to-be

And finally …

5 You work for a theater company, a musical organization, or a dance group.

a You want to attract larger audiences. Think about the information you want to find out. What questions can you ask?

b Try out your questionnaire on classmates and others. What interesting things do you find out?

Unit 12

Reading

1 **Read the text and choose the best answers to the questions on page 126.**

Poetic license

"The best poets read widely," says Wendy Cope. "Of course this will influence their work—but how else are they going to find out what makes a really superb poem?"

He was an elderly man and he had queued up with the people who were waiting for me to sign their books. When his turn came, he announced unapologetically, "I don't read poetry. I write it. I've brought you a copy of my book."

If he had been younger, I might not have been so polite. I smiled, took the book, and thanked him. Later on, a quick glance through his self-published volume confirmed what I already knew: the poems were no good. People who never read poetry don't write poems that are worth reading.

It's a free country, of course, and anyone can write whatever they like. However, if you are interested in writing well, in working at being a better poet, then the most important piece of advice that anyone can give you is that you have to read both recent poetry and the poetry of past centuries. That's how you learn. The elderly gentleman must have come across some poems at some point in order to have a concept of what a poem is. But vague memories of a few things you read at school are not enough.

It seems odd to me that anyone who hates reading poetry should want to write it at all. Are there amateur painters who never go to an art gallery? Or amateur musicians who never listen to music? Sometimes nonreading poets explain that they are afraid of being influenced. They don't understand that being influenced is part of the learning process. Some of my earliest (and unpublished) poems read like poor imitations of Sylvia Plath*. Others read like poor imitations of T. S. Eliot**. I was unaware of this at the time. Gradually, I worked my way through these and many other influences towards finding my own voice. Nowadays I hope I sound like myself in my poems, but I am still influenced by what I read, still learning.

I've spent a lot of time learning and practicing the piano, even though there was not the slightest possibility of my becoming a professional pianist. It is something I want to do for its own sake. So is writing poetry. It has to be. I've observed that people who are too focused on getting published tend not to get anywhere. If you have the urge to write poems, and to work at doing it better, good luck to you. I hope you will find the journey rewarding.

Sylvia Plath was an American poet whose life has been the subject of films and countless biographies. She wrote one novel (The Bell Jar) and many inward-looking and passionate poems that dealt with her childhood and later life. She committed suicide in 1963.
**T. S. Eliot was an American poet who moved to the UK at the age of 25. Among his greatest works are The Love Song of J Alfred Prufrock, The Waste Land, The Four Quartets, Murder in the Cathedral—and Old Possum's Book of Practical Cats.*

1 The elderly man was waiting in line
   a for an autograph.
   b to be unapologetic.
   c to buy a book.
   d to offer something for approval.
2 Wendy Cope
   a accepted a book because the man was old.
   b accepted a book even though she knew it was no good.
   c was not polite because she doesn't like that kind of thing.
   d was polite because the man didn't read poetry.
3 Wendy Cope thinks that if you want to be a better poet you should read
   a old poems.
   b poems from a range of different ages.
   c poems that were not written too long ago.
   d poems from your schooldays.
4 Wendy Cope
   a hopes she has her own individual style.
   b thinks that amateur musicians should listen to music.
   c tried to imitate poets like Sylvia Plath and T. S. Eliot.
   d worries that people might be influenced if they read other poets.
5 Wendy Cope
   a only thinks about a journey.
   b only thinks about getting her poetry published.
   c tries to be a better pianist for her own satisfaction.
   d wishes she could be a professional pianist.

2 **Complete the following sentences with what you think Wendy Cope's advice would be.**

a If you want to be a better musician, you should

....

b If you want to be a better artist, you should

....

Do you agree with her point of view about poets and reading poetry?

3 **Rewrite the following sentences using one of the phrases in the box. (See how they are used in the text.)**

find my voice	sound like
for its own sake	tend to
not enough	worth reading
part of the learning process	

a Reading poets from earlier times means your poems might be more or less OK.
b It is insufficient to have read a few poems in a magazine.
c When people are learning languages they often become frustrated.
d I hope I can write in my own style because then my poems will be my own.
e His songs have a remarkable similarity to the ones written by Nicole.
f You have to love music just because it is music—and then you might just succeed as a musician.
g Writers generally spend hours of their lives sitting by themselves.

And finally …

Team A picks a number 1–16 from a hat. A speaker from team B has to talk about the topic on that number card for 60 seconds with no hesitation or repetition. Team A can interrupt (for a point) if they hear either. A speaker from Team A continues for the remaining time. Team B can interrupt. The person who is speaking at the end of 60 seconds gets 2 points. Now Team B chooses a number and a speaker from Team A has to start …

1	detectives	9	music and dance
2	extreme sports	10	optical illusions
3	frightening animals	11	people with power
4	ghostwriting	12	poetry
5	artists who die young	13	prison life
6	immigration	14	sharks
7	Internet dating	15	virtual reality
8	megacities	16	learning English

Activity bank

1 (Unit 1)

Read the information about sharks and answer the questions in Activity 2.

Shark facts
- There are about 350 different species of sharks, and some of them are quite small.
- The first sharks appeared in ancient oceans 400 million years ago.
- Sharks are very successful predators, with sharp teeth, strong jaws, streamlined bodies, and very powerful senses.
- They are expert hunters but they don't hunt humans. They were feeding on something else a long time before humans arrived on the scene.
- Sharks are dangerous only if you invade their territory. And only about 10 of the 350 species are dangerous even then.

Now turn back to Activity 2 on page 6.

2 (Unit 2)

Activity 10

Look at these photos and discuss what they are. Make at least ten guesses. Use the expressions in Activities 6 and 7.

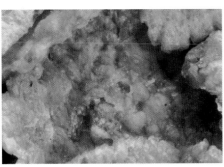

Now turn back to Activity 11 on page 16.

3 (Unit 2)

Activity 24

Now turn back to Activity 25 on page 19.

4 (Unit 2)

Activity 30 Student A

Find the sentence which explains the context of sentences a–e on page 19.

1 Her mom said she could go, but she didn't want to.
2 He doesn't have school tomorrow, so it's OK.
3 She's been taking lessons for ten years.
4 She really needs the iron. I'm always telling her, but she doesn't listen.
5 Mr. Gonzalez doesn't speak any English, so you have to.

Now compare your answers and use the meanings from Activities 27 and 29 to describe the meaning of the modal verb for each example.

5 (Unit 2)

Activity 25 Student A

You were an eyewitness to the robbery. Look at the photo and describe the robber to the detective (Student B).

Now turn back to Activity 25 on page 19.

6 (Unit 3)

Activity 2 Student B

Prison statistics from the United Kingdom

1   In the UK, the prison population is about 1 percent of the total population.
2   The UK prison population is currently about 85,000, about 90 percent higher than the prison population in 1993.
3   White males made up 83 percent of the male prison population of British nationals in England and Wales in 2006. Black British males accounted for 12 percent.
4   The number of female prisoners in UK prisons has risen at a faster rate than the number of male prisoners.
5   In 1993, when there were fewer than 45,000 prisoners, 53 percent were reconvicted within two years. In 2004, 65 percent of those leaving prison were reconvicted.

Now turn back to Activity 3 on page 22.

7 (Unit 3)

Activity 2 Student C

Prison statistics from Russia.

1   There are more than a million people in prison in Russia.
2   This represents 606 people per 100,000 population, the second highest percentage in the world.
3   One in four Russian men has been in prison.
4   The average time spent waiting for trial is two to three years, during which time prisoners share cells with prisoners who have been convicted.
5   In some Russian prisons, there are 120 prisoners in the same cell.

Now turn back to Activity 3 on page 22.

8 (Unit 3)

Prison statistics from China

1 One and a half million people are in prison in China. This does not include those awaiting trial and others who are held in "administrative" detention.
2 People held in administrative detention have usually had no trial or court hearing.
3 China's "reform through labor" penal system, known in Chinese as *laogai*, means that many Chinese prisons are also factories producing goods that are sold in China and other countries.
4 The prison population in urban areas is falling, as people who were imprisoned as political dissidents are being released.
5 China executes more people than the rest of the world put together. Execution can be the punishment not just for violent crimes but also for offenses such as bribery and embezzlement.

Now turn back to Activity 3 on page 22.

9 (Unit 4)

You went to a party after your last class, because your classmate was feeling down and you wanted to celebrate. Your cell phone wasn't working and you couldn't find a payphone. The party was fun and you forgot about the time. You also forgot that your family was having a special dinner for you. You waited half an hour for a bus and then eventually took a taxi. You arrived home four hours after you said you would be home.

Now turn back to Activity 20 on page 32.

10 (Unit 6)

Jacqueline du Pré (January 26th, 1945–October 19th, 1987) was an English cellist who is considered one of the best cellists the world has ever seen. In 1971 Jackie noticed that she was losing feeling in her fingers and her playing was suffering. She was diagnosed with multiple sclerosis in 1973 and she gave up concert performance. She died in 1987 and a book was written about her, which was then made into the Oscar-nominated movie *Hilary and Jackie*. She won several prizes during and after her life and left behind several wonderful recordings of her playing.

Now turn back to Activity 3 on page 46.

11 (Unit 6)

Activity 26

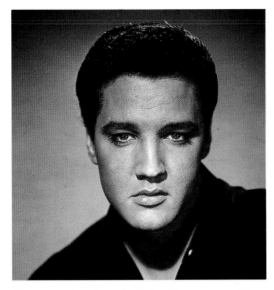

Now turn back to Activity 26 on page 51.

12 (Unit 7)

Activity 25 Student A

Read the sentences to your partner. Ask your partner to spell the word in bold.

a My hair was a mess but I didn't have a **comb**.
b She was working as a **maid** in a big hotel.
c We walked **through** the city and admired the bright lights.
d My sister had an operation on her **toe**.
e I got an excellent **report** from my English teacher.

Now turn back to Activity 26 on page 60.

13 (Unit 8)

Activity 6 Student C

You are Sherlock Holmes. You are going to be interviewed for an important case. Read the information about your character and make a note of your strengths and your preferred methods.

Dr. Watson describes Holmes as disorganized in his personal habits. Holmes is not averse to bending the truth or to breaking the law when it suits his purposes.

Holmes can be dispassionate and cold, but he becomes passionate when he is involved in an interesting case. He is a good actor and sets dramatic traps to catch a criminal. Holmes has enormous powers of deduction. He does not reveal his chain of reasoning and gives only cryptic clues. At the very end he explains his often surprising deductions.

Holmes loves danger. Indeed he remarks that it is this that attracted him to his profession. He is fearless and confronts dangerous criminals boldly. The only thing Holmes detests is boredom and he becomes quite irascible when he does not have a case to solve. These periods of inactivity led him for some time to use cocaine.

Now turn back to Activity 7 on page 63.

14 (Unit 12)

Activity 19

Two Cures for Love
1 Don't see him. Don't phone or write a letter.
2 The easy way: get to know him better.

Bloody Men
Bloody men are like bloody buses —
You wait for about a year
And as soon as one approaches your stop
Two or three others appear.

You look at them flashing their indicators,
Offering you a ride.
You're trying to read the destinations,
You haven't much time to decide.

If you make a mistake, there's no turning back.
Jump off, and you'll stand there and gaze
While the cars and the taxis and lorries go by
And the minutes, the hours, the days.

The Road Not Taken
Two roads diverged in a yellow wood,
And sorry I could not travel both
And be one traveler, long I stood
And looked down one as far as I could
To where it bent in the undergrowth.

Then took the other, as just as fair,
And having perhaps the better claim,
Because it was grassy and wanted wear;
Though as for that the passing there
Had worn them really about the same.

And both that morning equally lay
In leaves no step had trodden black.
Oh, I kept the first for another day!
Yet knowing how way leads on to way,
I doubted if I should ever come back.

I shall be telling this with a sigh
Somewhere ages and ages hence:
Two roads diverged in a wood, and I —
I took the one less traveled by,
And that has made all the difference.

In Two Minds
What I love about night
    is the silent certainty of its stars
What I hate about stars
    is the overweening swank of their names
What I love about names
    is that every complete stranger has one
What I hate about one
    is the numerical power it holds over its followers
What I love about followers
    is the unseemly jostle to fill the footsteps
What I hate about footsteps
    is the way they gang up in the darkness
What I love about darkness
    is the soft sighing of its secrets
What I hate about secrets
    is the excitement they pack into their short lives
What I love about lives
    is the variety cut from the same pattern
What I hate about pattern
    is its dull insistence on conformity
What I love about conformity
    is the seed of rebelliousness within
What I hate about within
    is the absence of landscape, the feel of the weather
What I love about the weather
    is its refusal to stay in at night
What I hate about night
    is the silver certainty of its stars

Now turn back to Activity 19 on page 98.

15 (Unit 12)

Activity 33 Student A

Read out the beginning of the joke. Use language from Activity 31. Which student (B, C, or D) has the punchline?

What did the fish say when it hit the wall?

Listen to B, C, and D's jokes. Say this punchline when you hear the right joke:

"I don't know. What does he look like?"

Now turn back to Activity 34 on page 99.

16 (Unit 1)

Activity 2 Student B

Read the information about sharks and answer the questions in Activity 2.

Shark facts
- You are ten times more likely to be struck by lightning than to be attacked by a shark, even if you live in an area where there is a shark population.
- Even in a bad year, fewer than ten people in the world are killed by sharks. In fact, Australian wild dogs kill more people each year than great whites have killed in 100 years.
- More than 12 million sharks are killed by people every year. Sharks are hunted for food and also for other useful by-products. Shark meat is high in protein, low in fat, and has no bones.
- Shark by-products are very useful, too. Shark oil, for example, is rich in vitamin A and is used in medicines, soap, cosmetics, and vitamins.

Now turn back to Activity 3 on page 6.

17 (Unit 2)

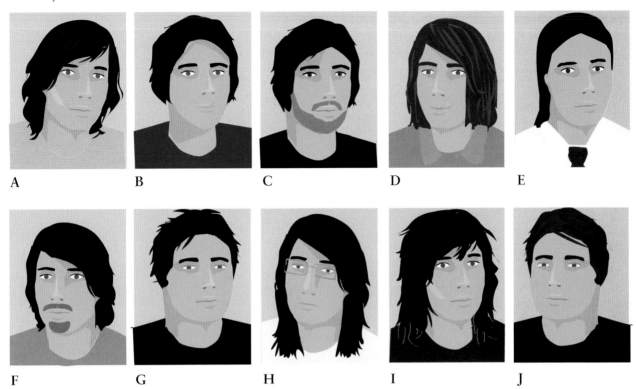

A   B   C   D   E

F   G   H   I   J

You are a detective.
1 Listen to Student A's description. Ask questions to get a clearer description.
2 Choose who Student A is describing and write down the letter.
3 Then show Student A the photos and write down the letter of the person Student A identifies.

Find out how many people identified the correct person.

Now turn back to Activity 26 on page 19.

18 (Unit 2)

Find the sentence that explains the context of sentences a–e on page 19.

1 Her car's not here, so she probably went out.
2 Or he may go to bed early—he hasn't decided yet.
3 But only for half an hour; then she has to do her homework.
4 You have lived in Spain for ten years, so you should be pretty good by now.
5 I told her to and she always does what I say.

Now compare your answers and use the meanings from Activities 27 and 29 to describe the meaning of the modal verb for each example.

19 (Unit 4)

Activity 19 Student B

You have prepared a special dinner for your brother/sister who was supposed to be home at 6 PM after her/his last class. It is now 10 PM and your brother/sister has just arrived home. You are very upset that your brother/sister did not phone you and that s/he arrived late and the dinner is ruined.

Now turn back to Activity 20 on page 32.

20 (Unit 6)

Activity 2 Student B

Bruce Lee (November 27th, 1940–July 20th, 1973) was an American-born martial artist, teacher, and actor who invented his own combat form, *Jeet Kune Do*. He was considered to be the most influential martial artist of the twentieth century as well as being a cultural icon. He was also the father of actor Brandon Lee (star of *The Crow*, who also died tragically at a young age) and of actress Shannon Lee. He was extremely disciplined and serious about his health, diet, and fitness and did an enormous amount of work to popularize martial arts around the world. He died accidentally after being given a painkiller for a headache that caused an allergic reaction. Today, Lee's influence can still be seen all over the world in the movies of stars like Jean-Claude Van Damme, Steven Seagal, and Jackie Chan, and in the growth of the bodybuilding industry.

Now turn back to Activity 3 on page 46.

21 (Unit 12)

Activity 33 Student B

Read out the beginning of the joke. Use language from Activity 31. Which student (A, C, or D) has the punchline?

A horse goes into a lounge and he walks up to the bar and he says, "Can I have a bottle of beer?"

"Certainly sir," says the bartender, ...

Listen to A, C, and D's jokes. Say this punchline when you hear the right joke:

"Damn!"

Now turn back to Activity 34 on page 99.

22 (Unit 6)

Activity 2 Student C

Eva Perón (May 7th, 1919–July 26th, 1952) was the second wife of President Juan Domingo Perón and served as the First Lady of Argentina from 1946 until her death in 1952. She was born Eva Duarte in rural Argentina in 1919, and at the age of 15 went to Buenos Aires to pursue a career as an actress. Eva met Colonel Juan Perón in 1944 and the two were married the following year. In 1946, Juan Perón was elected President of Argentina. During the next six years, Eva Perón became an influential advocate for workers' rights and for women's rights in Argentina. In 1951, Eva Perón accepted the nomination for the job of Vice President of Argentina. However, opposition from the military and the nation's elite, as well as her poor health, ultimately forced her to give up her nomination. She died of cancer at the age of 33, dearly loved by the ordinary people of Argentina. Many books have been written about Eva Perón as well as the famous musical *Evita*.

Now turn back to Activity 3 on page 46.

23 (Unit 8)

Activity 6 Student D

You are Hercule Poirot. You are going to be interviewed for an important case. Read the information about your character and make a note of your strengths and your preferred methods.

Hercule Poirot is a retired Belgian police officer. He is famous for his ability to solve the most complicated crimes using fairly conventional, clue-based detection methods that depend on logical thinking. He often likes to refer to "the little gray cells" and to "order and method" as his most powerful tools.

In his later life, Poirot gives up focusing on the traditional trail of clues in favor of a more psychological approach. He sees himself as a psychological detective who enquires into the nature of the victim and the murderer. He believes that particular crimes are committed only by particular types of people. He gets people to talk. He is sometimes a kind of confessor, especially to young women. Poirot is not afraid of lying to gain the confidence of people or to find a way to ask the questions he really wants to ask. One of his most frequent deceptions is to pretend he is more foreign and vain than he really is so that people relax and don't take him seriously: "It is true that I can speak the exact, the idiomatic English. But, my friend, to speak the broken English is an enormous asset. It leads people to despise you. They say, 'A foreigner – he can't even speak English properly.' [...] Also, I boast! An Englishman, he says often, 'A fellow who thinks as much of himself as that cannot be worth much.' [...] And so, you see, I put people off their guard."

Now turn back to Activity 8 on page 63.

24 (Unit 6)

Activity 2 Student D

Malcolm X (born Malcolm Little, May 19th, 1925–February 21st, 1965) was an American religious and political leader. He came from a humble background and, after spending time in jail, converted to Islam and became a strong proponent of equal rights for African-Americans in the United States. He was assassinated in 1965. Since his death, several books and movies have been made about him, including *Malcolm X* (1992). Today Malcolm X is seen as a hero by many and as a champion of equal rights.

Now turn back to Activity 3 on page 46.

25 (Unit 8)

Activity 6 Student E

You are James Bond. You are going to be interviewed for an important case. Read the information about your character and make a note of your strengths and your preferred methods.

Commander James Bond is an agent of the British Secret Intelligence Service (SIS), more commonly MI6. His important services to queen and country were rewarded when he was decorated as a Knight Commander.

Bond is a good-looking man but a certain cruelty around the mouth and a coldness in his eyes reveal his personality. He is brave and completely ruthless when he deals with his enemies. Betrayal and intrigue go hand-in-hand with his missions and Bond will stop at nothing to reach his objectives. Bond is a womanizer, susceptible to the charms of beautiful women, but he is also prepared to use them.

Bond relies on his charm, wit, and incisiveness to accomplish his missions, but also on intelligence gathered by the Secret Service. Exotic espionage equipment and vehicles are very popular elements of James Bond's missions. These items often prove critically important to Bond in completing his missions successfully. The espionage equipment is supplied by Q Branch of MI6. James Bond is "an anonymous, blunt instrument wielded by a government department" (Ian Fleming in a *Reader's Digest* interview).

Now turn back to Activity 8 on page 63.

26 (Unit 6)

Activity 2 Student E

Dian Fossey (January 16th, 1932–December 26th, 1985) was an American zoologist who carried out long-term research on mountain gorillas in Rwanda. She observed them daily from 1966 until her death and founded a research center dedicated to their study. She published extensively on her research and was very concerned that the animals should be allowed to live in their habitat naturally and not be taken to zoos. She opposed all forms of poaching and exploitation of the animals. She was murdered in her cabin in the Virunga Mountains in Rwanda. Thanks to Dian Fossey, far more is now known about gorillas and how they live. Fossey published a book about her life in 1983 which was made into a movie in 1990, starring Sigourney Weaver.

Now turn back to Activity 3 on page 46.

27 (Unit 11)

Activity 6

WOMAN: I'm going to say why I think home economics is—or should be—the most important subject in any school curriculum. *I'll start by* outlining my position. *Then I'll move on to* some statistics. *After that, if it's all right with you*, I'll deal with some possible objections to *what I'm going to say*, and then *I'll sum up*. I'll take questions, of course, when I have finished.

OK, then, *first of all let me say that I think that* home economics— *that is* learning to cook, learning how to manage the house—is a vital skill for any young person *if they want to* live a happy and successful life. I have two main reasons for saying this. Firstly, some households *run into trouble* because the homemakers don't understand *how to work with* a family budget. *But secondly—and this is, if anything*, my main reason for wanting home economics to achieve the importance it deserves—we are a nation sleepwalking into crisis, a health crisis of epic proportions. Child obesity has doubled in the last decade because people just don't eat right. And obesity brings future health problems that our nation will not be able to afford.

And that's why home economics—teaching girls and boys how to choose, manage, and cook their food—is so important. *We must act now, before it is too late.*

To those who say that people should be able *to* run their own lives without having to be educated into it *I would just say that* the evidence is against them. *Things are getting worse*, not better. *But anyway, let's just suppose* that such people are right; well, then *we might as well* not do anything about anything. But that would be wrong and irresponsible. *The fact is that* we do have a chance to *change things for the better* and *we'd better take that chance now*, because if we don't *we may just have* left it too late.

So that's it. If we want to help children learn how to manage their home lives as they grow older, and if we want to improve the nation's health, my contention is that home economics has to be a major subject on any school curriculum. I hope you agree with me. *Does anyone have any questions?*

Now turn back to Activity 6 on page 87.

Activity 30

Rehearse one of the scenes listed on page 92 from *O Go My Man*.
The complete extract is also on the CD, Track 31.

Sarah peers into the bright lights. She steps forward.

DIRECTOR: If you could just stay on the blue mark, please.

SARAH: Oh yes. Sorry. (*She takes a step back*)

DIRECTOR: Name, age, agent.

SARAH: Sarah Rafter. Thirty-four. The Actors, Agency.

DIRECTOR: Never heard of it.

SARAH: It's a cooperative.

DIRECTOR: I see. Profiles. Let's see your left and right profile. (*She turns slowly from left to right.*) Hurry it up a bit.

SARAH: Right. Sorry.

DIRECTOR: Smile.

SARAH: Sorry. I always find it difficult to smile if I've been told to. Could you say something funny?

DIRECTOR: Just smile.

SARAH: (*She smiles*)Mmm. That does it for me every time.

DIRECTOR: Have you done any ads recently?

SARAH: I've made quite a few but not for a while.

DIRECTOR: I see. Any cereal commercials?

SARAH: I did turn down an ad for Nestlé once—you know, because I didn't like them. I'm not sure I'd do that now.

DIRECTOR: Principles need finance.

SARAH: Yes.

DIRECTOR: Talk to me a bit about a pash. A hobby or something you are passionate about. You have thirty seconds. Go.

SARAH: Umm....ah ah...a pash? I...I'm passionate about acting. I can say that, can't I?

DIRECTOR: (*wearily*) Twenty-five seconds.

SARAH: (*speed talks*) I mean—acting is a vocation—that's not a cliché. It has to be. Why would you choose such a life? I did burn. I still burn but I don't know how much longer without burning out—you know? It's like having an affair—you wait for the phone to ring— (*Sarah's cell phone rings*) Sorry, I thought I'd turned it off.

DIRECTOR: You wait for the phone to ring—seven seconds—

SARAH: (*tries to ignore the ringing. She talks even faster.*) Yes. Frustration, bliss, pain, a kaleidoscope of possibility.
But is it an important job? (*Phone stops ringing*) If you consider the global nightmare that is elsewhere, I ask myself this question—does it matter? Do I?

DIRECTOR: Stop. OK. Do you have the sheet with the lines, yes?

SARAH: I know them. (*Her phone beeps loudly*) Sorry.

DIRECTOR: Well, I want you to deliver the monologue with that exact sense of discovery and passion.

SARAH: Ummm.....right...Right. Will I do it to you or to the camera?

DIRECTOR: To me.

SARAH: (*launches into the piece*) I work hard ...

DIRECTOR: Don't forget you are walking the dog and the children are running ahead.

SARAH: You mean act it out?

DIRECTOR: Exactly.

SARAH: I'm not sure I'd be reaching for the milk while walking the dog.

DIRECTOR: (*sighs*) You have a better idea, no doubt?

SARAH: I could be playing with them—in the house, I mean...

DIRECTOR: So play.

SARAH: I work hard. I play hard. Sometimes I just need a "regular" day. That's when I reach for the "All Brown." And some ice-cold milk—then I'm ready for anything life throws up.

DIRECTOR: On the "anything" the dog is pulling you. Just go from "I reach for ..."

SARAH: OK. I reach for the "All-Brown" and some ice-cold milk. And I'm ready for aaaaaaaaannnnyyyything the dog throws up.

DIRECTOR: Thank you.

SARAH: Sorry. Life throws up.

DIRECTOR: Thank you.

SARAH: Could I do that again?

DIRECTOR: Once was more than enough. Goodbye. (*Looks at his notes. He writes something. He looks up.*)

SARAH: I made an awful mess of that. I'd really like to have another go.

DIRECTOR: Oh, go on. Just get out.

SARAH: Are you talking to me?

DIRECTOR: Yes. You. Has-been. Never has been. Call yourself an actress? Out.

SARAH: What?

DIRECTOR: That was a terrible audition. Telephone ringing? You blew it by talking garbage. Acting is like having an affair? Global nightmare? I've never heard such garbage. Phuh. Now go on, get out. Get a job at Kroger's.

SARAH: Look you creep. I've had a number of four-star reviews in my time. I've come this close to being in a film with Kevin Spacey. I'm trying to give these stupid lines some dignity here. If you don't like what I'm doing you can take a running jump.

DIRECTOR: Why... you... you'll never work in this town again.

SARAH: Oh yeah? We'll see about that. (*She takes out her finger as if it's a gun and shoots the director.*) I am not an idiot. I just want to work. Bang! Bang! I am not an idiot. Bang! Bang! Bang! I am not an idiot. (*The director dies horribly, the bullets making him convulse as they hit.*)

Now turn back to Activity 30 on page 92.

29 (Unit 12)

. . . .

Activity 33 Student C

Read out the beginning of the joke. Use language from Activity 31 on page 99. Which student (A, B, or D) has the punchline?

A penguin walks into a bar and goes up to the bartender and says, "Have you seen my brother?" The bartender says ...

Listen to A, B, and D's jokes. Say this punchline when you hear the right joke:

"But that would make no sense!"

Now turn back to Activity 34 on page 99.

30 (Unit 12)

Activity 30

And the doctor says, "Don't worry sir, she's just having contractions."

Now turn back to Activity 30 on page 99.

31 (Unit 6)

Activity 2 Student F

Yuri Gagarin (March 9th, 1934–March 27th, 1968), hero of the Soviet Union, was a Soviet cosmonaut. On April 12th, 1961, he became the first human in space and the first to orbit the Earth. He received medals from around the world for his pioneering tour in outer space and became an instant celebrity. The Soviet Union was afraid of losing their hero and therefore he was not allowed to go into space again, but instead became a trainer for cosmonauts. He was training to become a fighter pilot when he died with his instructor during a routine training flight at the age of 34. He will always be remembered as the first man in space and the first person to orbit the Earth.

Now turn back to Activity 3 on page 46.

32 (Unit 12)

Activity 33 Student D

Read out the beginning of the joke. Use language from Activity 31. Which student (A, B, or C) has the punchline?

A dog walks into a post office and picks up a telegram form. He writes the following on it: "Woof Woof. Woof woof woof woof. Woof woof woof."

He hands the form to the woman behind the counter. She counts the words and says: "There are nine words here. You can have one more word for the same price. Do you want to write another 'woof'?" The dog looks astonished and replies: ...

Listen to A, B, and C's jokes. Say this punchline when you hear the right joke:

"But why the long face?"

Now turn back to Activity 34 on page 99.

Reader: Virtual Reality

An entertainment in six short chapters

1 *Tunnel*

When Natalie went through the exit barrier at the station, she was feeling pleased with herself. Despite her tunnel phobia she had traveled by train from Paris to London, and this had included 26 minutes in the tunnel under the English Channel. She had hated every minute of it, of course, but she had done it anyway, and although she could still remember the discomfort she had felt as the train rushed through that dark cylinder, now she felt good and strong and ready for anything.

Natalie Finch was in her mid-twenties. She had short, well-cut brown hair. She wore jeans and a simple olive green top, with a fashionable leather jacket hanging over her shoulder. Green snake earrings were perhaps the only unusual things about her. But if you looked at her carefully, you would notice a keen intelligence that seemed to emanate from her striking eyes.

She stood in the station concourse looking around. The new terminal was even more exciting than she had imagined—all shiny rails and platforms, and even a long champagne bar. This was reality, she thought, the real world, not some virtual arrivals area, but the modern Eurostar terminal at St. Pancras Station in the heart of London, one of Europe's great capital cities.

Someone bumped into her as they ran past, rushing toward the barrier. She started to lose her balance and tried to stay upright, but the knapsack on her back slipped and she fell, sprawling, on to the ground as the crowd surged around her. The breath was knocked from her body. For a moment she lay there sensing the pain in her leg and wondering if she was badly hurt.

"Are you all right down there?" There was an old man, his coat tied with string, staring down at her with interest. He had a long, untidy beard, and his face looked as if whole families had been living there for centuries. But he didn't seem unpleasant. His voice was surprisingly strong. "Here, let me help you," he said, and, despite his age, he pulled her to her feet.

"No real damage?"

"No, I don't think so." Her knee felt sore, and she suspected she would soon have a bruise on her left thigh. She brushed herself down and adjusted her knapsack.

"That was bad luck!"

"Yes." And, she didn't tell him, it was the second time today. At the Gare du Nord in Paris three hours before, just before she got on to the train, a woman with dramatic red hair and a long coat had run straight into her, muttered an apology, and then disappeared into the crowd.

"Come to see your boyfriend?" the old man said, walking by her side as she limped out of the station. She was about to tell him to mind his own business, but when she looked at him he was smiling in such a friendly way that she couldn't.

"Well, he's not actually my boyfriend. At least, I don't think he is."

"Oh, it's like that, is it?" He was making fun of her, she thought, and was about to get angry. But he doubled over, coughing uncontrollably, and she felt guilty.

They had reached the taxi stand. Saying goodbye to the coughing man, she got into a taxi, closed the door beside her, and wondered what to tell the taxi driver. All she knew was that her "not actually" boyfriend (if that was what he was) lived in a 24-story building called "Lion's Gate." It was south of the river near the Globe Theater. If she ever went there, he had told her, she should ask for Kate.

* * *

"How do you expect me to find this Lion's Gate place if you don't even know the address?" the taxi driver said angrily, as they drove around the South Bank, but she gave him her sweetest smile, and finally they saw the building right in front of them.

She paid the driver and gave him a generous tip. She felt him watching her as she crossed the road.

Inside the building a woman was sitting at a desk, reading a newspaper. The word "security" was taped to her chest. She looked up as Natalie approached.

"Yes?" she said.

"I'm looking for a friend of mine."

"What's his name?"

She was about to say "Tiger Tim," but she stopped herself just in time.

"You must know his name," the security guard said in an exasperated voice.

"Well, it's just … Look …," Natalie said, "he told me to ask for someone named Kate."

"Oh, right. That's OK, then. Kate rang down earlier. Said to expect a young woman, twenty-something, brunette she said, and you seem about right for that."

"Well, I …"

"Take the lift to the twenty-fourth floor—that's

where all the computers are, but you should ignore them. Walk up an extra flight of stairs till you come to a door. It will be opened for you."

Natalie turned away.

"Don't thank me!" (She hadn't.) "Just go and see if you can find your Mr. Mysterious." And the security guard went back to the paper she had been reading.

The door at the top of the stairs opened with a hissing sound as Natalie approached it. She found herself looking out on to a flat roof and, in the distance, half of London glinting in the afternoon sunshine. She walked out. At first it was just a roof. But when she walked around, behind the stairwell she had just walked up, it was a different story. There were wire cages, and some kind of tank, and what looked like a chicken coop. In the middle of London? On a roof?

There was a movement behind the tank. She saw a hat, a familiar wide-brimmed hat moving, as if by itself, along the top of the tank on the other side. Then a figure appeared. But it wasn't the boyfriend she had been expecting. It wasn't even a man. She found herself looking at a young girl with long brown hair, wearing overalls, a bucket in her hand.

"Have you brought it?" the girl asked without saying hello.

"Brought what?" Natalie walked over to the tank. She peered in. There was something large, too large, in the water. She couldn't believe her eyes. It looked like a crocodile. Its head was just visible, and it was watching her with cold, unfriendly eyes. It was almost too big for the tank.

She went closer and looked down at the almost prehistoric animal in front of her. The crocodile half rose out of the water, opening its hideous mouth. She saw rows of teeth and felt a sudden stab of fear.

"Saltwater crocodile," said the girl, "one of the most dangerous animals on earth. I'd be careful if I were you. The saltwater ..." But suddenly Natalie couldn't hear her any more as the sky was full of the deafening *whumpa whumpa whumpa* of engine noise, and a helicopter shot up above the roof from below.

"Give it to me. Quickly."

"Give what to you?"

"Oh, forget it," the girl screamed. "Run for it, run!" And she was gone.

The crocodile thrashed in its tank. Claustrophobia, poor thing, Natalie thought in one crazy moment. We all have our phobias! She couldn't understand what was happening.

Hardly had she recovered from the shock than a voice boomed: "Drop everything. Hands above your head. Stay right where you are!" She looked at the helicopter, black and menacing. She saw a man with a rifle pointed directly at her, and another man, gun in hand, jumping from the helicopter and running toward her.

"On the ground," he was shouting, "on the ground," and with her heart suddenly lurching with fear, she fell to her knees. To her left she saw a movement, a wide-brimmed hat disappearing beneath a trapdoor in the roof, and then they had her. The two gunmen dragged her toward the clattering helicopter and threw her in. Before she could say anything, they had ripped off her knapsack, tied her hands behind her with plastic wire, and pulled a smelly bag over her head. With a great leap, the helicopter rose into the sky.

2 *The jungle*

"Empty your pockets!"

For a moment she didn't understand what they were saying. The light was still too bright, since they had pulled the dark hood from her head. The gunman who had brought her to this place was standing beside her, leaning on the counter, watching her a little bit like the crocodile who had stared at her half an hour before. Three other people, a man and two women, were standing around. They were pretending they weren't interested.

"I don't keep anything in my pockets," she said to the man in uniform behind the counter. He was looking at her with an interest that made her uncomfortable.

"We'll see about that, shall we?" he said, and leaned over the counter towards her.

"No, it's OK. I'll do it. If you untie my hands." She felt the gunman reach behind her, and a knife blade went through the plastic cord. She reached into her jeans pocket. There was something there.

"Don't keep anything in your pockets?" the uniform said, unpleasantly. "So what have you got there?"

Natalie looked at what she had in her hand. It was a USB flash drive for a computer. She had never seen it before in her life. "I ... that is ... this isn't mine ... I don't … " "Save it!" said the man behind the counter, angry now. "We're not interested in your stories, understand? Now, let's see what we have here." He took her handbag (they must have picked it up from the roof) and emptied the contents on to the counter. Now everyone could see how chaotic she was, that she smoked—even though it was no longer fashionable—and a number of other private things about her life. She turned her face away. The man in uniform was staring at her in a way that made her feel uncomfortable.

"Can I have my phone?" she asked hopelessly. The policeman turned to one of the women. The woman rolled her eyes and shook her head.

"You're joking! Phones? You!" he said. "People like you ..."

"Enough," said the woman. "Get on with it."

"You're coming with me," the man in uniform barked, and even though she turned to the women for help, she found herself gripped by the gunman and the man in uniform and marched down a corridor. She could hear people shouting somewhere in the distance, and there was a disagreeable smell.

They came to a door and, without letting go of her, the man in uniform opened it with a key that was hanging from his waist. He opened the door and thrust her through the opening. "Your new residence," he said. "I do hope you'll like it. Bucket over there." He slammed the door and she heard him turn the key in the lock.

A little window opened in the door. She saw him looking in, a nasty smile on his red face. "And don't do anything silly, because I'll be watching you, OK?" With a harsh crack the window was closed. She was in some kind of prison, and she was alone.

* * *

Natalie hadn't meant to become addicted to the computer. It was just that she had been going through a bad patch. Her boyfriend, who she was seriously in love with, had left her; she had been feeling lonely, and her life didn't mean much to her at all. True, she had her classes to keep her busy, and Bucharest was a city she was beginning to like. Besides which, she was a popular teacher. She had natural empathy with her students and seemed to understand how difficult it was for them to learn English. She had a good sense of humor, too, and came up with original ideas for lessons, which her students found challenging and engaging. Her colleagues were impressed by the way she bounced down the corridor, heading to class as if it were the most exciting job in the world. If nothing else, Natalie knew how to look enthusiastic, to look as if she was having the time of her life.

But after Razvan left her, saying he wanted to travel, and that he wasn't ready to be tied down—he wanted to experience "things" (though he didn't make it clear what they were)—she found it more and more difficult to really enjoy her work, and suddenly, when she was in her little apartment on the Boulevard Lascar Catargiu on her own, she felt alone. Just alone.

And that's when she started using the Internet. At first it was just the newspapers from back home, and social sites like Facebook, and searching out her favorite music tracks on YouTube, but then she discovered Second Life. She was reading some Internet articles about love and dating ("Why am I torturing myself?" she remembered asking herself at the time, "and why am I being tortured like this?"), and her eye was caught by a story about people who had met in some "virtual reality," some special place where people could be anyone they wanted. Apparently you could "go there" ("there" was just images on your computer screen), make a new character for yourself, and meet all sorts of other people who were doing the same. It sounded too good to be true. So one night, after a long session with her advanced class that made her feel miserable (because all her students looked so happy), she came home to her empty apartment and downloaded the software that she needed. Then she chose a name for herself—"Beata Vir"— because she had once studied Latin, and because it was a satisfying mixture of masculine and feminine and meant "blessed one." She chose what she would look like in her new virtual world, too—long, black hair, fashionable sunglasses, and a smart, black suit. Beata Vir was ready to go out and discover a new world.

At first she had trouble learning how to walk and how to fly (you could do both by using the controls on the computer keyboard), but soon she stopped bumping into trees and ending up in the water. She could make out other avatars like her wandering around the site, and soon she could see them talking to each other, their words appearing in little speech bubbles above their heads.

She found "Tiger Tim" in a location called "the jungle." He was dressed like an explorer, a "raiders-of-the-lost-ark" adventurer in a khaki shirt. He seemed to be tall and thin and very handsome (well, anyway, his avatar was). He had a leather jacket (rather like one Natalie herself owned in her "first life") and a wide-brimmed hat. There was something about him that she liked, and after a few days she no longer felt alone. They "talked" about everything; she told him about her life in Bucharest and he told her that he lived in London.

It was vacation period in Bucharest so she had weeks without classes. She didn't know what to do or how to occupy her time. Tiger Tim seemed to have disappeared—at least he was never online. Natalie went to Paris and stayed with her aunt and her new husband, a software engineer from Madrid named Sergio (a computer genius, her aunt said, looking lovingly across at him).

The night before she left, her aunt had organized a special dinner. Sergio had invited a friend of his named Tony. He was the same age as her father would have been, if only ... Natalie had liked him because he was cheerful and friendly, but occasionally his smile vanished, and he exchanged strange glances with his friend. He seemed strangely familiar, though she couldn't think why.

She had told them all about her new plan; she was going to travel to London and try to find someone she had met in Second Life. Sergio hadn't said much. The man named Tony had laughed. He had been fascinated by all the details. He said it all sounded very romantic. Her aunt said she was crazy.

Now, twenty-four hours later, Natalie lay back on the hard concrete bed and looked around her bare cell. She was very, very frightened and very confused.

Her aunt had obviously been right.

3 *The end of the world*

In a back street in Taipei, Han-Gyong Park was singing his favorite song. The members of his Taiwan team were listening with the usual mixture of attention and adulation. When he had finished, they would shower him with flowery congratulations. As he read the lyrics off the sheet in front of him, he felt his heart swell with pride.

Every time he came to Taiwan from his home in Seoul, Korea, Han-Gyong came to this, his favorite, karaoke bar. Here, instead of machines playing the songs, and the words dancing across a TV screen like the karaoke bars he went to in Japan and back home, a Chinese woman sat at an electronic keyboard. As far as he knew, she could play any tune in the world—Chinese, Japanese, American, British, or Korean. And if the singers forgot the words, or found them too difficult to read, she would sing along with them and put them at their ease—or offer sweet harmonies to accompany them. He never ceased to be amazed by her musical brilliance, but when he tried to talk to her, she just smiled and kept her distance. Perhaps it was better that way.

Here it was again, that beautiful refrain, and he sang it with a lachrymose intensity because it was, after all, some kind of lament for all those beautiful people who blaze like stars and then die young, their light forever lost in the cold darkness of endless space.

"So, bye-bye, Miss American Pie
Drove my Chevy to the levee
But the levee was dry
And them good old boys were drinkin'
  whiskey and rye
Singin' this'll be the day that I die
This'll be the day that I die."

Yes, he knew that people had been arguing about the lyrics of the song for more than forty years. It was about the death of the great American singer Buddy Holly, who died in a plane crash when he was young ("The day the music died," according to the song), and it seemed to be about other singers who never made it to old age. At least, he thought comfortingly, their music lives on so that people like him could sing it. Whatever the song was really about, people were still singing it in bars and clubs all over the world. And best of all, it had six verses and a chorus, so if you liked performing in karaoke bars, you got to sing for eight and a half minutes or so instead of the usual three.

He looked over at his team. They were gazing at him with reverence and awe. He let his glance linger on the beautiful Li-Hua. Her face was impassive, but he thought he detected something a bit like scorn in her opaque eyes. He felt his mood begin to change. He had reached the line in the song "my hands were clenched with rage" when suddenly he felt a deep sense of anger and frustration. What was the point of power if you couldn't have what you wanted? Li-Hua was his employee. He had brought her here from a village in Sichuan where she had worked for a wildlife organization, protecting pandas. She should have fallen in love with him when he asked her to. He was the boss, after all, the biggest beast in this particular jungle. But every time he tried to suggest that they might spend time together, she had refused. She had a boyfriend, he knew, but he was just a young British man named Michael, who worked for an educational publisher based in Taiwan. This Michael couldn't be as interesting as *he* was. Damn. Surely he could force her to love him. Perhaps he should get someone to make the British man disappear. He had done that kind of thing before. But with Li-Hua it was different. He needed her to like him, to *want* to be with him, and he didn't know how to make it happen. It was just one more thing that wasn't going his way right now. In fact, nothing was going his way. Kate, Holland's daughter, had been in touch. There had been a raid at Lion's Gate. Helicopters, men with rifles. They had seized a young woman who had been there, Kate said, but Holland himself was in France at the time, so he hadn't been taken. Then she started screaming at him, saying that he had betrayed her father, and that she was "coming to get him." He tried to tell her that it wasn't true, but the line went dead.

Han-Gyong Park smuggled exotic animals—among other "business" interests. It was against the law. If they had raided the London end of the operation, he was in real trouble. But why had they needed helicopters and gunmen? Was there something Holland had not been telling him?

He realized that he had stopped singing, and the Chinese keyboard player had taken over from him. "This'll be the day that I die," she sang in echo to his own performance some minutes before. She looked at him helpfully, encouraging him to rejoin the song, but his mood had changed. He suddenly realized that his team hated to hear him sing. They just pretended to think he was good. How could he ever have thought otherwise?

He threw the microphone on to the music stand and strode from the little stage. Calling his driver and his bodyguard, he marched out of the bar, the door crashing behind him as he left.

* * *

On the other side of the world Natalie was trying to stop herself from feeling so scared. It seemed that she was in a police station, but when she thought of police dramas she had seen on television, she just felt more and more worried. Her captors didn't seem like ordinary policemen or women. This felt more like a secret organization, or an army. And how did you ever escape from people like that?

After she had been in her cell for hours, someone in a balaclava (man or woman, she couldn't tell: she could only see the eyes through slits in the material) opened the window and pushed through a sandwich and a cup of milky tea. Natalie tried to talk to her: "Why am I here? What's going on? I want to see a lawyer!" But the moment she had spoken, she realized how stupid it was because the hooded figure just turned and walked away as if she hadn't spoken at all.

After she had eaten the tasteless sandwich (it was probably supposed to be cheese, she thought) and drank the by-now tepid tea, Natalie lay down again on the hard bench, and thought that she would try and sleep—or just doze—if only to pass the time. But the moment she had closed her eyes, a fierce light lit up the cell, and the walls echoed with the enormous, ear-splitting noise of what sounded like the ugliest rock band in the world. She covered her ears, but there was nothing to stop the brightness of the light from burning into her eyes, however hard she tried to close them tight. It was like being in someone's vision of hell, and she had no idea how she would be able to stand it. She hunched into a corner, crouching on the stone-cold floor, and tried to concentrate on something nice, a good memory, a happier time.

Like the night she and Razvan had sat in a restaurant in the old town in Bucharest talking about love and death and poetry, in the way that all romantics do at some time or another.

"Some say the world will end in fire," she started, hoping to surprise him with her favorite poem, but before she could go on, he had supplied the next line: "Some say in ice" (he had studied English literature), and it was like that the whole of that perfect evening. They were in complete harmony and she was in love.

The end of the world! Fire and ice. Oh! please, she screamed inwardly, don't let it end like this. But the light blazed on, the music hammered into her ears until her whole body vibrated, and she felt that if it did not stop soon she would lose her mind.

4 *Prayer is better than sleep*

It stopped as suddenly as it had begun, perhaps twenty-four hours later, perhaps longer. Natalie's cell was plunged into darkness. Her ears were bursting with pain, her eyes hurt from the effort of clenching them tight against the glare, and she had not slept. But before she had had time to readjust to this new reality, her cell door opened, a hood was thrown over her head, and she was dragged out into the corridor. It all happened so fast that she could not keep up, and her feet bounced along the floor behind her. She was bundled into a car, driven at breakneck speed through city streets, lifted out of the car, and taken into a lift (she thought), which rose at a stomach-churning speed. All this time nobody said a word, and the darkness beneath her hood was as terrifying as the atrocious light and deafening music had been only a few minutes before.

Then they were in a room and she was forced to sit down. The hood was snatched from her head. And when her sore eyes had adjusted to the light, she could hardly believe what she saw. She was in some kind of luxury flat. There was an imitation fire burning in the grate, and two people sat facing her on a large leather sofa. She stared at them as if they were from outer space. The man was wearing a dark suit with a pink tie and a matching handkerchief poking out of the top pocket of his jacket. A woman in her thirties in an elegant dress was sitting beside him. For some reason, Natalie's attention was drawn to the string of pearls around her neck. The couple looked like the kind of people her parents might have liked. No, she thought, her mind wandering as she tried not to lose her sense of reality, they looked like the kind of people her grandparents might have liked. She stared at them stupidly.

"Ah," said the woman, "it's nice to meet you, Miss Finch."

Natalie found it difficult to speak. She wanted to sleep.

"Are you the police, or what?" she managed finally.

"Government," said the woman, "not police exactly. That's all you need to know."

"I'll tell you what," the man said in a clipped accent that few people used nowadays, except perhaps for the Queen of England and her immediate family, "let's play detectives, shall we?"

"Yes, let's," said the woman.

"I don't know what any of this is about. Why am I here?"

"Nice try, Miss Finch, but it won't work here. We want to know who you are, why you were on that roof, why you were carrying …"

"Carrying what? What's this all about?"

"We suggest you cooperate," said the man.

"Yes," agreed his companion, "and we hope, that is, we think, you will be amenable. We expect, you see, that you might possibly be influenced by the thought of that cheerful cell we have just brought you from. We could always get our plain-clothes officers to take you back there if you wish."

Natalie looked from one to another. Their smiles were as cold as ice. She started to talk.

* * *

A few weeks before Natalie arrived in London, Razvan Balitiu had a terrible dream. It went on and on, and he wanted it to stop. Of course, he knew it was just a dream, but he couldn't get out of it, however hard he tried. What was it that woman had said in the airport at Casablanca two weeks ago? "When you're having a bad dream, you ask God's help or, if you cannot believe in God, touch something and the dream will go away." But it hadn't gone away. Everyone he loved was leaving him, and he was alone in an empty house that had once been his home. He heard police sirens and smelled fire. He desperately wanted to be with his family and friends. There was a blessed one he had lost, someone seemed to be telling him, but he didn't know who it was or who was speaking to him.

The woman who had talked to him about dreams was from Sierra Leone, his conscious mind informed him. He had spoken to her because they were both waiting for a flight that had been delayed. He had seen her talking to an airline official who had appeared at the desk for no more than two minutes and had then disappeared. He had gone to ask her what she had found out. They had started chatting then, and somehow she had told him about dreams and the evil spirits that haunted her, and about the advice a priest had given her.

Back in the dream, he found that he couldn't leave the house, only now it wasn't his own home anymore, though it was supposed to be, but it was more like the flat where Natalie had lived, except that his dead grandmother was there, but she did not recognize him. If he could just touch the sheet, like that woman had said, or touch the light switch beside his bed ... But his hand was being controlled by the dream. He couldn't move it. His conscious thought was of no avail. And in the dream he was the only person left in a cold, desolate landscape.

And then suddenly from beyond the window of his hotel room, from beyond the hallucinatory world that had ensnared him, he heard it, a voice, piercing the air, rising above the traffic that still roared along the Corniche el-Nil: *Allāhu Akbar* ..., Allah is great ...; he began to recognize what he could hear dimly: *Hayya 'alāṣ-ṣalāh* ..., make haste to prayer ...; he turned on his back: *Aṣ-ṣalātu khayru min an-nawm* ..., prayer is better than sleep... He opened his eyes. The clock by his bedside showed 5:24 AM. He was awake, and behind him the dream was vanishing, rushing screaming into the darkness of his unconscious. By the time the morning call to prayer had stopped resonating from the loudspeakers at the top of one of Cairo's biggest mosques, the nightmare had completely disappeared, and he had only a hazy idea of what it had all been about. All he knew was that it had been important, and as he lay there he felt terribly alone, more alone than he had ever been—as if he had lost something precious, something he might never have again.

And for a second he, too, prayed that the darkness would pass, and that the nagging dread he felt would dissipate with the morning. Then, when he thought that perhaps it already had, he fell back to sleep and didn't wake up until the sun was pouring through the hotel window, and the megacity noise of Cairo was blasting his ears with a cacophony of shouts, revving engines, police sirens, and the blare of horns, as the boats twisted, fighting the current on the River Nile, the longest and most impressive of the world's waterways.

Razvan stretched, refreshed and no longer haunted by the distant memory of an uncomfortable dream. This was his last day in Africa's biggest city, with more than seventeen million people (if you counted the whole of "Greater Cairo")—the rich and the poor, businessmen and beggars, the religious and the hedonists, weaving their way through the impossible tangle of traffic and overcrowded streets. He hated its indescribable noise and loved its vivid chaos. There was life here. Since he had arrived two weeks ago, he had taken in the sights and museums like any other tourist. It might be some kind of a cliché, but you couldn't come to Egypt and not see the pyramids.

But now it was time to go to Sharm el-Sheik on the Red Sea. He had a date for a scuba diving course, something he had always wanted to try. And after that, who knows, he might go and have a go at paragliding in Turkey.

His brother had accused him of running away when he had taken him to the airport in Bucharest: "... running away from that English girlfriend of yours, running away from being an adult. But it's time to grow up, Razvan." Older brothers! Just because Nicolai had a wife and two small children, he thought he knew everything.

5 *The folded lie*

I never meant to be an English teacher, Natalie was saying to the two old-fashioned-looking English people in front of her. "I studied interior design at college; well, that is, I was studying interior design when my parents were killed in a road accident, you see…"

"How tragic." It was the suited man with a tie who spoke, sarcasm dripping from his mouth like icy poison. "But, Miss Finch. Much as we are fascinated"—he elongated the vowel-sound on the first syllable as if he were an American comedian—"by your touching life story"—his voice dropped to a nasty growl—"what we are interested in, what we have repeatedly asked you, is why you went to that roof, and what your connection with…"

Natalie should have been frightened of him by now, but her recent experiences had been so absurd, and her senses had been so violently assaulted, that suddenly she no longer cared.

"It's my story," she said amiably enough, "and if you want anything from me, you're going to have to listen to it, whether you like it or not."

The man's eyes flashed cold fire, but the woman was looking at her with something that could almost be construed as genuine interest.

"And when your parents are killed suddenly, it sort of messes you up a bit. I know that's a bit of an understatement, but it has always helped to talk about it like that. You see …,"—she was getting into her stride now—"it sort of takes away everything you thought was sure and certain, so you just go a bit wild. I know I did. My tutors were all very sympathetic, of course, and they wanted me to continue my studies. So I told them I was going off around the world to study design. And I went. My friends thought I was crazy. My aunt begged me to stay where I was for a bit until I got over what had happened, but I didn't listen to her. I just had to get away."

"Miss Finch, I'm warning you …"

"Oh, just shut up!" Natalie heard herself say, and then she laughed in a kind of hysterical way that didn't sound like her, and the man gestured to some people behind her. Oh no, she thought, not that cell again, all that hideous noise, that excruciating light!

"OK, OK." She tried to control herself. "We'll get to the roof, OK? But first you have to picture me, going from one airport to the next, hopping around the world, burning up the money from my parent's inheritance—which wasn't much. They were teachers, after all. And I did go and look at design, in a way. Have you seen the incredible woven 'paintings' of the Huichol Indians in northwestern Mexico? No? They call themselves the *Wixáritari*. I spent a few happy, hazy months there before I headed south. I partied in Caracas, and learned how to dance *salsa* and the *regaton* and the *merengue*. Shall I show you? No? Have patience." She held up her hand. Incredibly, given the situation, she was enjoying herself now. "I stood with my feet on both sides of the equator in Ecuador, and I walked the Inca trail to Machu Picchu in Peru. I even …"—she couldn't stop herself now—"… saw whales off the coast of Patagonia in southern Argentina, and got a bad case of sunburn on the roof of a hotel overlooking Copacabana Beach in Rio de Janeiro. And that's where it happened, I suppose. I just stopped. Ground to a halt. I had no idea where I was, or what I was going to do. When anyone spoke to me, I would fly off the handle. I guess finally, I sort of went out of my mind. But luckily—and it really was lucky—I met a guy who had some private English students, and he passed one or two of them over to me, and I quite enjoyed teaching them. This guy, Bill, had a spare room in the flat he shared with Roberto, so I lived with them, and I began to calm down and think about what I wanted. We would talk late into the night about that, Bill, Roberto, and me. They must have been so bored with my whining about my life, but they never said so, and after about four months I decided to go home, and I came here to London, multicultural London, where you can meet anyone from anywhere, and where we all get along with each other pretty much, and the English spoken is English from everywhere in the world, and where you can eat food from anywhere. Well, it's a great place isn't it?"

"Not if your friend is trying to destroy everything, it isn't!"

Natalie didn't hear, and she was so wrapped up in her story that she didn't see the warning glance the man gave his companion.

"And I got a flat just off Brick Lane, and tried to learn Bengali—not very successfully as it happens—and I did a teacher training course at a fantastic school in Piccadilly, and took to teaching like a duck to water. I did really well on that course, and the first real job offer I got was at a school in Romania, and I was good—I am good—at teaching, you know, and then I met Razvan …." Now suddenly, for the first time since she had started, she felt as if she might lose control. "And I thought he might be the one; well he was, he is the one, you know, but he upped and left me, so I went on Second Life and met Tiger Tim—this is so ridiculous—and decided to come and visit him in London, even though I don't even know his real name. I went to the building where he said he lived, and there were animals in cages and tanks, and the next thing I know, there's a huge helicopter and men with guns, and I'm being treated worse than a terrorist."

"Your friend's real name," the woman said before her companion could stop her, "is Anthony Holland. And unless we can find him and stop him, he and his associates will do so much damage that we will all witness something very much like the end of the world as we know it."

* * *

When his instructor told him to start, Razvan ran headlong to the edge of the mountain. Then the wind took him, and suddenly he was flying, paragliding down towards the beach of Oludeniz, one of the most beautiful places in Turkey, or, he thought, looking down at the intense blue of the sea, anywhere in the world. This was his first solo paragliding attempt, and he felt a sense of elation as he floated free in the currents of air that swirled around him. This was his first really extreme sport; more extreme than scuba diving or waterskiing, more frightening and more exhilarating than anything he had tried so far. This felt good. His life was perfect.

And then it happened. The wind changed and backed, and turbulence rippled through the canopy above him. The wing was beginning to lose its shape, and he was falling, screaming, through the blue Aegean air. Desperately he tried to remember what his instructor had told him to do if anything like this happened. He pulled the risers frantically and tried to regain control, but the beach was getting closer and closer. In that second he thought he was going to die. He suddenly realized that he had made a terrible mistake, and that if he survived this, he wouldn't stop until he had put things right. As he fell toward the ground, some lines from his favorite English poem came rushing into his brain: "All I have is a voice/to undo the folded lie …" How did it end? Oh yes—*Dumnezeule Mare*! Why was he thinking about this when everything was about to end? "We must love one another or die." It seemed that he was regaining control of the wing, but the ground was rushing toward him, and it looked as if he had left it too late.

6 *Puzzle*

As Li-Hua went through the security check at Taoyuan airport, she couldn't stop crying. She needed the love and support of her mother and father, and the company of her friends. They were the only ones who could help her. How could she have been so stupid? How come she had not known that Michael needed more from her than just a relationship? True, from the moment they had met, she had had a vague idea that something wasn't quite what it seemed, but she thought that was just because he was British.

Coming to Taiwan, she realized now, had been a mistake. She loved Taipei, of course, and she had made many friends. But then she had found out that Mr. Park was just a crook, an animal smuggler among other things and, worse, an old man who kept looking at her in an unhealthy and unattractive way. That was why Michael made her feel so secure; somehow she believed she was safe as long as everyone thought she was his girlfriend. Except, she realized now, she never had been, not really. He had been working for British intelligence or something, and if she hadn't seen the email on his computer screen in his flat that night, she might never have known. When she challenged him, he hadn't denied that he had been using her to get information about Mr. Park (how could he?). So she had bought a ticket home to Sichuan, and here she was, on her way out of this mess, back to working for the protection of wildlife, not its exploitation. She heard the announcement for her Asiana flight and started the walk to the gate.

* * *

Han-Gyong Park sat in his flat twenty-three floors above the busy Seoul traffic and knew that it was over. The police would be coming for him and he had nowhere to run. Maybe he could bribe someone. That was his only hope.

It wasn't himself he was worried about, though; it was the effect on his children. Mi-Sook was working at the national security headquarters. Her specialty was protecting the Internet against computer viruses, like the one called ICE 1, which had caused so much damage six months before by freezing thousands of computer systems. Now there were rumors of ICE 2—something far, far worse which would bring the whole computer-based world to a complete halt. But apparently no one knew where it would come from or when. It was up to people like Mi-Sook to build a defense against it. And quickly, before it was too late.

Park Junior (he smiled when he thought of that name; at least something would live on) had just graduated from the Juilliard School of Music in New York, and was already being described as one of the great pianists of his generation. His children, in other words, were everything that Korea could be proud of. If only their mother had lived to see this. But then she would have had to witness his own disgrace.

The door buzzer sounded. "This is it!" he thought, expecting that the police had come to get him. But when he opened the door, there was just a young girl standing there. Kate Holland. She was holding a gun, and it was pointing straight at him.

* * *

Finally they believed her. Despite all their threats and menaces, it was obvious that she knew nothing. They returned her things.

They wouldn't let her go, though. "Just a bit longer," the woman said, and nodded to one of the guards standing by the door. A few minutes later a new man entered the room. He was tall and wore jeans and a loose sweater over his angular frame. "Hello, Sam," said the man whom Natalie had come to hate over the last few hours. "This is Miss Finch."

"Ah, Miss Finch, a pleasure to meet you." He coughed.

"I know you, don't I? We've met before, right?"

The man, Sam, coughed again. And suddenly she remembered.

"You were the old man who helped me at St. Pancras, weren't you?"

"Oh, dear. Three years at drama school and all those years on stage, and I can't even fool someone, even with my best make-up and costume. I thought it was rather a good performance, actually. Pity."

"It was, honestly. I really thought you were old."

"That was the only part that wasn't acting," he laughed ruefully.

"Can we get on with it?" the man in the suit said.

"Sure, sorry. Look, Miss Finch …"

"Natalie, please." She liked him.

"Have a look at this film clip, Natalie." He inserted a CD into the computer that he had brought into the room with him. When the footage started, she saw a crowd of people on a station platform. The camera zoomed in and she saw herself at the Gare du Nord in Paris. A woman in a long coat brushed against her. Sam fiddled with the computer keys and this time the pictures were enlarged, so that she saw it, the woman's hand slipping something into the pocket of her jeans. The woman with red hair!

"That USB flash drive! That's where it came from. I knew it wasn't mine. What was on it?"

"A computer code—well, half of one," the woman in the pearl necklace said, "for one of the most dangerous computer viruses in the world."

"That's quite enough, Hermione," said the man in the suit. But she seemed to want to go on.

"We received a threat, a warning that unless we paid an enormous ransom, the virus would be put on to the Internet. And if that happened, it would stop this world in its tracks."

"We traced the threat to Anthony Holland— that's who you were taking the USB to. Well, to his daughter, at least."

"But if you have half of the code…," Natalie said, thinking quickly now.

"Oh, they have the complete code somewhere. They just don't want to launch it from only one place."

"And the animals? That crocodile?"

"Yes, well, we've been watching Holland—he was involved in an operation smuggling exotic animals. It was run from Korea. He was using it as a cover, a bluff."

"But why me?"

"Yes, that's a puzzle. Perhaps he was lonely. His wife had just left him. Perhaps he was just playing—" Natalie shuddered—"or perhaps he always intended you to come over, so that they could use you as a courier—safer because no one would be watching you, they thought. But we'd been watching that red-haired woman, and we saw what happened at the Gare du Nord. What we can't work out is how they knew you were coming."

She hadn't even told "Tiger Tim" Holland that she was going to see him. She had only decided to go to London when she was in Paris. The only people she had told were…—suddenly she realized how she had become involved in this whole story. Because the short form of the name Anthony is…

Her phone started ringing. She looked at the screen. It just said "Call 1."

"Answer it," said the man in the suit.

"Some say the world will end in fire…"

"Some say in ice," she said without thinking. She noticed the man and the woman lean forward suddenly, their expressions hard and questioning.

"Natalie?"

"Razvan? Where are you? Why are you calling me?"

"I'm in the hospital. In Istanbul."

"Why? What's happened to you?"

"An accident. Paragliding. I thought I could escape."

"Escape from what? Razvan, you're not making any sense."

"From you. From commitment. From everything. From the family, from normal life. But it didn't work. I want to come back. If you'll have me."

"Razvan!"

"Miss Finch, put down that phone. We need to talk."

"Razvan, do you mean that? Do you really mean that?"

"Miss Finch? Miss Finch?"

But she didn't hear them. Their voices were like echoes from some alien planet, some crazy computer-generated virtual world. They were unreal, their story bizarre and uninteresting. It was Razvan who was real, and who she wanted to be with more than anything.

"Razvan. Stay there. I'll buy a ticket. I'm coming."

And she stood up to leave.

Reader activities

Chapter 1: Tunnel

1 Character profile Copy and complete the chart with only information about the characters that is given in Chapter 1.

Age	
Nationality	
Appearance	
Occupation	
Other information	

Now add your own thoughts to the chart (including what they look like, what personality traits they have, what kind of life each one leads, etc.).

2 Word attack Look at the following words. Divide them into two lists (words I know/words I don't know).

emanate   exasperated   hissing   menacing
muttered   knapsack   shock   sprawling   stab
striking   surged   sweetest   thrashed   upright

Now say what part of speech the "words I don't know" are, as used in the text (noun, verb, etc.). Replace the words with your "best-guess" synonyms.

Check the meaning of the "words I don't know" using a dictionary or any other source. How good were your guesses?

3 Word check Complete the following chart with words and phrases from the list below. Use a dictionary or any other source to look up the meanings of words and phrases of which you are unsure.

breath   bruise   bumped into   clattering   coughing
cylinder   discomfort   doubled   fell to her knees
generous   heart   hideous   ignore   keen   limped
lose (her) balance   lurching   menacing   mind (his)
own business   overalls   rose into   visible

I have seen the word/phrase before and I know what it means.

I don't think I have seen the word/phrase before but I think I know what it means.

I don't think I have seen the word/phrase before and I don't know what it means.

Put a check mark [✓] next to words or phrases from Activities 2 and 3 if you think you would like to use them yourself.

4 Headline summary Choose the best six-word summary of Chapter 1.
(Note: headlines are often written in the present simple and omit things like articles and auxiliary verbs because they have to be short.)

a Woman arrested on Lion's Gate roof
b Visit to boyfriend ends in arrest
c Woman snatched in helicopter rooftop raid
d Crocodile clue to rooftop arrest mystery

Can you write a better summary than your first choice?

5 Research tasks Using any means, including the Internet, find out more about:

a the English Channel
b Eurostar and the Channel Tunnel

6 Prediction games What is your answer to the following questions?

a Which of the characters in Activity 1 are we likely to meet again in the story? What will they be doing?
b Why has Natalie been captured by the men in the helicopter? What is going to happen to her?

SPM score Mark the "story pleasure" meter depending on whether the story interests you a lot (very hot) or not at all (very cold).

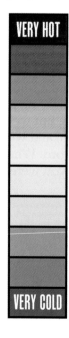

Chapter 2: The jungle

1 **Character profile** Make a chart for the man in uniform, Razvan and Tiger Tim like the one you completed for the characters in Chapter 1. Use only information given in Chapter 2.

Now add your own thoughts to the chart (including what they look like, what personality traits they have, what kind of life each one leads, etc.).

2 **Word attack** Find these words in Chapter 2. How could you figure out their meaning even if you did not recognize them at first?

avatar   bounced   counter   hood   occupy
torturing   wide-brimmed

3 **Word map** Find (forms of) the following words in the text. Make a word map (see example below) for at least four of them. You can use a dictionary or any other source.

blade   challenge   chaotic   cheerful   crack
empathy   end up   enthusiastic   experience
genius   grip   hang   image   interest   lean
patch   roll   slam   tied down   torturing
uniform   vanish   wander

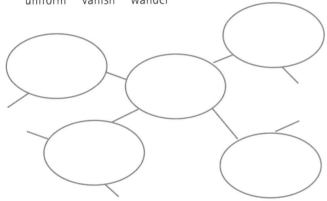

Put a check mark [✓] next to words or phrases from Activities 2 and 3 if you think you would like to use them yourself.

4 **Conversations** Create (all or part of) the "conversations" that took place between:

a Beata Vir and Tiger Tim
b Natalie and her aunt, Sergio, and Tony at dinner in Paris.

5 **Research tasks** Using any means, including the Internet, find out more about:

a what most people keep in their handbags
b love and dating on the Internet

6 **Prediction games** What is your answer to the following questions?

a How long is Natalie going to be in her "prison"? Why do you think she has been taken there?
b When and where might Natalie meet Tiger Tim?

Chapter 3: The end of the world

1 **Character profile** Make a chart for Han-Gyong Park, Li-Hua, the keyboard player, and Michael like the one you completed for the characters in Chapter 1. Use only information given in Chapter 3.

Now add your own thoughts to the chart (including what they look like, what personality traits they have, what kind of life each one leads, etc.).

2 **Word attack** Look at the following words. Divide them into two lists (words I know/words I don't know).

adulation   balaclava   beast   bodyguard
brilliance   crouching   doze   fierce   harmonies
lachrymose   linger   lyrics   opaque   refrain
shower   slits

Now say what part of speech the "words I don't know" are, as used in the text (noun/verb, etc.). Replace the words with your "best-guess" synonyms.

Check the meaning of the "words I don't know" using a dictionary or any other source. How good were your guesses?

3 **Word check** Complete the following chart with words and phrases from the list below. Use a dictionary or any other source to look up the meanings of words and phrases of which you are unsure.

awe   beautiful   refrain   blaze like stars   crouching
flowery   congratulations   hooded   hunched
impassive   intensity   keep her distance   lament
put them at their ease   reverence   scorn   slits
sweet harmonies   swell with pride   take over from
vibrated

I have seen the word/phrase before and I know what it means.

I don't think I have seen the word/phrase before but I think I know what it means.

I don't think I have seen the word/phrase before and I don't know what it means.

Put a check mark [✓] next to words or phrases from Activities 2 and 3 if you think you would like to use them yourself.

4 **Headline summary** Write a six-word summary of:

a the scene in the karaoke bar in Taipei
b Natalie's ordeal in the cell

5 **Research tasks** Using any means, including the Internet, find out more about:

a the song "American Pie." What are (1) a Chevy and (2) a levee? What is the song all about?
b karaoke bars. How did they start? Where can you find them?

6 **Prediction games** What is your answer to the following questions?

a Which of the characters in Activity 1 are we likely to meet again in the story? What will they be doing?
b What is the importance of Natalie's favorite poem for the future of the story?

SPM score Mark the "story pleasure" meter depending on whether the story interests you a lot (very hot) or not at all (very cold).

Is your temperature the same as for the previous two chapters?

Chapter 4: Prayer is better than sleep

1 **Character profile** Make a chart for the man and the woman in the luxury flat like the one you completed for the characters in Chapter 1. Use only information given in Chapter 4.

Now add your own thoughts to the chart (including what they look like, what personality traits they have, what kind of life each one leads, etc.).

2 **Word attack** Look at the following words and phrases. What other words or information in the text would help you to figure out their meaning even if you did not recognize them at first?

bounced   breakneck   bundled   churning   clipped
deafening   forced   indescribable   matching
nagging   plunged

3 **Word map** Find (forms of) the following words in the text. Make word maps (see page 157) for at least five of them. You can use a dictionary or any other source.

adjust   amenable   burst   cacophony   clench
conscious   current   desolate   drag   dream
ensnare   glare   grate   hallucinatory   hedonist
imitation   loudspeaker   music   overcrowded
precious   rise   sore   stare

Put a check mark [✓] next to words or phrases from Activities 2 and 3 if you think you would like to use them yourself.

4 **Inner thoughts and outer mails** Choose one of the following tasks:

a What is going on in Natalie's mind? What is she thinking? What does she think is going on? Write her inner thoughts, or record them on an audio track.
b What is Razvan thinking? Write the email that he sends to a British friend of his who lives in Bucharest, or the Skype Messenger conversation they have.

5 **Research tasks** Using any means, including the Internet, find out more about:
a the queen of England and her immediate family
b Cairo and Sharm el-Sheik

6 **Prediction games** What is your answer to the following questions?
a What is Razvan going to do when/if he gets to Turkey?
b Why was Natalie on that roof? What do the man in the suit and the woman with pearls want to know?

Chapter 5: The folded lie

1 **Character profile** Make a chart for Natalie and Razvan like the one you completed for the characters in Chapter 1. Use only information given in Chapter 5.

2 **Word attack** Look at the following words. Divide them into two lists (words I know/words I don't know).

absurd   assaulted   backed   canopy   construed
elation   elongated   excruciating   flashed
floated   patience   rippled   risers   sarcasm
touching   trail   whining   woven   wrapped up

Now say what part of speech the "words I don't know" are, as used in the text (noun/verb, etc.). Replace the words with your "best-guess" synonyms.

Check the meaning of the "words I don't know" using a dictionary or any other source. How good were your guesses?

3 **Word check** Complete the following chart with words from the list below. Use a dictionary or any other source to look up the meanings of words and phrases of which you are unsure.

a bad case of   a bit of an understatement   assaulted
backed   begged   elation   burning up the money
getting into (her) stride   go a bit wild   grind to a halt
growl   headlong   inheritance   interior design
like a duck to water   messes you up   swirled   tragic
turbulence   upped and left

I have seen the word/phrase before and I know what it means.

I don't think I have seen the word/phrase before but I think I know what it means.

I don't think I have seen the word/phrase before and I don't know what it means.

Put a check mark [✓] next to words or phrases from Activities 2 and 3 if you think you would like to use them yourself.

4 **Conversations outside the story** Given what you know about Natalie and Razvan, think of conversations they might have in the following situations:

a Natalie with Bill and Roberto in a restaurant in Rio de Janeiro
b Razvan with an American scuba diving instructor. It is his last day at Sharm el-Sheik just before he sets off for Turkey.

Choose a topic. Think of three things that either Natalie or Razvan might say about each other to Bill and Roberto or the instructors.

5 **Research tasks** Using any means, including the Internet, find out more about two of the following:

a the Huichol
b popular dances in Venezuela
c Mitad del Mundo, Ecuador
d Machu Picchu
e paragliding

6 **Prediction games** What is your answer to the following questions?

a Who is Natalie's friend and how is he trying to destroy the whole system?
b What is going to happen to Razvan?

Chapter 6: Puzzle

1 **Character profile** Look back at the charts you completed for Chapters 1–5. What can you add to what you have written? What do you want, or need, to change?

2 **Word check** Look at the following list of words and phrases and cross out the ones that you already know.

angular   bizarre   bluff   bribe   challenged
costume   cover   crook   denied   disgrace
echoes   escape   exploitation   freezing   generation
graduated   hard   intended   launch   ransom
support   threats   unhealthy   witness   zoomed in

Using a dictionary or any other resource, check on the meaning of the words you have not crossed out. Put a check mark [✓] next to the remaining words or phrases if you think you would like to use them yourself.

3 **Headline summary** Write an eight-word summary of Virtual Reality.

....

....

....

Now write four more summaries, adding four more words each time.

....

....

....

4 **Conversations** Create (all or part of) the conversations that took place between:

a Kate Holland and Han-Gyong Park
b Li-Hua and her mother (an English version of this)

5 **Film** If you were making a film of Virtual Reality, which actors would you cast in the main parts and why?

6 **Research tasks** Using any means, including the Internet, find out more about the following:

a the poem that includes "the folded lie" (see Chapter 5) and who wrote it
b computer viruses

7 **And they all lived happily ever after?** What happened,

finally, to the following, in your opinion?

a Natalie and Razvan
b the Ice 2 virus
c Tony Holland

What, if anything, still confuses you about Virtual Reality?

SPM score Mark the "story pleasure" meter depending on whether you enjoyed Virtual Reality a lot (very hot) or not at all (very cold).

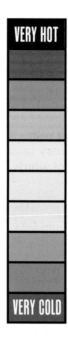